How Capitalism Saved America

How Capitalism Saved America

*The Untold History of Our Country,
from the Pilgrims to the Present*

Thomas J. DiLorenzo

THREE RIVERS PRESS • NEW YORK

Grateful acknowledgment is made to the following for permission to reprint previously published material.

Alfred A. Knopf: Excerpts from *Of Plymouth Plantation 1620–1647* by William Bradford, edited by Samuel Eliot Morison. Copyright © 1952 by Samuel Eliot Morison and renewed 1980 by Emily M. Beck. Reprinted by permission Alfred A. Knopf, a division of Random House, Inc.

Dom Armentano: Excerpts from *Antitrust and Monopoly* by Dom Armentano. Reprinted by permission of the author.

Copyright Clearance Center, Inc.: Excerpts from *Myths of Rich and Poor: Why We're Better Off Than We Think* by W. Michael Cox and Richard Alm. Excerpts from *Political Pilgrims: Western Intellectuals in Search of the Good Society*. Reprinted by permission of the Copyright Clearance Center, Inc.

Libertarian Press, Inc.: Excerpts from *Anti-Capitalistic Mentality* by Ludwig von Mises. Reprinted by permission of Libertarian Press, Inc., www.libertarianpress.com.

Lew Rockwell: Excerpt from *America's Great Depression* by Murray N. Rothbard. Reprinted by permission of Lew Rockwell.

Originally published in hardcover in the United States by Crown Forum, an imprint of the Crown Publishing Group, a division of Random House, Inc., New York, in 2004.

Library of Congress Cataloging-in-Publication Data
DiLorenzo, Thomas J.
How capitalism saved America : the untold history of our country,
from the Pilgrims to the present / Thomas J. DiLorenzo.
Includes bibliographical references and index.
1. Capitalism—United States—History. I. Title.
HB501.D522 2004
330.12'2'0973—dc22   2004000975

ISBN 978-1-4000-8331-2

Design by Robert C. Olsson

First Paperback Edition

146122990

To Ludwig von Mises, the twentieth century's most dedicated and accomplished champion of free markets, individual liberty, and the free society

CONTENTS

Contents

The Untold Story

> *Ignorance, as well as disapproval for the natural restraints placed on market excesses that capitalism and sound markets impose, cause our present leaders to reject capitalism and blame it for all the problems we face. If this fallacy is not corrected and capitalism is even further undermined, the prosperity that the free market generates will be destroyed.*

> —Congressman Ron Paul, "Has Capitalism Failed?" (July 9, 2002)

THE WORD *capitalism* was coined by none other than Karl Marx, who hoped that it would help in his crusade to denigrate the system of private property and free enterprise and to promote socialism. Marx insinuated that the only beneficiaries of capitalism were the capitalists. Of course, nearly every one of Marx's assumptions (government would wither away under communism, capitalism would make workers poorer, etc.) turned out to be wrong, including this one. Free-market capitalism, based on private property and peaceful exchange, is the source of civilization and human progress. Human beings have a natural propensity to "truck, barter, and exchange," as Adam Smith said more than two centuries ago, and free-market capitalism is by far the best-known means by which this can be accomplished.

In his famous treatise *The Wealth of Nations*, Smith neatly summed up the essence of how capitalism works: "Give me that which I want, and you shall have this which you want."[1] In other words, commerce is what economists call a "positive-sum game." The act of buying and selling always benefits both buyer and seller; otherwise they wouldn't trade with each other. Voluntary exchange in the free market is *mutually advantageous.*

Unfortunately, this simple fact of economic life is misunderstood or ignored by many commentators who cling to the discredited Marxist notion that one person gains in business at the expense of someone else. This nonsense is spread throughout the popular culture. It was on display in the movie *Wall Street,* for instance, in the now-famous "greed" speech, when Michael Douglas's character explained that business "is all a zero-sum game: somebody wins, and somebody loses." Nothing could be further from the truth, but Hollywood is full of movie scripts that spread silly, neo-Marxist propaganda such as this. And it is not just movies that perpetuate these myths. Many American universities are quite hostile toward capitalism, and during the twentieth century an entire class of intellectuals, journalists, television executives, private foundations, and others coalesced to form what might be called the anti-industry industry. Anticapitalist ideas and institutions are alive and well in the United States. Indeed, author and filmmaker Michael Moore has become a wealthy man by making outrageous and unsupportable claims about supposedly evil capitalists and by promoting socialism, and he is just one of many people spreading myths about capitalism.

These myths are inflicting great costs on the American economy and society. The more Americans feel that capitalism needs to be reined in, or that the public has no say in an economy that is largely in the hands of "plutocrats," the more the government is called on to regulate the economy. Congressman Ron Paul, Republican of Texas, is exactly right: Because of a widespread misunderstanding of what capitalism is, our leaders—and also much of the general public—incorrectly blame capitalism for any economic problems we face. Consequently, they are all too quick to recommend bigger government as the "solution."

Sure enough, in the wake of the corporate accounting scandals that became public starting in the late 1990s, anticapitalist demagoguery has become pervasive. Pundits, politicians, and intellectuals have argued that such fraud is an inherent and unique feature of capitalism and that, therefore, the government needs to impose *more* regulations on financial markets, the accounting profession, and corporations in general. But fraud is *not* a feature unique to capitalism: we find wrongdoers not just in the corporate world but also in government, in charities, in religion, and everywhere else. In addition, there are laws against fraud, and those who commit fraud quite often end up in jail; thus it is ridiculous and irresponsible to wage a general political campaign against capitalism when the laws already in place address the problem of wrongdoing.

Nor is the threat of a jail sentence the only deterrent to corporate fraud. The anticapitalists who call for more government regulation also ignore what Congressman Paul calls "the natural restraints placed on market excesses that capitalism and sound markets impose." Businesspeople have great incentives not to commit fraud because they know that sooner or later no one would want to do business with them if they were somehow manipulating the market, and that they would ultimately lose money or even go bankrupt. And these "natural restraints" are much weaker, perhaps even nonexistent, in the government sector. Thus, if fraud were a problem it would probably be a much bigger problem in the government regulatory agencies than in the businesses they are supposed to be regulating.

The most important point that the anticapitalists overlook or ignore is this: overwhelming evidence indicates that the more regulations, controls, taxes, government-run industries, protectionism, and other forms of interventionism that exist, the poorer a country will be. Big government invariably causes higher unemployment, higher prices, shortages of goods and services, and myriad other problems that can be eliminated only by more, not less, voluntary exchange on the free market—that is, by capitalism. Excessive government controls are precisely why the countries of western Europe lag so far behind the United States economically.

And the opposite is also true: the more economic freedom a nation has—the more economic opportunity there is—the more vibrant that country's economy will be.

A careful review of our nation's history reveals a long series of myths that demonize capitalism—and just how pernicious such myths are. Capitalism supposedly harmed the working class during the industrial revolution; is prone to monopolization; harms consumers with dangerous products; generates macroeconomic instability; harms the environment; exploits the Third World; breeds discrimination; is a cause of war; and on and on.

This is all untrue. In this book, we will learn about the *realities* of capitalism in the United States: how, from the very beginning, capitalism has been vital to America's growth, and how excessive government interference in the economy has only exacerbated economic problems and stifled growth.

THE REAL STORY ABOUT CAPITALISM IN AMERICA

Today there is so much confusion about capitalism that what politicians and pundits often label "capitalism" is just the opposite: interventionism. A good example of how commentators wrongly blame capitalism for causing problems occurred in August 2003, when the American Northeast experienced an electric power blackout. On Sunday, August 24, 2003, just over a week after the blackout, the *New York Times* ran a front-page story announcing in the opening paragraphs that the electricity grid "was an afterthought during the decade-long process of deregulating the power industry" and that "deregulation increased the vulnerability of the grid." But the article flatly contradicted itself in the third paragraph, where the *Times* admitted that "deregulation is actually a misnomer" because, even though the generation of electricity had been partially deregulated in the United States, the "transmission of electricity over high-voltage lines and the distribution into homes and buildings [that is, the power grid] remained regulated."[2] Those who read only the headline or the first couple of paragraphs of the *Times* article went away believing that "deregulation," or a move in the direction of capitalism, in the electric power industry was the source of the problem. In fact, however, the opposite was true: the problem was excessive government regulation.

This book is meant to correct such mistaken beliefs about capitalism. Whether the source is the *New York Times* or Michael Moore, so much of what we hear about capitalism is confused or deliberately misleading. That is why Chapter 1 cuts through the common, inaccurate discussions to explain how capitalism actually works. As we will see, the fact is that true capitalism—that is, capitalism absent excessive government regulation and taxation—has not existed to any significant degree in America in many, many years. The United States has suffered under excessive government intervention in the economy in large part because of the anticapitalist movement, which will be explored in Chapter 2.

But nothing debunks the claims of the anticapitalists better than a close examination of the role capitalism has played throughout American history. As the last ten chapters of this book reveal, time after time American capitalism has actually *solved* the problems that generations of pundits, politicians, and intellectuals have blamed it for.

Indeed, Chapter 3 shows how, long before the term *capitalism* came into use, the adoption of one of the defining characteristics of capitalism—private property—literally saved the Pilgrims and the other early American settlers from starvation.

Chapter 4 explains how the American Revolution of 1776 was, at base, a *capitalist* revolution. Most Americans know that the American Revolution was fought against the tyrannical King George III of England, but they are less aware that King George imposed his tyrannical restrictions on the American colonists in an attempt to enforce England's interventionist, anticapitalist system of mercantilism. Chapter 5 is the first of several that dispose of a number of myths about American capitalism—in this case, that government financing was necessary for the building of the nation's transportation infrastructure of roads, canals, and railroads. The truth is that early American transportation entrepreneurs succeeded marvelously while government-subsidized transportation was a flop and a scandal.

Shelves and shelves of books have been written on how capitalism supposedly harmed the American working class, which needed to be "rescued" by government, with its minimum-wage/maximum-hour laws and child labor legislation, and by labor unions. Chapter 6 explains why this, too, is a myth. Capitalism is the source of the generational increase in the American standard of living; both government and unions have been a drag on living standards.

Chapter 7 disposes of another common myth: that of the robber baron. The accepted wisdom is that all the railroad entrepreneurs of the nineteenth century, for example, were robber barons. But such a claim unfairly lumps together those who succeeded on the strength of their own talents, intelligence, and innovations and those who did in fact gain an unfair advantage over competitors (and consumers). The true capitalists—in the railroad industry and other industries—were the so-called market entrepreneurs. In contrast, the real robber barons—the political entrepreneurs—were not capitalists but corporatists, or, to use a term that Adam Smith employed in *The Wealth of Nations*, mercantilists. These political entrepreneurs gained an unfair advantage through special privileges created by government intervention (direct subsidies, regulations that harmed their competitors, and much more). The critics are right to condemn these business/government partnerships, but they are wrong to label them as capitalism.

Every student of American business history knows that the late nineteenth century was a period of "rampant monopolization," when trusts operated by the likes of John D. Rockefeller had an unfair advantage over competitors and exploited consumers. The government's antitrust laws were supposedly implemented to tame these trusts and force them to operate in the public interest. Chapter 8 shows why this, too, is a myth.

Most Americans also know that the 1920s were a period of extreme laissez-faire and that the "excesses of capitalism" caused the Great Depression of the 1930s. Chapter 9 shows how the administration of Herbert Hoover (1929–1933) was in fact the most interventionist peacetime administration in American history up to that point. It was those interventions—especially those of the Federal Reserve Board—that spawned the Great Depression.

Perhaps the most powerful of all American political myths is the Roosevelt myth, which has fostered the widespread belief that the government needs to intervene in any sort of economic downturn. Franklin D. Roosevelt supposedly saved capitalism, and the country as a whole, by responding to Hoover's alleged laissez-faire policies with massive government intervention. In reality, however, America never got out of its Depression economy until after World War II. In actuality, as Chapter 10 shows, FDR's New Deal policies unequivocally prolonged the Great Depression and made it more severe than it would otherwise have been because the New Deal crippled capitalism.

Ever since Roosevelt's New Deal created the expectation that government intervention is necessary to "fix" capitalism, government regulations have grown out of control, and we only hear demands for further regulation. A major event that triggered further calls for government regulation of capitalism was the energy crisis of the 1970s. At the time, many believed that the "greedy oil companies" (capitalists) had caused the crisis and that the natural solution therefore was massive government intervention. As a result, the government imposed price controls, rationing, and mandatory speed limits, created a federal Department of Energy, and employed thousands of government bureaucrats to administer all the new regulations. But Chapter 11 details how all of this massive interventionism made the energy crisis worse, not better. Worse, excessive government regulation is still causing problems today in American energy markets, for, as we saw in the blackout of August 2003, many still blame capitalism, or deregulation, for the problems that the government's intervention in free markets has caused.

The final chapter is about the never-ending war on capitalism. The recklessness in the way that today's politicians impose more and more regulatory restrictions and taxes on American businesses has already been extremely harmful to our standard of living. If a climate of opinion more favorable to capitalism and capitalists is not created, then the political process will create more economic stagnation and more misery.

Capitalism has made America the most prosperous nation on earth. But if the anticapitalists have their way and continue to put roadblocks in the way of economic freedom, the capitalist system that has continually saved this country will be eliminated forever, and all Americans will suffer for it.

CHAPTER ONE

What Is Capitalism?

*Free-market capitalism is a network of free and voluntary
exchanges in which producers work, produce, and exchange
their products for the products of others through prices voluntarily arrived at.*

—Murray N. Rothbard, "Capitalism versus Statism" (1972)

*Capitalism is a social system based on the recognition of
individual rights, including property rights, in which all
property is privately owned.*

—Ayn Rand, *Capitalism: The Unknown Ideal* (1962)

S o How has the United States gotten so far from true capitalism?
How have so many pernicious myths about capitalism come to
be so prevalent?

The answer is that too many Americans are ignorant of how
capitalism really works—though with some of the most ardent anticapitalists, the ignorance is willful. To counter such ignorance, it
is useful to return to the first great treatise on capitalism, Adam
Smith's *The Wealth of Nations,* published in 1776, the same year the
American colonies declared their independence from Britain. Smith
described the basic workings of capitalism succinctly:

In civilized society [man] stands at all times in need of the cooperation and assistance of great multitudes, while his whole life

is scarce sufficient to gain the friendship of a few persons. . . .
Man has almost constant occasion for the help of his brethren,
and it is in vain for him to expect it from their benevolence
only. He will be more likely to prevail if he can interest their
self-love in his favour, and show them that it is for their own
advantage to do for him what he requires of them. Whoever
offers to another a bargain of any kind, proposes to do this.
Give me that which I want, and you shall have this which you
want, is the meaning of every such offer; and it is in this manner that we obtain from one another the far greater part of
those good offices which we stand in need of. It is not from the
benevolence of the butcher, brewer, or the baker, that we expect our dinner, but from their regard to their own interest. . . .
Nobody but a beggar chuses to depend chiefly upon the benevolence of his fellow citizens.[1]

Here Smith clearly explained some of the most important elements of capitalism—the division of labor, social cooperation, and
free exchange. The division of labor is a natural, and beneficial, consequence of the fact that each human being is unique in a thousand
different ways—in motivation, intelligence, interests, physical at-
tributes and abilities, preferences, goals, skill levels, age, formal and
informal education, worldly experiences, family history and culture, psychology, and much more. So, for example, people who happen to live in a fertile part of the world are more inclined to
specialize in farming than, say, people who live in the arid Middle
East. But because of this specialization, we rely daily on thousands
of people whom we don't even know for the basic necessities of
life. This breeds social cooperation. The farmer in the American
Midwest can sell food to Middle Easterners and use some of the
money he earns from that to purchase, for instance, petroleum

products that are generated in the Middle East. Imagine how poor we would all be if we were to live under what is called economic autarky—where we all had to grow our own food, build our own houses, make our own clothing, manufacture and fuel our own cars, and so on.

Free exchange allows us to avoid the economic desperation of autarky. It also provides powerful incentives to continue educating ourselves and improving our skills so we can provide our fellow man with better and better (and less expensive) goods and services in return for money. This notion of serving one's fellow man is central to any capitalist economy. In fact, the economist and syndicated columnist Walter Williams refers to dollars (and other currencies) as "certificates of performance," for one can only earn money by providing one's fellow man with a good or service that he values more than the money he pays for it.

Nevertheless, as Smith observed, capitalism does not operate on the principle of altruism or "benevolence"; a basic fact of human nature is that we all have an instinct for self-preservation and personal advancement. Capitalism succeeds precisely because free exchange is mutually advantageous; each party serves his own self-interest, or what Smith called "self-love." Cattle ranchers in Montana, for instance, rise at 4 A.M. and work until well after dark at a number of physically demanding jobs not out of love for their fellow man but because they want to earn a living for themselves and their families. Yet the marvelous advantage of capitalism is that it captures this motivation and channels it in a way that encourages human cooperation and betterment.

In a capitalist economy the primary means (the only means, for most people) of improving one's standard of living is, in Adam Smith's formulation, giving others that which they want. Indeed, most exceptionally wealthy people amassed their fortunes precisely because they provided valued products to millions of people all around the world. This is what Bill Gates did with Microsoft and what Henry Ford, Andrew Carnegie, and many other well-known industrialists did before him. The clothing industry, the grocery industry, mechanized agriculture, and many other industries have created multimillionaires or billionaires because these individuals have vastly improved the standard of living of the masses. A common myth spread by anticapitalists is that the wealthiest capitalists profit at the expense of the rest of the society, particularly the working classes. But it is amazing to consider the innovations and improvements that entrepreneurs have brought to everyone. As the Austrian economist Ludwig von Mises wrote, "Every advance first comes into being as the luxury of a few rich people, only to become, after a time, the indispensable necessity taken for granted by everyone. Luxury consumption provides industry with the stimulus to discover and introduce new things."[2] Indeed, the most successful capitalists have brought to the masses products and services that were once considered luxuries available only to the rich. The result is that the average American working person today lives better in many ways than kings did several hundred years ago, with his automobiles, central heating and air conditioning, swimming pools and hot tubs, inexpensive food, and all the other "necessities" of modern life that those kings would have considered miracles. All of this is the product of capitalism. The economist Joseph Schumpeter summed up how capitalism benefits the masses:

> The capitalist engine is first and last an engine of mass production which unavoidably also means production for the masses. . . . It is the cheap cloth, the cheap cotton and rayon fabric, boots, motorcars and so on that are the typical achievements of capitalist production, and not as a rule improvements

that would mean much to the rich man. Queen Elizabeth owned silk stockings. The capitalist achievement does not typically consist in providing more silk stockings for queens but in bringing them within reach of factory girls.[3]

These are the facts that the neo-Marxist propagandists ignore when bashing capitalism as a zero-sum game in which "somebody wins, somebody loses."

CONSUMER SOVEREIGNTY

We all observe corporate executives, bankers, and businesspeople in general managing the day-to-day affairs of business, from the smallest dry cleaner to the largest multinational corporation. This has led many to believe that they—the public—have no say in their economy, which is largely in the hands of these "plutocrats." But this is a myth, for as Mises pointed out:

> Neither the entrepreneurs nor the farmers nor the capitalists determine what has to be produced. The consumers do that. If a businessman does not strictly obey the orders of the public as they are conveyed to him by the structure of market prices, he suffers losses, he goes bankrupt. . . . Other men who did better in satisfying the demand of the consumers replace him. . . . The consumers . . . make poor people rich and rich people poor. They determine precisely what should be produced, in what quality, and in what qualities. They are merciless egoistic bosses, full of whims and fancies, changeable and unpredictable. . . . They do not care a whit for past merit and vested interests. . . . In their capacities as buyers and consumers they are hard hearted and callous, without consideration for other people.[4]

Every business depends on repeat sales, and for this reason the consumer really is the captain of the economic ship, as Mises called it. True, some businesses treat consumers poorly, but such behavior is always harshly penalized (by consumers) with lower profits or bankruptcy. Meanwhile, the opposite kind of behavior is rewarded. This goes not only for businesses that deal directly with consumers but for all of their suppliers and workers as well. The demand for labor on the part of businesses, for example, is said to be a "derived demand" in that it is derived from the consumer demand for the product. Thus, if consumers prefer more Bibles and less booze, fewer workers will be manufacturing booze and more will be publishing Bibles. This is why it is ultimately the consumers who pay everyone's wages in a capitalist economy. People who acquire skills producing goods and services for which there is stronger consumer demand will, all other things being equal, be paid more than those who work in industries in which consumer demand is weaker.

In this sense consumers are "voting" with their dollars. Consumer sovereignty under capitalism is truly a form of economic democracy. But it is much more efficient than political democracy. In political democracies the majority rules and the minority can be largely ignored. In an "economic democracy" everyone's dollar vote counts the same. That is why, for example, businesses compete fiercely for niche markets with relatively small pockets of customers.[5]

THE CENTRAL IMPORTANCE OF PROPERTY RIGHTS

As the quotation of Ayn Rand at the beginning of this chapter denotes, private property is the most important distinguishing feature of capitalism. The only alternative is communal or governmental ownership—that is, socialism. And socialism is economic poison wherever it is implemented.[6] Private ownership of the means of production is the only way to ensure a workable system of human cooperation and division of labor.

The American founding fathers were students of the British philosopher John Locke, whose famous *Second Treatise of Government* proclaimed that individuals are willing to join in society with others, and form governments, primarily for the mutual preservation of their "lives, liberties, and estates [that is, property]." This was the major function of government, as Locke saw it, and America's founders agreed. Protection of private property at the very least will minimize political conflict, for the political allocation of resources (as opposed to the market allocation that occurs under capitalism) is primarily legal plunder—one coalition or group uses the power of the state to take from another group. Modern governments actually spend relatively little on programs and systems that benefit all citizens, such as national defense or the judicial system; mainly they are concerned with infringing on the property rights of one (less politically powerful) group of citizens for the benefit of another (more politically powerful) group.

The benefits of private property to a capitalist economy are crucial. In a system with private property, individuals are free to choose different occupations, consumption patterns, or lifestyles as long as they don't interfere with the freedom of others to do the same. This establishes the supremacy of consumer sovereignty: people are free to choose their occupations, but subject to the demands of consumers.

Private property under capitalism also creates a wide dispersal of economic power. No matter how wealthy any one person becomes, his power is severely limited by the fact that he is just one of millions of property owners. Even Bill Gates is constantly pressured to reinvest his wealth in a way that will please consumers—if he wants to hold on to it. Ludwig von Mises explained:

Private property creates for the individual a sphere in which he is free of the state. It sets limits to the operation of the authoritarian will. It allows other forces to arise side by side with and in opposition to political power. It thus becomes the basis of all those activities that are free from violent interference on the part of the state. It is the soil in which the seeds of freedom are nurtured and in which the autonomy of the individual and ultimately all intellectual and material progress are rooted.[7]

Private property also provides powerful incentives for wise stewardship of property. Property owners who do not take good care of their property bear the full cost of their actions when their property—that is, their wealth—depreciates in value. The opposite is also true: those who take care of and improve their property reap the rewards when their property value goes up. This is why private homes are so much better maintained than government housing projects, for example, or why private lakes and streams are carefully maintained while government-owned ones are often overfished and overused, or why private forests that are harvested are often replanted with trees that mature in twenty-five years while public forests are not.

With well-enforced property rights people have the ability to sell goods and services to others as a means of improving their own standards of living. Consequently, secure property rights (minimal or nonexistent levels of governmental confiscation through taxation, for example) create incentives to develop greater skills and abilities to produce goods and services for others and to profit from that. And because they create the ability to profit from one's own productive endeavors, property rights are the keystone of modern capitalism and of civilization itself. (That's why Marx and Engels wrote in big capital letters in *The Communist Manifesto* that a prerequisite for socialism was ABOLITION OF PRIVATE PROPERTY.)

Another reason private property is essential to a well-functioning capitalist economy is that any such economy is extraordinarily vast and complex. No individual or central planning authority could possibly have command of all the information necessary to keep a complex economy working smoothly and efficiently.

One of the more famous demonstrations of the complexities of an economic system came in an essay about what goes into making a seemingly simple product: a pencil. In "I, Pencil," Leonard Read, the founder of the Foundation of Economic Education in Irvington, New York, discussed the many materials necessary to produce a pencil: wood, metal, zinc, rubber, paint, and dozens of other things.[8] But that is just the beginning, for there is an entire industry to produce each of those materials—a lumber industry to get the wood, a mining industry to get the zinc, and so on. Moreover, engineering and tool-making businesses are required to supply all of those industries. Finally, neither the pencils themselves nor the various elements needed to manufacture pencils could be transported without the oil and shipping industries.

All told, making the most simple of objects, a pencil, involves thousands of people who possess very detailed knowledge and information about their day-to-day jobs, whether they are in the lumber industry, the rubber industry, or elsewhere. And these people come from all over the world. No central planner or "pencil czar"— even with access to the most powerful computer imaginable—could possibly possess and utilize all the detailed and constantly changing information that goes into making pencils. And yet we still have our pencils. How? Because of private property and the free-market capitalism it enables. Under a free-market system, all of these thousands of people, very few of whom actually know one another, have an economic incentive to cooperate with one another under a division of labor and produce pencils. There's no magic or invisible hand involved. It is the common sense of everyday life under capitalism. As long as there is a consumer demand for pencils—and thus the potential for profit—people will cooperate with others to figure out a way to produce and market pencils. Consumers get the pencils they want, and the people who produce them improve the standard of living for themselves and their families. Property rights and the capitalist system make all of this possible.

The more complex an economy becomes, the *more* essential it is to rely on free-market capitalism. Indeed, Leonard Read's pencil example emphasizes just how misguided government planning of the economy is: no group of experts could possibly possess the knowledge required to produce a simple pencil, let alone "plan" an entire economy. The delusion that a single person or group of government planners could possibly possess such information and manage an entire economy is what Nobel laureate economist Friedrich Hayek called the "pretense of knowledge" or the "fatal conceit."[9] Central planning inevitably leads to economic chaos.

Private property and capitalism also provide strong incentives to preserve resources for the future, whereas political resource allocation under democracy tends toward immediate gratification. Whenever the present value of using a resource in the future is larger than the value of current use, that resource will be preserved. For example, tree farmers often replant their land with trees that will not mature for thirty to fifty years, long after the farmers are retired or dead. They do this because, as long as property is transferable, such plantings will enhance the value of their land. When one of these farmers sells his land, he can get a higher price for it and capture the value of his investment; the buyer, meanwhile, benefits from being able to harvest the trees in the future.

It is in this way that free-market capitalism has a conservation ethic. After all, elementary economics teaches that a business can maximize profits by minimizing costs, and the way for any business to minimize costs is to use as few resources as possible in producing its goods or services—to conserve, in other words. Corporations spend large amounts of money on research and development trying to figure out ways to increase their profits by using fewer resources. Coca-Cola, for example, uses considerably less aluminum in its cans than it did several decades ago. Coca-Cola did this not because it became more environmentally sensitive but because it wanted to increase its profits.

One of the most striking demonstrations of the importance of property rights is the fact that the *absence* of property rights protections is a major cause of world poverty. As Hernando de Soto notes in his book *The Mystery of Capital,* many of the poorest countries in the world possess enormous amounts of capital, but their ownership is insecure because of faulty or nonexistent property law or property rights protections.[10] The value of private savings in the "poor" countries of the world, says de Soto, is forty times the amount of foreign aid they have received since 1945. The problem is that the citizens of poorer countries

> hold these resources in defective forms: houses built on land whose ownership rights are not adequately recorded, unincorporated businesses with undefined liability, industries located where financiers and investors cannot see them. Because the rights to these possessions are not adequately documented, these assets cannot readily be turned into capital, cannot be traded outside of narrow local circles . . . , cannot be used as collateral for a loan, and cannot be used as a share against an investment.[11]

In the West, by contrast, "every parcel of land, every building, every piece of equipment, or store of inventories is represented in a property document that is the visible sign of a vast hidden process that connects all these assets to the rest of the economy."[12] In the United States, for example, the single most important source of collateral for a small business loan is the mortgage on the small business owner's house. Because government in poorer countries has failed to enforce property rights, the people of these countries lack the ability, on any large scale, to create capital and become entrepreneurs. And without capital there can be no capitalism.

It is no coincidence, then, that capitalism grew from the fifteenth century onward after the creation of commercial law and commercial law courts designed to enforce and protect property rights. Nathan Rosenberg and L. E. Birdzell, Jr. explain this development in their book *How the West Grew Rich: The Economic Transformation of the Industrial World.* For instance, talking about eighteenth-century England, they write:

> Mercantile transactions, insurance policies, and credit instruments subject to English law seemed more secure, more calculable in their consequences, less subject to the vagaries of sovereigns and changes of heart by one party or the other. . . . Other Western countries sought to emulate these advantages by adopting commercial codes and establishing commercial courts. . . . Thus, systematic law added to the ability to predict the behavior of others. . . . It thereby reduced the risks of trading and investing with them. . . . This . . . was an important element in the development of capitalist institutions.[13]

ENTREPRENEURSHIP

When it comes down to it, what are being traded in a capitalist economy are property rights—the ownership rights in goods and services. Trade and exchange will be minimal without reasonably secure property rights. And it is these trades and exchanges (supply and demand) that determine free-market prices. Prices in a capitalist economy reflect the relative scarcity of a good or service as well as the amount and intensity of consumer demand. Free-market prices are the only viable means of rational economic calculation. If a good or service becomes in shorter supply, for whatever reason, its price will rise, all other things being equal. The higher price will give consumers the proper incentive to do what is needed whenever anything becomes scarcer: conserve, or cut back on consumption. At the same time, the higher price gives producers an incentive to supply more to the market (since it is more profitable to do so), while others are given financial incentives to create and market substitutes for the higher-priced item.

On the other hand, if a product catches on and more consumers want to buy it, they will bid up the price of the product. That in turn will once again provide the correct incentive to producers: to produce more. More entrepreneurs will enter the business, as long as there are no government-imposed barriers to competition, such as protectionism, monopoly franchises, and onerous licensing regulation—all things that, as we will see in the next chapter, *impede* capitalism. The additional production and competition will eventually bring the price back down, perhaps even to a lower level than the original price. The process of competition also tends to improve the quality of the product, benefiting the consumer even more.

The other effect of competition is that the entrepreneurs who were among the first to meet the consumers' demands—and may have made a killing doing so—will see their profits fall. Competition never lets entrepreneurs rest on their laurels. The entrepreneur must always be on the lookout for the next opportunity to serve consumers better than the competition if he is to have a long career.

Another way of putting this is that the successful entrepreneur is one who recognizes profit opportunities before others do and acts on it. The goal of the entrepreneur is, obviously, to have revenue exceed costs—to know that all the investment in resources (land, labor, capital, technology, ideas, and so forth) has created a product or service that consumers value more than the resources themselves.

Not all entrepreneurs are successful, of course; many lose money and go bankrupt. But this is another strength of free-market capitalism, where the consumer is king. If one capitalist uses his resources in a way that does not please consumers and therefore cuts back on resources or goes out of business, more successful entrepreneurs will take up those resources and use them more efficiently. Indeed, in many cases a company that goes bankrupt is purchased by a more successful competitor in the same industry who knows better how to manage those resources and produce products and services that are more to the liking of consumers. The freedom to fail is an important ingredient of capitalist success.

Entrepreneurial freedom in general is a prerequisite for capitalist success. It is entrepreneurs who take risks, invest their money, start up new businesses, create new products, and employ most of the workforce in the United States. Entrepreneurs have created whole new industries by filling market niches that were ignored by other businesses. They have created competition for older, more established businesses, which is always good for the consumer. Entrepreneurs are also the main source of experimentation in the business world, for in trying to find profit opportunities that others have missed they are constantly experimenting with newer products. These products sometimes become revolutionary, as in the case of personal computers, the automobile, and thousands of other products and services.

It is also entrepreneurs who turn technological innovations into real products available for sale to consumers. The key ingredient of entrepreneurship is a *vision* of how to serve consumers better than others have previously done, as Israel Kirzner, the preeminent theorist of the economics of entrepreneurship, has explained:

> The important feature of entrepreneurship is not so much the ability to break away from routine as the ability to perceive new opportunities which others have not yet noticed. Entrepreneurship . . . is not so much the introduction of new products or of new techniques of production as the ability to *see* where new methods of production have, unknown to others, become feasible.[14]

We who live in capitalist countries tend to take all of this—property rights, free-market pricing, entrepreneurship—for granted, but every socialist country that has ever existed in the world has taken away these key ingredients of capitalism and has consequently created an economic catastrophe. Still, as we will see in Chapter 2, governments—including, too often, our own—persistently interfere with the free-market economy with regulations that cause economic distortions and cripple the economy.

THE IMPORTANCE OF ECONOMIC FREEDOM

Economic freedom in general is a necessary prerequisite for the success of capitalism. That is, citizens must be free to engage in commerce with whomever they want as long as they don't interfere by violent means with the equal rights of others to do so. People must be free to pursue whatever occupation they think is best for them as well, and the fruits of their labor cannot be confiscated by the state's tax collectors.

Any discussion of economic freedom must consider *degrees* of freedom, for neither the United States nor any other nation has ever had an economy that was genuinely free of government interference— that is, free of taxes and regulations. But overwhelming evidence indicates that the more economic freedom a nation has, the more economic opportunity there will be and the more vibrant that nation's economy will be. And the opposite is also true: the more regulations, controls, taxes, government-run industries, protectionism, and other forms of interventionism that exist, the poorer a country will be. The strongest evidence comes from several annual "economic freedom indexes" calculated and published by the Fraser Institute in Canada and by the *Wall Street Journal* and the Heritage Foundation in the United States.[15] These indexes show a strong correlation between the degree of economic freedom in a country and economic growth. And in fact the studies show more than just a correlation; they explain why a higher degree of economic freedom (that is, a more capitalistic society) *causes* more prosperity.

The seven components of the Fraser Institute's index (which are virtually identical to those of the *Wall Street Journal*/Heritage Foundation index) are size of government, extent of government control of markets, degree of price stability, freedom to use foreign currencies, protection of property rights, freedom of international trade, and freedom of capital markets.

The overall size of government as a percentage of an economy is important because every dollar that government spends must necessarily come from the private sector. If the government taxes, it takes money out of the pockets of consumers; if it borrows, it crowds out private borrowers (individuals, families, and businesses) and puts upward pressure on interest rates, which makes borrowing more expensive for private citizens; and if it prints money to finance its programs, it creates inflation, which reduces the value of all privately held wealth. Except for spending to protect property rights, enforce the law, and protect citizens from foreign aggressors, all government spending crowds out private spending and weakens the vitality of capitalism.

Taxation, price controls, regulation in general, and government control of production with government-run enterprises all shrink the private sector as well. When the government causes inflation it makes it difficult for capitalists to make economic calculations. After all, the entrepreneur must assess whether his investment in resources is producing a product or service that consumers value more than the resources themselves—that is, whether his revenues exceed his costs. And inflation complicates this critical calculation, which harms capitalism.

The freedom to engage in international commerce expands the size of markets in a capitalist economy and makes competition more vigorous. This, in turn, generally leads to higher-quality and lower-priced products for consumers.

Perhaps the most important element of the Fraser Institute's index is "Legal Structure and Property Rights," by which it means the relative security of property rights and the viability of contracts across countries. The more stable property rights are, the stronger a nation's economy will be.

Each annual publication of the economic freedom indexes produces stronger evidence of the correlation between the degree of economic freedom and prosperity. As one measure of this correlation, the 2003 Fraser Institute report showed that the freest countries in the world had more than seven times the per capita income as the least free countries (see Table 1.1).

A similar correlation existed between the economic freedom index ratings and the *growth rate* of gross domestic product (GDP) across the 123 countries, as seen in Table 1.2. Quite simply, the index reveals that there is no better solution to poverty than capitalism. And looking at the United Nations Human Poverty Index only con-

TABLE 1.1: ECONOMIC FREEDOM AND INCOME

ECONOMIC FREEDOM INDEX (QUINTILES)	PER CAPITA INCOME
Bottom	$3,251
4th	$3,803
3rd	$7,316
2nd	$12,666
1st	$22,922

Source: Fraser Institute, *Economic Freedom of the World, 2003 Annual Report* (Vancouver, B.C.: Fraser Institute, 2003), 11.

firms the point that with more economic freedom comes less poverty (not to mention longer life expectancy). The countries in the bottom quintile of the Fraser Institute's economic freedom ranking had an average UN Poverty Index ranking of 36.62—about two and a half times the ranking of the freest countries (14.6).[16]

As these studies clearly convey, capitalism is the best-known source of upward economic mobility. And, despite the oft-repeated claims of anticapitalists, capitalism actually reduces income inequalities within a nation as well. While there will always be inequalities of incomes—this is only natural, for every human being has different aptitudes, priorities, and interests—the *economic opportunity* in a capitalist economy enables those at the bottom of the economic ladder to ascend to the middle and the top. Over time, income inequalities diminish as more and more people take advantage of job opportunities, work hard, learn skills, educate themselves, save their money, get married and raise families, and start up their own busi-

TABLE 1.2: ECONOMIC FREEDOM AND
ECONOMIC GROWTH

ECONOMIC FREEDOM INDEX (QUINTILES)	REAL GDP GROWTH PER CAPITA
Bottom	-0.57%
4th	1.51%
3rd	1.76%
2nd	1.88%
1st	2.34%

Source: Fraser Institute, *Economic Freedom of the World, 2003 Annual Report* (Vancouver, B.C.: Fraser Institute, 2003), 11.

nesses. This is exactly what happens in the United States, as we will see in more detail in Chapter 6. Numerous studies have documented the remarkable degree of upward income mobility in the United States, but to realize just how much opportunity this country offers, one need think only of the countless stories of penniless immigrants who have come to America and become affluent entrepreneurs.

BACKLASH

Capitalism's record is truly extraordinary. It has brought incredible economic opportunity to countless people, has lifted many out of poverty, has allowed consumers to be in control of the economy, and so much more. Nevertheless, the success of capitalism has always bred a certain number of malcontents who, among other things, believe that they are insufficiently rewarded by the capitalist system, are envious of others' success, have a compulsion to use politics to control other people's behavior (and their wealth), deny the reality of human inequalities, believe that personal freedom is overrated, and resent the power that ordinary consumers have over the economy. Many of these anticapitalists are ignorant of basic economics, but that does not stop them from assaulting capitalism at every opportunity. During the twentieth century an entire class of intellectuals, journalists, television executives, private foundations, and others coalesced to form what might be called the anti-industry industry. The next chapter will explore some of the sources of this anticapitalistic mentality as well as its effects on American society.

CHAPTER TWO

Anticapitalism

A nation is the more prosperous today the less it has tried to put obstacles in the way of the spirit of free enterprise and private initiative. The people of the United States are more prosperous than the inhabitants of all other countries because their government embarked later than the governments in other parts of the world upon the policy of obstructing business. Nonetheless, many people, and especially intellectuals, loathe capitalism.

—Ludwig von Mises, *The Anti-Capitalistic Mentality* (1956)

DESPITE the remarkable success of capitalism in alleviating poverty, raising living standards, expanding economic opportunity, and generally enabling scores of millions to live longer, healthier, and more peaceful lives, a large segment of the intellectual class has long been critical of it. Many intellectuals still advocate socialism even though it is well known that socialism has been economic poison everywhere it has been implemented. As Nobel laureate economist Friedrich Hayek has written:

> Socialism has never and nowhere been at first a working-class movement. It is by no means an obvious remedy for the obvious evil which the interests of that class will necessarily demand. It is a construction of theorists, deriving from certain tendencies of abstract thought with which for a long time only

the intellectuals were familiar; and it required long efforts by the intellectuals before the working classes could be persuaded to adopt it as their program.[1]

Anticapitalist ideas begin with the intellectual class but are transported to the public through what Hayek called "professional secondhand dealers in ideas." These secondhand dealers include journalists, public school teachers, ministers, priests, radio and television personalities, novelists, cartoonists, artists, columnists, editors, and many others. These people decide what opinions about capitalism reach the public, which ones are important, and how they are to be presented; the average person depends on whatever information comes through this filter.

Having been educated in a university system that is dominated by socialists, these secondhand dealers in ideas are overwhelmingly critical of capitalism and supportive of socialism and socialistic ideas. Their knee-jerk sentiment is typically to blame capitalism for all the world's ills, from poverty to pollution to inadequate health care, while urging government interventionism in the form of more regulation, taxation, and government spending.

ANTICAPITALIST INTELLECTUALS

Why are intellectuals so disposed to socialism? Hayek offered the most generous explanation: they are generally ignorant of the economic world and of economic theory. Hayek never questioned his opponents' intentions; they were guilty, in his eyes, of nothing more than egregious intellectual error. But whether they do so intentionally or unintentionally, anticapitalists offer a view of economics that is wholly inaccurate.

Perhaps the single most important reason why the intellectual class favors socialism is that it denounces the material inequality it sees as intrinsic to a capitalist economy. The socialist intellectuals' ideal is material equality—*why should some be better off financially than others?* Hayek captured how dogmatic these intellectuals are on the point of material equality when he wrote, "That a particular measure tends to bring about greater equality has come to be regarded as so strong a recommendation that little else will be considered."[2] In fact, however, these intellectuals seem interested only in whether public policies are *intended* to bring about greater material equality, for as economist Thomas Sowell has pointed out, even when government policies that are supposed to produce greater material equality turn out to do exactly the opposite, the socialist intellectual class usually either ignores the evidence or denounces those who present it.[3]

Besides, the anticapitalists fail to acknowledge that capitalism per se is not responsible for material inequality. Rather, the disparities in income and standard of living in any economy reflect human nature itself—that is, individuals pursue different paths and achieve different levels of financial reward precisely because no two people are the same in terms of ambition, aptitude, intelligence, skill, and so much more. These natural human differences are present in any kind of economy—capitalist, socialist, or anything else—and will generate material inequalities. In fact, the most socialistic countries of the world—the former communist countries of the Soviet Union and Eastern and Central Europe—were also the most inequitable: a political elite lived very well while all the ordinary citizens lived in grinding poverty. Moreover, a capitalist economy thrives because it enables all members of society to benefit from the many advances that capitalist leaders bring.

The Iron Law of Oligarchy holds that in any society a certain minority will be more able, interested, or motivated than the rest and will form what Thomas Jefferson called a "natural aristocracy." Capitalism does not attempt to block this natural aristocracy but rather allows it to flourish, and consequently allows everyone to benefit. These individuals will be the leaders in all fields of endeavor, and they will provide us with new and better products and services for lower and lower prices. They are the ones who turn luxury goods that were once the exclusive playthings of kings and millionaires into the everyday "necessities" of common working families.

The anticapitalist critiques of material inequality are also misguided because, as seen in the last chapter, capitalism is the only system that can provide the economic opportunities to seriously erode material inequalities over time. For all that anticapitalist intellectuals embrace socialism, socialist governments have always failed to effect material equality, because egalitarianism, or government-enforced material equality, is nothing less than a futile revolt against human nature. Worse, even while these intellectuals condemn the supposed evils of capitalism, they refuse to acknowledge what the twentieth century's many experiments with socialism proved: as Murray Rothbard has put it, "An egalitarian society can only hope to achieve its goals by totalitarian methods of coercion."[4]

A second reason why intellectuals tend to be enamored with socialism and government planning of economies, according to Hayek, is that they believe, falsely, that engineering techniques, which have created such great improvements in the human condition, can apply to "social engineering." For example, nearly everyone has heard: "If we can send a man to the moon, why can't we eliminate poverty [or racism, or unhappiness, or obesity, or hunger, and on and on]?" The fact is, however, that the United States has poured hundreds of billions of dollars and millions of hours into government programs that for decades have done nothing but make social problems even worse. For instance, poverty programs that pay people as long as they do not work, save their money, or marry have discouraged work, saving, and marriage, the three key ingredients in poverty reduction. It is not surprising, then, that progress against poverty in America stopped and reversed itself at precisely the moment when the federal government declared "war" on it.[5]

Government-directed social engineering fails mainly because human beings cannot be manipulated like so many mathematical symbols. Human beings are rational, thinking actors who react to changes in government policy. Thus the government's social engineering often follows the Law of Unintended Consequences. Rent-control laws, for example, are designed to help the poor by holding down the price of housing, but these laws artificially stimulate the demand for rental housing while reducing its supply, which causes housing shortages. And usually the poor suffer most from such shortages. Likewise, minimum-wage laws designed to help low-income workers force wages up above the levels set by supply and demand, which makes it uneconomical for employers to keep those low-income workers. The result is higher unemployment and more poverty.

Still, so-called intellectuals continue to advocate the fantasy of social planning or engineering.

UTOPIANISM

Intellectuals deal mainly in abstract ideas, including ideas about how to reconstruct entire societies to their liking. As such, they are predominantly utopians. Laissez-faire capitalism has little or no role in utopian planning, for such a system calls for no central planning authority (which the advising intellectual class should guide, of course). Under pure capitalism individuals constantly plan, but they do so voluntarily and in a way that best serves *their own interests, as they see them,* which are not necessarily the same as the would-be government planners' interests. This is another reason why the intellectual class is predominantly socialistic: under a regime of economic freedom and laissez-faire capitalism there is no role for intellectuals to advise to the state on how to best plan everyone else's affairs.

In the field of economics this utopianism has manifested itself in what Hayek described as "the contrast between an existing state of affairs and that one ideal of a possible future society which the socialists alone held up before the public."[6] For many years, economics students were taught that a genuinely competitive capitalist economy was one in which: (1) all businesses in an industry produced the exact same physical product; (2) every business charged exactly the same price; (3) consumers had "perfect information" (that is, were omniscient) about all available products; (4) businesses also had "perfect information" about how to manufacture their products at the minimum cost; and (5) it was cost-free to enter into or exit any industry. Of course, this "perfect competition" could never be achieved in the real world. Nevertheless, generations of American college students, beginning in the 1940s, were taught that anything short of this was evidence of "imperfect competition" or "market failure," and that the government must tax, regulate, and control capitalism to perfect it.[7] UCLA economist Harold Demsetz called this approach the "Nirvana Fallacy": when one compares real-world markets (or anything else) to a theoretically perfect world (Nirvana), then of course—indeed, by definition—the real world will appear imperfect. Such are the fantasies of the socialist intellectual class. And the economics profession is generally less utopian than other academic disciplines.

The utopian fantasies of the anticapitalist intellectual class were entertainingly catalogued by sociologist Paul Hollander in his book *Political Pilgrims: Travels of Western Intellectuals to the Soviet Union, China, and Cuba*.[8] Hollander wrote of how, beginning in the 1920s, Western anticapitalist intellectuals traveled to various communist utopias and returned home to write about how "wonderful" life was there compared with the capitalist hell of America. "Almost invariably," said Hollander, "they contrasted the defects of their own societies with the virtues of those visited."[9] More than that, these supposedly critical intellectuals somehow found the totalitarian regimes of Stalin, Mao, and Castro to be "appealing—their defects so easy to ignore," and "strikingly superior" to their own societies.[10] They were typically inclined to "give every benefit of doubt" to the communist regimes they were visiting while remaining harshly critical of the capitalist systems of their own countries, denouncing their "capitalistic greed and wastefulness," poverty, unemployment, "impoverishment of human relationships," "lack of community," "the vulgar noises of advertising," the "crudeness of commercial transactions," and countless other sins.[11] These intellectuals also complained about their dissatisfaction with American capitalism's supposed lack of spirituality, inequality of both income and political power, racism and colonialism, and "irrationality."[12]

When the first wave of anticapitalist intellectuals visited the Soviet Union in the 1920s they were "wildly enthusiastic over all they see but not always logical," wrote the American journalist William C. White.[13] American public school teachers traveled to communist Russia and came back praising its educational regimentation; health-care workers praised it as a land of health and hygiene; ministers adored the atheistic "political missionaries" in Stalin's government; and social scientists, said Hollander, "found themselves singularly at home in a society which was guided by fellow social scientists who aimed to build a rational, planned world."[14] Quakers were among the most notorious Western idolaters of totalitarian communism. One of them, D. F. Buxton, wrote of how "the Communist view of human nature seems to me far more inspired by Faith, Hope and Charity than our own. To them the prime cause of evil . . . is the poison of wealth."[15] Although the rulers of the Soviet empire lived like kings while millions of their fellow citizens lived in squalor and starvation, Buxton was of the mistaken impression that "the simple unostentatious life of Russia's rulers represents a notable advance in *real* civilization."[16] Theodore Dreiser agreed, writing of how "the rooms of Lenin in the Kremlin . . . offer perhaps a classical example of the simplicity and frugality of the present day rulers of Russia."[17]

Whenever they were confronted with the pervasive inequalities that did in fact characterize Russia's socialist paradise, American intellectuals responded with hundreds of implausible excuses for them (inequality works better under socialism; it is always for the good of society anyway; Russian inequalities, unlike inequalities in the United States, are consistent with "social justice"; and many others). In general, the intellectuals sugarcoated every negative aspect of Soviet communism. Dreiser noted that "in Moscow there is poverty" and that "there are beggars in the streets," but he proclaimed, "Lord, how picturesque! The multi-colored and voluminous rags of them!"[18]

Buxton also praised Soviet communism for its "sense of moral advance" and "the emphasis they place on the spirit of service," which had supposedly "taken to heart some of the most important maxims of the New Testament. . . . Their society is a more Christian one than ours."[19] John Dewey, one of the founders of the American public school movement, concurred, gushing that Soviet communism was "intrinsically religious" and had "the moving spirit and force of primitive Christianity."[20]

Another clergyman, Hewlett Johnson, returned from Russia to write of how American capitalism supposedly "lacks moral basis," creates a "divergence between principles and practice of Christian people, which is so damning to religion," and is responsible for an "irrational wastage of wealth, the artificially induced shortage, the poverty amidst plenty."[21] In contrast, Soviet communism was supposedly a society in which "co-operation replaces competitive chaos and a Plan succeeds the rot of disorder. . . . The elimination of the profit-motive makes room for the higher motive of service."[22]

Such economic nonsense is repeated literally verbatim by many of today's American religious leaders. Their ignorance is even more egregious than Johnson's, however, since they have the benefit of hindsight: socialism was a colossal economic and social failure, as has been amply documented. Socialism creates economic chaos, grinding poverty, and all the social pathologies that religious leaders are so concerned about. Government bureaucrats are notoriously unconcerned about providing quality "service" to their fellow man, but capitalists *must* provide such service if they are to survive economically.

Literally millions starved during the Russian famines of the 1920s and 1930s because of the inherent futility of collectivized agriculture. But Walter Duranty of the *New York Times* falsely reported to his American readers that Russian granaries "were overflowing with grain" and that the cows were "plump and contented." Contrary to all reality, George Bernard Shaw insisted that "there was not, and could not be, a food shortage in the USSR."[23] Stalin's forced collectivization in the Ukraine in 1932 caused the deaths of six million people in less than a year.[24]

Many of these intellectuals praised Soviet prisons, made excuses for Stalin's purges (that is, murder) of political opponents, and waxed eloquently about Soviet communism's "wise and caring leaders." W. E. B. Du Bois, for example, thought Stalin was a perfect gentleman who "asked for neither adulation nor vengeance. He was reasonable and conciliatory."[25]

Western intellectuals were particularly impressed because fellow intellectuals were so prominent in the Soviet government. The literary critic Edmund Wilson gushed, "There has been in our times no parallel . . . to the position of Gorky in the Soviet Union. In the past a close friend of Lenin, he is at present a kind of Commissar of Literature; and is perhaps closer to sharing the glory of Stalin than any one public man."[26] In reality, Gorky was Stalin's censor; he ensured that the government's propaganda apparatus was a more or less airtight operation. If such an office were a part of the U.S. government at the time Wilson was writing, his literary criticisms certainly would have been censored, his career ruined.

America's anticapitalist intellectuals have found a new socialist utopia in communist Cuba. Just as earlier generations of intellectuals praised the Soviet Union's government-run schools and its health and hygiene, more recent anticapitalists have lauded Cuba's education and health-care systems, among many other things. The journalist Jonathan Kozol, who has spent decades arguing that Americans should adopt the Cuban communists' government-schooling model, stated that "each of my two visits to Cuba was a pilgrimage and an adventure."[27] Scholar Saul Landau declared that "Cuba is the first purposeful society that we have had in the Western Hemisphere for many years . . . where human beings are treated as human beings."[28] The American Marxist economist Paul Baran described communist Cuba as a "paradisiac garden" where "agricultural problems would melt away" with a "gigantic" economic surplus.[29] Baran's associate, fellow Marxist Paul Sweezy, was just as effusive, saying that you come away from Cuba's communists "with your faith in the human race restored" because of their "purifying and liberating experiences."[30] The American writer Theodore Draper admitted that Cuban economic policy was "murderous, mendacious . . . brutal and arbitrary," but it should still be admired because, after all, "it is still socialist."[31] Many other American intellectuals were of the same opinion.

The anticapitalists' blind devotion to Cuba has also meant embracing the totalitarian dictator Fidel Castro. PBS executive Frank Mankiewicz interviewed Castro for the PBS audience and also wrote a book heaping praise on the dictator.[32] Norman Mailer swooned over Castro and his dictatorship, writing, "So Fidel Castro, I announce to the City of New York that you gave all of us . . . some sense that there were heroes in the world. . . . You were the first and greatest hero to appear in the world since the Second World War."[33] Many other American intellectuals described the brutal Cuban dictator as a Christ-like figure. To Marxist economist Paul Sweezy, even though Castro tortured and murdered his political opponents, including thousands of ordinary citizens, he was nevertheless "a passionate humanitarian." To Saul Landau of the Institute for Policy Studies, he was "a man who has been steeped in democracy," even though Cubans under Castro never enjoyed a single day of democracy. Senator George McGovern described Castro as some kind of genius who "responds knowledgeably on almost any subject from agricultural methods to Marxist dialectics."[34]

It is easy to understand why so many American intellectuals have idolized Cuban totalitarian communism: it snuffed out capitalism. Plus, as Hollander observed, "the position of intellectuals in Cuba was by itself among the major attractions of the regime in the eyes of the visiting intellectuals."[35]

While Cuba remains a favorite, America's anticapitalist intellectuals are constantly on the lookout for new socialist utopias. For a while they were fixated on communist Albania and Mozambique. Tom Wicker wrote in the *New York Times* that the people of Mozambique found "hope and discipline" once communists took over the government; the communists were "working toward a new society" that Wicker obviously approved of.[36]

Anticapitalist intellectuals and opinion makers loved communist China, naturally, but are less enamored of it today because capitalism is becoming more prevalent there. When Chinese communism was in its heyday under Mao, however, David Rockefeller said that he was "impressed immediately by the sense of national harmony . . . and pervasive dedication to Chairman Mao and Maoist principles.

Whatever the price of the Chinese Revolution, it has obviously succeeded not only in producing more efficient and dedicated administration, but also in fostering high morale and community of purpose. General economic and social progress is no less impressive."[37]

THE ANTICAPITALISTIC MENTALITY

In 1956 Ludwig von Mises published his classic analysis of anticapitalism, *The Anti-Capitalistic Mentality*.[38] In this monograph he catalogued various reasons why so many intellectuals (and others) harbor an anticapitalistic bias.

First on the list of reasons for anticapitalistic bias is that many people refuse to accept the reality that those who accumulate wealth in a capitalist system do so by pleasing large numbers of fellow citizens. There is such a thing as business luck, of course, but for the most part wealth can be accumulated only by pleasing consumers better than one's competitors do. Mises explained the law of "economic democracy": "Those who satisfy the wants of a smaller number of people only collect fewer votes—dollars—than those who satisfy the wants of more people. In money-making the movie star outstrips the philosopher."[39]

Many people believe that they should be judged by some absolute standard, as opposed to the dollar votes of their fellow citizens. Consequently, they are frustrated that people whom they view as frivolous or unworthy are rewarded more than they are in the capitalist marketplace. A contemporary example of this phenomenon is the bitter hatred that so many computer software engineers have publicly expressed toward Bill Gates and his Microsoft Corporation. The standard complaint is that the Windows operating system is technologically inferior to other ones (the ones invented by the complaining software engineers, of course), yet some 90 percent of computer users have the Windows system. For whatever reasons, the vast majority of consumers have chosen Windows, based on their own preferences. If *they* were convinced of the software engineers' arguments, then they would switch brands; Bill Gates would lose market share and money, and the producers of the alternative products would become richer. In a capitalist marketplace the choices of consumers matter most, even more so than the opinions of the "experts."

The "resentment over frustrated ambition," said Mises, can be pervasive: "Capitalism grants to each the opportunity to attain the most desirable position which, of course, can only be attained by a few. . . . Such is the attitude of the tramp against the man with a regular job, the factory hand against the foreman, the executive against the vice-president, the vice-president against the company's president, the man who is worth three hundred thousand dollars against the millionaire and so on."[40] The unsuccessful, lazy, and incompetent feel humiliated and often express "hate and enmity against all those who superseded them."[41] Intellectual and political demagogues take advantage of this truth and appeal to the hatred and enmity that the less successful feel toward the more successful. This is the basis of the economic class conflict on which generations of American politicians have built their careers by promising to take from "the rich" and redistribute their wealth to "the poor."

It is a natural inclination for many human beings to search for scapegoats for their own inadequacies (which we all have). Consequently, many people rationalize to themselves that those who have exceeded them financially did not do so by merit or public service but by some nefarious, unscrupulous, or illegal means. Of course, some businesspeople do get ahead by underhanded means, but such underhanded people are found not just in business but in all walks of life, including government, the clergy, and the charitable sector. The overwhelming majority of successful businesspeople succeed because they have pleased large numbers of customers.

This doesn't matter to those who seek scapegoats, however, which is why it has always been so easy for intellectual and political demagogues to demonize businesspeople. As Mises wrote, "The fool releases these feelings in slander and defamation. The more sophisticated . . . sublimate their hatred into a philosophy, the philosophy of anti-capitalism, in order to render inaudible the inner voice that tells them that their failure is entirely their own fault."[42] This attitude is pervasive among American intellectuals—those who influence public opinion—which is why there is so much anticapitalistic bias in nearly everything they say.

For decades, America's entertainment industry—particularly theater, television, and film—has demonstrated the most intense dislike of capitalism. Today, movies and television programs of all kinds have anticapitalist themes. Businesspeople are rarely, if ever, portrayed as social benefactors and are much more likely to be seen as crooks, conmen, clowns, swindlers, adulterers, and murderers. The Media Research Center in Washington, D.C., conducted a "content analysis" of several weeks of network television to analyze how businesspeople were portrayed. The researchers found that more than 90 percent of all murderers on television are businessmen, when in reality businessmen commit less than 1 percent of murders.

Mises offered an intriguing analysis of why Hollywood and Broadway are so anticapitalistic. Like all businesses in a capitalist society, movies, television, and the theater depend on consumer sovereignty. In manufacturing businesses, if a product catches on with consumers the producers can be confident that a market for their product will exist for quite a while. But with entertainment the consumer is much more fickle:

> People long for amusement because they are bored. And nothing makes them so weary as amusements with which they are already familiar. The essence of entertainment is variety. The

patrons applaud most what is new and therefore unexpected and surprising. They are capricious and unaccountable. . . . A tycoon of the stage or the screen must always fear the waywardness of the public. He awakes rich and famous one morning and may be forgotten the next day.[43]

The instability of fame and fortune, said Mises, is what makes so many entertainers and entertainment industry executives critical of capitalism. What they are really complaining about, of course, is the fact that their livelihoods depend so crucially on the dollar votes of the masses, who can indeed be capricious and unaccountable.

There is also a powerful anticapitalist bias in literature. Again, Mises offered an explanation: capitalism gives the masses exactly what it wants, and the average citizen does not enjoy the highest-caliber literature. "Trash novels" outsell serious nonfiction books by orders of magnitude; grocery-store tabloids sell far more papers than does the *Wall Street Journal*. "The tycoon of the book market is the author of fiction for the masses," observed Mises.[44] Many of the intellectuals who write sophisticated books resent the fact that their works sell far fewer copies than the latest diet book or detective mystery. They don't blame themselves, however; capitalism is supposedly responsible for their mediocre financial situation.

MERCANTILISM

The long campaign against capitalism has had profound effects. Today, most businesspeople are not even capitalists. In a free-market system, individuals and groups pursue profit by providing consumers with goods and services, and the rule of law and a code of morality protect the rights of property, contract, and association. But some people always try to operate outside the bounds of free-market capitalism by securing special favors from government. This is how the prevailing economic system operated in Europe during the seventeenth and eighteenth centuries. This system, known as "mercantilism," was an elaborate scheme of state-sponsored monopolies and protections from competition (through protectionist tariffs, for example). It was mercantilism that Adam Smith railed against in his classic defense of capitalism, *The Wealth of Nations*. As Smith astutely wrote:

> In the mercantilist system, the interest of the consumer is almost constantly sacrificed to that of the producer. In the restraints upon the importation of all foreign commodities which can come into competition with those of our own growth, or manufacture, the home-consumer is evidently sacrificed to that of the producer. It is altogether for the benefit of the latter, that the former is obligated to pay the enhancement of price which this monopoly almost always occasions.[45]

Despite Smith's emphatic and persuasive attacks on mercantilism, a strong mercantilist lobby has existed in the United States since its inception. Alexander Hamilton and his followers were the first to push for special privileges from the government, as they advocated a more centralized government that would centrally plan the economy primarily for the benefit of business interests. They advocated tariffs to protect American businesses from foreign competition, tax-funded subsidies for certain businesses ("corporate welfare"), and a central bank that could print paper money to pay for these schemes. Later, from the 1830s to the 1850s, the special business interests who advocated bringing the corrupt European mercantilist system to America supported the American Whig Party, and then they backed the Republican Party. They finally prevailed when, during the War Between the States, all of these policies were finally put into place.[46] The election of Abraham Lincoln was, among other things, the triumph of mercantilism in America. The American economy has featured what might be called creeping mercantilism ever since.

Anticapitalists of all varieties have always praised mercantilism. As Murray Rothbard wrote, government intervention–minded Keynesian economists "hail mercantilists as prefiguring their own economic insights; Marxists, constitutionally unable to distinguish between free enterprise and special privilege, hail mercantilism as a 'progressive' step in the historical development of capitalism; socialists and interventionists salute mercantilism as anticipating modern state-building and central planning."[47]

Today, many corporations support interventionist or anticapitalist policies like trade protectionism or corporate welfare because they hope to benefit from the policies at everyone else's expense. Mercantilist policies usually backfire, however, as regulations inevitably create cost burdens on the businesses that initially favored the policies. In some cases, though, large corporations with substantial cash reserves support expanded government regulation of their industries because they understand that costly regulations will harm their smaller competitors more and will deter other potential competitors from entering the business altogether. All corporations make a rhetorical stand in favor of competitive capitalism, but they too often want special privileges and protections from competition.

During the 1980s and early 1990s mercantilist policies were given a new name: "industrial policy." Neomercantilists called for "collaboration" between business, government, and unions to plan the economy. Fortunately, after a decade-long political battle at the national level, such a plan was dismissed. So-called industrial policies ultimately failed to take hold because it was widely recognized that under any such policies politically powerful businesses would inevitably be subsidized at the expense of their competitors and of taxpayers. This neomercantilist scheme also fell into disrepute because politicians with no financial stake in investments could not possibly do a good job of picking which industries to invest in. Private investors make mistakes all the time, but at least the incentives are in the right direction: wise investments (those that please consumers the most) will be rewarded with profits, whereas poor investments will be punished with losses. When politicians use tax dollars to invest in business there is no such feedback mechanism. Usually the government puts more and more money into bad investments to disguise the fact that it has once again squandered taxpayer dollars.

The government can never subsidize any one business or industry without simultaneously harming others, since the money to pay for the subsidies has to come from another part of the economy, usually through taxes. Thus, the very idea that mercantilism, corporate welfare, industrial policy, or whatever these policies might be called can stimulate overall economic prosperity is a myth. Nevertheless, businesses seeking taxpayer subsidies have worked tirelessly to try to confuse the public on this issue by manufacturing myths—for example, that government is capable of managing an entire economy, that reducing competitive pressures through protectionism is good for consumers, that politicians can leave politics aside when subsidizing selected businesses, and so on. Armed with such myths, anticapitalist business interests (mercantilists) continue to be the enemies of free-market capitalism.

In fact, even though the U.S. government did not adopt industrial policy, it has in recent decades intervened more and more in the economy, which has only stifled capitalism. The interventions have taken many forms, the most common being price and wage controls. These measures are always instituted for political reasons and almost inevitably create even greater problems than the ones they were supposed to fix.

When the government imposes a price ceiling—that is, mandates prices that are below what the free market would generate—it artificially boosts consumer demand while reducing incentives for supply, which causes shortages. To see the negative consequences of price ceilings, one need look no further than the electric power catastrophe in California that began in 2000. The state government placed price controls on electricity and at the same time (to pander to the environmental lobby) enacted regulations that effectively prohibited electric companies from generating new power. It doesn't take much more than common sense to realize that this was a sure-fire recipe for the electric power shortages that have plagued California (though the anticapitalists insist on blaming the shortages on "deregulation," even when the electric power industry is still heavily regulated).

Government-mandated price floors have the opposite effect, but, just like price ceilings, they create major problems because they interfere with the workings of the free market. When the government sets a minimum price on something, it artificially boosts supply while reducing consumer demand—a recipe for surplus. Price floors have been common in the agriculture sector since the 1920s, when U.S. politicians, in an attempt to win votes and campaign contributions from farmers, began enacting various "price-support" programs to force prices up above free-market levels. Sure enough, these programs induce farmers to produce more and consumers to cut back somewhat on their consumption. The resulting surpluses are rarely put to good use: even while some people do not have enough to eat, the farmers and the government stockpile tons and tons of grain, corn, cheese, and other commodities, much of which is simply wasted.

Minimum-wage laws have a similar effect on labor markets by artificially reducing the demand for labor on the part of employers. It doesn't make economic sense for a fast-food restaurant to pay a sixteen-year-old more than, say, $5 an hour if he or she doesn't produce at least $5 an hour in profits for the restaurant. If the minimum wage is set at $6 an hour, then the restaurant would lose $1 for every hour the teenager is employed. Since restaurants are not in business to lose money, they will not employ such teenagers. Minimum-wage laws are supposed to help low-income workers, but in fact they only lead to further unemployment.

Then, of course, the government can interfere with free-market capitalism by printing money. This monetary policy creates inflation, and the uncertainties that come with general price inflation make it difficult (even impossible, in extreme cases) for capitalists to determine whether their investments are paying off—quite simply, whether they are profiting. Price controls can similarly make it difficult to calculate profits and losses because they artificially prop up or hold down the prices of goods used in production.

In sum, government regulation sabotages the free-market pricing system in a capitalist economy. It makes us all poorer, and sometimes it leads to true economic catastrophes.

THE ANTI-INDUSTRY INDUSTRY

Because government interventionism harms the economy, it makes sense that it is driven by political considerations. The anticapitalist intellectuals and their secondhand dealers in ideas constantly call for further government regulation of the economy, and often politicians eager for votes cave in to these demands. Consequently, the most politically active anticapitalists can exert extraordinary influence over the economy.

Consider the influence of the so-called environmentalists. Environmentalists are not conservationists, who devote time and money to improving fish and wildlife habitats; planting trees; cleaning up parks, streams, and neighborhoods; and doing much else. Rather, the environmental movement—which is composed of intellectuals, journalists, think-tank "policy wonks," government bureaucrats, politicians, lobbyists, and others—try to use politics to block the production of goods and services.

Environmentalists claim that the world has a finite amount of natural resources and that more production (that is, more capitalism) will use up those resources. They usually predict cataclysmic consequences, based on false projections that we're running out of clean air, water, forests, minerals, or anything else. Hence, for decades the environmental movement has waged political campaigns against all forms of energy: nuclear, coal, hydroelectric, natural gas, petroleum. Energy is the lifeblood of industrial capitalism, and the environmental movement obviously believes that if it can use politics to deprive industry of energy, it can effectively destroy much of that industry and move society in the direction of some kind of environmentalist utopia. In truth, if this movement were to succeed, society would look more like a stone age civilization than utopia.

But the fundamental premise on which environmentalism is based is mistaken. Capitalism does not deplete a finite amount of resources; human intelligence in a capitalist economy has always been the key to creating *economically useable* natural resources. As economist George Reisman explains, in a capitalist society

> large numbers of the most intelligent people devote their lives to science, technology, and business. All are highly motivated to increase the supply of economically useable natural resources by the prospect of earning a personal fortune for every significant success they achieve in this regard. No greater guarantee of mankind's ability to enjoy a growing supply of natural resources could be found.[48]

Unfortunately, says Reisman, environmentalists have "no conception of the role of human intelligence in the creation of economically useable natural resources" and they confuse "the present supply with all the natural resources present in nature." Thus they "naively believe that every act of production that consumes natural resources is an act of impoverishment, using up an allegedly priceless, irreplaceable treasure of nature. On this basis, they conclude that the pursuit of self-interest by individuals under economic freedom leads to the wanton consumption of mankind's irreplaceable heritage, with no regard for the needs of future generations."[49]

This is why environmentalists advocate government intervention designed to conserve natural resources by blocking economic development, whether it is in the form of regulatory moratoria on home building in an area, or on drilling for oil in Alaska or in the ocean, or on the building of dams, or on the expansion of manufacturing industry. It is also why the environmental movement has come up with an endless stream of false claims about catastrophes that will supposedly befall us unless we stifle industrial production—from acid rain, to the hole in the ozone layer, to global cooling (popular in the 1970s), to global warming, to numerous cancer scares.

In reality, capitalism has built-in incentives to *conserve* natural resources, as discussed in Chapter 1. Everyone agrees that capitalists seek to maximize their profits, and basic economics teaches that minimizing costs is an important means of maximizing profits. One way of minimizing costs is to figure out how to manufacture a product with the least possible resources. In the telecommunications industry, for example, the developed countries of the world have gone from using relatively expensive copper wire, to extremely inexpensive sand (silicon chips), to even less expensive satellite signals. Enormous natural resources (copper) have been conserved not because of environmental sensitivity but because of profit seeking in a competitive, capitalist economy. Thousands of similar examples could be cited, though environmentalists ignore these.

The environmental movement also ignores the basic economic

truth that private property provides the right incentives for conservation. When people own their own home, lake, forest, whatever, they tend to take better care of that property. Pride of ownership is one factor, but the financial motivations are also powerful: the better one takes care of one's property, the more valuable that property is. When government owns any property, individuals have no incentive to see to that property's maintenance. Still, instead of fighting for the enforcement and protection of property rights, environmentalists advocate *more* government ownership of resources, which only leads to further environmental degradation.

The environmentalists' perspective is so backward that they don't push for sound liability laws, which provide businesses and individuals with powerful incentives to avoid damaging the environment. Liability laws, an important part of any capitalist economy, can hold a person or group accountable for harming others by dumping refuse or polluting the air or water, for example.

Not only do environmentalists ignore the positive environmental record of capitalism, but they also fail to look at what happened to the environment in the former communist countries of the Soviet Union and Eastern Europe, where profit seeking was outlawed for decades and where the government controlled almost all natural resources. According to the environmentalists' logic, one would expect these countries to have been environmentally pristine. But in reality, after the fall of communism in the late 1980s the world learned of some of the worst environmental disasters imaginable— rivers so polluted that they caught on fire; forests turned into deserts; soil so polluted with chemical fertilizers that nothing would grow; floating islands of untreated sewage a mile long and three miles wide in the Soviet Union's Lake Baikal; dangerously polluted air; sinkholes the size of football stadiums caused by overmining in coal regions; and worse. Under communism, these resources belonged to the state; in other words, they belonged to *no one,* which is why they were exploited so ruthlessly. In the case of Soviet deforestation, for example, each household had an incentive to chop down as many trees as possible before everyone else did, so as to not risk being caught without sufficient fuel for fires during the long Russian winters.

Obviously, despite the environmentalists' mantra that the pursuit of profit is the root cause of pollution problems, this was not the problem in the communist world. Indeed, the pursuit of profit is perfectly compatible with environmental conservation in a regime of private property and sound liability law—that is, under free-market capitalism. Socialism destroys the environment just as it destroys economic opportunity and so much else.

SETTING THE RECORD STRAIGHT

Environmentalists are just a small part of what has become a massive anticapitalist movement. But examining their claims against the actual record is instructive, for it offers a clear example of how so many of the anticapitalists' arguments are utterly false. Everywhere we hear and read assaults on capitalism, and the false notions peddled by anticapitalist intellectuals and their supporters can have devastating consequences for American society. To further their case that the government should take an ever more active role in directing the American economy, the anticapitalists have foisted on the American people a number of myths about capitalism's role in this country's history. Many of their bizarre claims have, unfortunately, become an accepted part of the history of our country. It is time to debunk these myths.

CHAPTER THREE

How Capitalism Saved the Pilgrims

The Pilgrims had encountered what is called the free-rider problem [which] is difficult to solve without dividing property into individual or family-sized units. And this is the course of action that William Bradford wisely took.

—Tom Bethell, *The Noblest Triumph* (1998)

WHEN THE first settlers came to America in the early seventeenth century, the word *capitalism* had not yet been coined. But the most important ingredient of capitalism—private property—was responsible for their very survival, and indeed for the creation of America. As Tom Bethell explains in *The Noblest Triumph: Property and Prosperity Through the Ages*, the American settlers originally adopted communal ownership of land and property, and as a result most of them starved to death or died of disease—a problem endured in later centuries by virtually every communist country that adopted collectivized agriculture.[1]

The first American settlers arrived in Jamestown in May of 1607. There, in the Virginia Tidewater region, they found incredibly fertile soil and a cornucopia of seafood, wild game such as deer and turkey, and fruits of all kind. Nevertheless, within six months, all but 38 of the original 104 Jamestown settlers were dead, most having succumbed to famine.[2]

Two years later, the Virginia Company sent 500 more "recruits" to settle in Virginia, and within six months a staggering 440 were dead by starvation and disease. This was appropriately known as the "starving time," which one eyewitness described as follows (in old English): "So great was our famine, that a Savage we slew and buried, the poorer sorte took him up againe and eat him; and so did divers one another boyled and stewed with roots and herbs."[3] This man understood the crux of the problem when he remarked on the irony of such massive starvation occurring amidst such plenty—game, fish, fruits, nuts, and so forth. The cause of the starvation, he said, was "want of providence, industrie and government, and not the barennnesse and defect of the Countrie, as is generally supposed."[4]

How could there be a lack of "industrie"? After all, the Virginia Company had not chosen a group of indolent and lazy people to settle the Virginia colony. The problem was that all of the men were indentured servants who had no financial stake in the fruits of their own labor. For seven years, all that they produced was to go into a common pool to be used, supposedly, to support the colony and to generate profits for the Virginia Company. Working harder or longer was of no benefit to them, and they responded as anyone would, by shirking. Having been given free passage to the new world, these settlers were supposed to compensate the Virginia Company through their labor, so they were effectively reneging on their contracts.

Bethell points out that scholars have long recognized the link between the workers' lack of effort and the absence of property rights among the early American settlers. In the late nineteenth century, for example, historian Philip A. Bruce wrote of the Jamestown colonists: "The settlers did not have even a modified interest in the soil. . . . Everything produced by them went into the store, in which they had no proprietorship."[5] As a result, Bruce wrote, the men idled over their tasks or refused to work altogether. Even men who were generally known to be among the most energetic by nature were derelict. The absence of property rights—and of the work/reward nexus that such rights create—completely destroyed the work ethic of the settlers.

Economic historians Gary Walton and Hugh Rockoff aptly describe how such indolence can occur when workers have no property rights:

> Consider 10 workers, who share ownership of the land and who collectively produce 100 bushels of corn, averaging 10 bushels each for consumption. Suppose that one worker begins to shirk and cuts his labor effort in half, reducing output by 5. The shirker's consumption, like the other workers', is now 9.5 (95/10) bushels thanks to the shared arrangement. Though his effort has fallen 50 percent, his consumption falls only 5 percent. The shirker is free riding on the labors of others. The incentive for each worker, in fact, is to free ride, and this lowers the total effort and total output.[6]

In 1611, the British government sent Sir Thomas Dale to serve as the "high marshal" of the Virginia colony. Dale noted that although most of the settlers had starved to death, the remaining ones were spending much of their time playing games in the streets and he immediately identified the problem: the system of communal ownership. He determined, therefore, that each man in the colony would be given three acres of land and be required to work no more than one month per year, and not at planting or harvest time, to contribute to the treasury of the colony. The farmers would be required to pay the colony a lump-sum tax of two and a half barrels of corn.[7]

Private property was thus put into place, and the colony immediately began to prosper. There was no more free riding, for each individual himself bore the full consequences of any reductions in output. At the same time, the individual had an incentive to *increase* his effort because he directly benefited from his own labor. As historian Mathew Page Andrews writes, "As soon as the settlers were thrown upon their own resources, and each freeman had acquired the right of owning property, the colonists quickly developed what became the distinguishing characteristic of Americans—an aptitude for all kinds of craftsmanship coupled with an innate genius for experimentation and invention."[8]

The new system produced other benefits as well. The Jamestown colonists had originally implored the Indians to sell them corn, but the Indians looked down on the settlers because they were barely capable of growing corn, thanks to their communistic economic system. After the introduction of private property and the resulting transformation, however, the Indians began coming to the colonists to acquire corn in return for furs and other items. That is, the colonists and the Indians began to engage in peaceful market exchange based on the division of labor. The mutual advantages of such a system are always conducive to peace as well as prosperity, as many of the colonists realized, for it makes little sense to make war on one's neighbor if one can prosper by trading.

Sir Thomas Dale's decision to give small three-acre plots of land to the Jamestown settlers worked so well that the private property system was soon expanded. As Walton and Rockoff explain:

As private landholdings replaced common ownership, work incentives improved; the full return for individual effort became a reality, superseding output sharing arrangements. In 1614, private landholdings of three acres were allowed. A second and more significant step toward private property came in 1618 with the establishment of the headright system. Under this system, any settler who paid his own way to Virginia was given 50 acres and another 50 acres for anyone else whose transportation he paid. In 1623—only 16 years after the first

Jamestown settlers had arrived—all landholdings were converted to private ownership.[9]

It was a remarkable turnaround, one that the settlers owed to the institution of a capitalist system.

"GOD IN HIS WISDOM SAW ANOTHER COURSE FITTER FOR THEM"

Jamestown was financed by the British aristocracy (who lost the equivalent of some $20 million in today's dollars), but the other original American colony, in Plymouth, Massachusetts, was largely a product of individual adventurers and investors who were not aristocrats. They knew about the debacle at Jamestown in the early years, but they did not immediately make the connection between the starving time and collectivized farming. The investors in the *Mayflower,* which arrived at Cape Cod in November of 1620, were taking a huge financial risk, since the Jamestown investors had lost so much of their investment. Unfortunately, they made the same mistake that the Virginia Company had at Jamestown: they established collective land ownership. As Tom Bethell has written, the *Mayflower* investors must have

> worried that if the Pilgrims—3,000 miles away and beyond the reach of supervision—owned their own houses and plots, the investors would find it difficult to collect their due. How could they be sure that the faraway colonists would spend their days working for the company if they were allowed to become private owners? With such an arrangement rational colonists would work little on "company time," but would reserve their best efforts for their own gardens and houses. . . . Only by insisting that all accumulated wealth was to be "common

wealth," or placed in a common pool, could the investors feel reassured that the colonists would be working to benefit everyone, including themselves.[10]

Thus the investors in the *Mayflower* wrongly assumed that common property ownership would be the most profitable arrangement, when in reality it was—and always has been—poisonous to profit making. (Some have argued that the Pilgrims adopted communal land ownership for religious reasons, but this is not so: it was purely a profit-driven decision, wrongheaded as it was.)

About half of the 101 people who arrived on Cape Cod in November of 1620 were dead within a few months. Over the next three years another 100 settlers arrived from England, but they were barely able to feed themselves. They ate fish and game but had no bread. As William Bradford, the governor of Plymouth Colony, wrote in his classic *Of Plymouth Plantation*, the Pilgrims of Massachusetts were so destitute that

> many sold away their clothes and bed coverings [to the Indians]; others (so base were they) became servants to the Indians, and would cut them wood and fetch them water for a capful of corn; others fell to plain stealing, both night and day, from the Indians. . . . In the end, they came to that misery that some starved and died with cold and hunger. One in gathering shellfish was so weak as he stuck fast in the mud and was found dead in the place.[11]

The chief *Mayflower* investor, London iron maker Thomas Weston, arrived in the colony disguised as a blacksmith to examine firsthand "the ruin and dissolution of his colony."[12] But Bradford was soon to solve the problems in Massachusetts in the same way that Sir Thomas Dale had in Jamestown. As Bradford explained in his now-famous passage on private property in *Of Plymouth Plantation,* after "much debate of things" it was decided that the Pilgrims

> should set corn every man for his own particular, and in that regard trust to themselves; in all other things to go on in the general way as before. And so assigned to every family a parcel of land, for present use . . . and ranged all boys and youth under some family. This had very good success, for it made all hands very industrious, so as much more corn was planted than otherwise would have been by any means the Governor or any other could use, and saved him a great deal of trouble, and gave far better content. The women now went willingly into the field, and took their little ones with them to set corn; which before would allege weakness and inability; whom to have compelled would have been thought great tyranny and oppression.[13]

Setting "every man for his own particular" meant establishing private plots of land. Immediately, those who had been lazy and indolent became "very industrious," so much so that women who had previously pleaded frailty worked long and hard—once they saw how they and their families could benefit from such hard work.

Bradford went on to blame the disastrous policy of collectivism on "that conceit of Plato's"—the Greek philosopher's advocacy of collective ownership of land, an idea that Aristotle had refuted. Those who mistakenly believed that communal property could make people "happy and flourishing," wrote Bradford, deluded themselves into thinking they were "wiser than God."[14] He fully understood how the absence of property rights destroyed the work incentive:

> For the young men, that were most able and fit for labour and service, did repine that they should spend their time and

strength to work for other men's wives and children without any recompense. The strong, or man of parts, had no more division of victuals and clothes than he that was weak and not able to do a quarter the other could; this was thought injustice. . . . And for men's wives to be commanded to do service for other men, as dressing their meat, washing their clothes, etc., they deemed it a kind of slavery, neither could many husbands brook it.[15]

Communal land ownership certainly caused problems for the Pilgrims, but, Bradford noted, "God in His wisdom saw another course fitter for them"—and that course was private property.[16] The "common course" was abandoned. By 1650 privately owned farms were predominant in New England.

Some have argued that the Pilgrims were exploited by British capitalists such as Thomas Weston,[17] but these critics simply do not understand (or at least do not acknowledge) that the true conflict was not between the colonists and the investors but among the colonists themselves. Under communistic land ownership each worker attempts to exploit his fellow workers through free riding. This was the problem that initially plagued the Pilgrims, just as it had plagued the Jamestown settlers; only a capitalist system saved the suffering American settlers.

THE KEY TO THE COLONISTS' SUCCESS

Securing property rights not only saved those fledgling settlements but also made it possible for other colonies to flourish. The American colonies had economic freedom—secure property rights and only minor taxation—and as a result they thrived economically. This economic freedom allowed the colonists to harness America's abundant natural resources and take advantage of its fertile soil in a way that the earliest settlers had been unable to in their communal arrangements.

Each region recognized and made the most of its comparative advantages. In New England, for example, the settlers became fur trappers, farmers, and most of all fishermen. Once fishermen devised means for preserving cod and mackerel with salt and exporting it to Europe, commercial fishing became a major industry. In fact, by the time of the Revolution of 1776, fish comprised 90 percent of the exports to Europe from Massachusetts and 10 percent of all American exports.[18] New Englanders also developed a new industry—whaling—and whale oil would become the chief source of home lighting for the next century. They became master shipbuilders, as well, and by 1776 New England had the third largest maritime fleet in the entire world and was building ships for England.[19] The expansion of the American shipbuilding industry opened up new and bigger markets for myriad American merchants, entrepreneurs, artisans, and farmers. Europe became a key market, but the development of the American merchant marine also enabled a more vigorous trade among the colonies themselves.

While most colonists in New England engaged in subsistence farming because the land was only marginally fertile, farming was critical to the economies in other regions. The southern colonies excelled at growing such staples as cotton, rice, wheat and other grains, indigo, corn, and especially tobacco. They also raised prodigious amounts of livestock for consumption and exportation to other colonies. The "middle states" had a comparative advantage in the growing of wheat and other grains, such as rye, oats, and barley. Farmers from all regions also became craftsmen and artisans who manufactured their own farm implements and sold them on the free market as well. Clothing, shoes, and other items were also manufactured by America's growing merchant class.

The American colonies thrived, in short, because of a burst of entrepreneurship. Economic historians Jeremy Atack and Peter Passell sum up what such entrepreneurship had produced over the first century and a half of America's existence:

> The American economy was at least ten times larger [in 1775] than it had been in 1690 and a hundred times larger than in the 1630s. Moreover, the colonists in 1775 enjoyed a measurably higher material standard of living than their grandparents and great grandparents. A per capita income averaging about $60—equivalent to perhaps $750 or so today—made them among the richest in the world at the time.[20]

In addition, many Americans were also able to accumulate wealth. The average merchant in 1774 was worth approximately 497 British pounds (or about $2,500 in 1994 dollars), while the average farmer was worth 410 British pounds (or about $2,100 in 1994 dollars).[21] As Atack and Passell point out, these figures indicate that Americans were quite well off compared with others of that era; some colonists had even accumulated enough wealth to be millionaires by today's standards.

Americans were also taller, on average, than their British counterparts, a measure of their success in overcoming dietary deficiencies. They had gone from starvation to an even healthier diet than was enjoyed by those who had stayed behind in England.

But the American colonists were becoming increasingly concerned that their prosperity was being threatened by the British government, particularly by its growing attempts to impose mercantilism on the colonies. As we will see in the next chapter, the American Revolution was, to a very large extent, a capitalist revolution.

CHAPTER FOUR

America's Capitalist Revolt

From the time when the British tried to tax us in 1764, to the adoption of the income tax amendment in 1913, our combative anti-tax character led from one rebellion to another.

—Charles Adams, *Those Dirty Rotten Taxes* (1998)

A MERICANS WHO have studied the Revolution of 1776 are aware that it was a revolution against the tyranny of King George III of Britain, who was harshly criticized in the Declaration of Independence as the perpetrator of a "train of abuses." "The history of the present King of Great Britain," Thomas Jefferson wrote in the Declaration, "is a history of repeated injuries and usurpations, all having in direct object the establishment of an absolute Tyranny over these States." Jefferson denounced the king for prohibiting consent of the governed when it came to the colonists, for obstructing justice, for depriving many colonists of trial by jury, for conscripting them into his armies "to become the executioners of their friends and brethren," and for essentially establishing arbitrary government, or dictatorship. The colonists were promised the rights of Englishmen, and they believed they were being denied those rights.

To be sure, economic issues were a major concern for the Americans, as the Declaration of Independence reveals. It is telling that among the many complaints listed in the Declaration were a number of important *economic* grievances. Complaining of the king's tax collectors, Jefferson wrote, "He has erected a multitude of New Offices, and sent hither swarms of Officers to harass our People, and eat out their substance." The Declaration also condemned the king for his protectionist trade policy toward the colonies—"For cutting off our Trade with all parts of the world." And of course, the king was denounced "For imposing taxes on us without our Consent."

Even beyond these specific economic grievances, however, economics proved central to setting the American Revolution in motion. The tyranny against which the colonists revolted had come about because the king had wanted to forcefully impose British mercantilism on the colonies. As the colonists resisted these attempts, the British government instituted more and more stringent measures to bring the Americans into compliance. The American Revolution was, at base, an antimercantilist—and thus procapitalist—revolution.

SMOTHERING THE COLONIAL ECONOMY

As discussed in Chapter 2, the main purpose of mercantilism is to employ economic policy in a way that will aggrandize the state, not to serve consumers. Thus, British mercantilism involved high tariffs and import quotas or prohibitions to "protect" domestic industry, with the side effect of limiting the outflow of gold and silver. Mercantilists believed that wealth was created not by entrepreneurship and trade but by the accumulation of precious metals like gold or silver. The British, seeing how the Spanish empire had long been financed by its discoveries of gold, equated gold with political and military power.

The British government looked to the American colonies merely to enrich the empire with their plentiful resources. While they certainly hoped to discover gold or silver in the colonies, the British also knew that anything the colonies provided—timber, sugar, tobacco, and much more—would not have to be purchased from foreign countries in exchange for gold or silver.[1] The colonies could also serve as a market for British-made goods that were shut out of other countries because of the retaliatory trade wars that British protectionism inevitably spawned. The idea was that if, say, the French responded to British import restrictions by prohibiting the importation of certain British-made goods into France, these goods could be dumped on the American colonists.

Beginning in the eighteenth century, then, the British government tried to rein in the Americans' trade to preserve the colonies as a depot for the empire. One of the first mercantilist laws imposed on the colonists was the Molasses Act of 1733, which placed a high tariff on imports of molasses from the French West Indies.[2] The act was not very effective, however, because of American ingenuity in the smuggling trade. Indeed, the most famous signatory of the Declaration of Independence, John Hancock, was a renowned smuggler. Adam Smith, the father of modern economics, praised smugglers like Hancock as popular heroes for defying mercantilist restrictions on trade and providing consumers with cheaper goods.

A series of laws known as the Navigation Acts went a long way toward imposing British mercantilism on America; these laws were an important cause of the Revolution. To protect the British shipping industry from competition, the Navigation Acts prohibited any ships built outside the British Empire from engaging in trade with the colonies; ships involved in colonial trade were also required to employ a crew consisting of at least three-fourths British subjects.[3]

A second aspect of the Navigation Acts was a long and constantly changing list of "enumerated goods" produced in the American colonies (e.g., sugar, tobacco, indigo, furs) that could be shipped only to England. Even if the goods were traded elsewhere in Europe, they had to go to England first and then be reshipped. This made shipping more costly to the colonists, and less profitable as well. On the other hand, it was an indirect subsidy to the British shipbuilding, shipping, and port industries at the colonists' expense. An entire warehousing industry sprang up in England to store goods shipped from the colonies before they were reshipped. The owners of these businesses soon became powerful supporters of the laws from which they handsomely benefited at the expense of the American colonists (and of the ultimate consumers of goods shipped from the colonies).[4]

In an attempt to limit smuggling, the British government also placed restrictions on imports into the colonies such that all "enumerated imports" were required to go to England first, be placed on British ships (where a stiff tariff was imposed), and then finally be shipped to the colonies. This scheme obviously benefited British shipping interests, and it provided additional tariff revenue to the British government while increasing the cost of imported goods to the colonists.

Finally, the Navigation Acts entailed a byzantine bureaucratic system of regulations and subsidies. For example, the colonies were prohibited from exporting such things as textiles and fur hats, even from one colony to another. A citizen of Massachusetts, for example, was breaking the law if he sold a fur hat to a neighbor over the border in Rhode Island.

As the Declaration would later state, "swarms" of bureaucrats were employed to enforce such measures, which must have been a constant annoyance to the colonists. In 1750 England established the Council of Trade, managed by British trading companies, to "oversee" the implementation of mercantilism in the colonies. While certain colonists benefited from Britain's mercantilist policies—for example, government subsidies allowed the indigo industry to flourish in South Carolina, and the Navigation Acts protected the New England shipbuilding industry from competition—many others were harmed economically. And the constant meddling in American merchants' day-to-day affairs began to build up resentment and animosity toward Britain.[5] The degree of mercantilist meddling in the colonies increased quite significantly with the end of the Seven Years War in Europe in 1763. Though Britain had been victorious in its war with France, it was left with a huge war debt and a vast empire that was becoming increasingly costly to police. More and more, the British viewed the American colonies as mere subject provinces waiting to be economically exploited. The Navigation Acts and other mercantilist regulations were enforced with a renewed vigor, which generated even greater animosity toward the British government. In addition, a series of new tax-raising measures were imposed on the Americans not for their benefit (that is, to finance their protection from foreign invaders through the presence of the British army and navy) but to subsidize the empire and aggrandize the British state.

In 1764 the British government imposed the Sugar Act, which levied higher taxes on sugar imports. Like all import taxes, the Sugar Act led to more smuggling, and in response the British sent even more bureaucrats to enforce the act and instituted a series of regulations to help with this enforcement. British enforcers could board all vessels, large and small, and confiscate the entire vessel and its cargo if it was determined to have run afoul of the new tax law.[6] Pro-British "Kangaroo courts" were established in Halifax, Nova Scotia, to deny the accused a fair trial, and informers were given one-third of the confiscated goods. In other words, the Sugar Act created a war-on-drugs-style bureaucracy with powers to confiscate private property on the mere suspicion of committing the "grievous" offense of not paying enough sugar tax. And, like the modern war on drugs, it relied heavily on paid informants, many of whom were probably sugar smugglers themselves who informed on their competitors to get rid of them. Thus, the Sugar Act was an attack on freedom of commerce.

Even more controversial was the Stamp Act of 1765, which affected Americans at nearly every step of their lives. The act required a government stamp to be placed on every paper transaction in the colonies—marriage licenses, property titles, and so forth; to purchase the stamp, Americans had to pay a tax to the British. Americans thus found themselves paying a very visible tax (as opposed to a hidden tax, such as an import tariff). The stamp tax was probably more of an annoyance than a serious financial burden, but the American colonists also realized that the king's attitude toward them had changed. If he could impose a tax such as this, where would it all end? What other plans did he have for further arbitrary taxation? Many of them viewed the stamp tax as nothing less than legalized theft. Colonial state legislatures held emergency sessions to denounce the Stamp Act, and the tax led to numerous town meetings and protests, and even mob violence.[7] Leading many of the protests were merchants—that is, the growing American capitalist class, which could not abide such assaults on its freedom of commerce.

The first American continental congress was formed in direct response to the Stamp Act. The Stamp Act Congress coined the phrase "no taxation without representation" and expressed such outrage over the precedent the tax established that the British Parliament was pressured to repeal the act in 1766.[8]

The Townshend Acts of 1767 came on the heels of the abolition of the hated Stamp Act and imposed a series of new import tariffs on goods imported from England. Many Americans saw this as an underhanded means of reinstituting the Stamp Act taxes in slightly different form. The acts had a "quartering" provision, which required colonists to "support British troops" in America.[9]

Once again, American merchants led the protests, in this case by boycotting British goods. The boycotts apparently had enough of an effect that they bankrupted a number of British businesses and caused unemployment in England to rise. The British government was forced to repeal the Townshend Acts.

In 1773 the British government yet again pressed for tax increases on the colonists. This time it was the Tea Act, which imposed higher tariffs on tea and promised to increase the policing of tea smuggling (some 750,000 pounds of tea were being smuggled annually).[10] In other words, more British bureaucrats were on the way to harass John Hancock and his fellow smugglers, who were the backbone of the growing American entrepreneurial class. The Tea Act was a direct assault on this class, for it exempted the East India Company from the tariff and gave grants of monopoly to distribute the cheaper East India Company tea to "loyal British merchants" in the colonies.[11]

The American tea merchants believed that this tax would ruin them economically, so on December 16, 1773, a group of merchants including Paul Revere orchestrated the famous Boston Tea Party, in which they dressed as Indians and dumped tons of tea into Boston Harbor. Though merchants again led the protests against the British, they were eventually joined, as business historian Larry Schweikart writes, by "Virginia planters, Pennsylvania farmers, Connecticut woodsmen, and New England seafarers," who all viewed British mercantilism as a threat to their livelihoods.[12]

Thus it was that in 1776, when Jefferson wrote the Declaration of Independence, so many of the acts of tyranny that King George III was accused of had as their objective the implementation of British mercantilism in the colonies. This point tends to get lost if one merely familiarizes oneself with the Declaration without understanding the *economic* context within which it was written. The charge of depriving the colonists of consent of the governed was primarily a protest of taxation without consent.

A NEW NATION PROTECTS ECONOMIC LIBERTIES

After fighting a revolution at least in part because the king of England had tried to exploit the colonists economically through mercantilism, the Revolutionary generation adopted a government that would safeguard economic liberty. That is, the American founders wanted to protect capitalism (though the word was not even coined at that time). Several key parts of the Constitution, adopted in 1789, provided important safeguards. The Contract Clause, for example, prohibited any laws abridging freedom of contract ("No state shall . . . pass any . . . law impairing the Obligation of Contracts"). Though it is no longer very well enforced—minimum-wage laws, rent control laws, virtually all of employment law, antitrust regulation, and the American regulatory state in general all violate the clause—this perversion of the law took many decades to accomplish. For the founders, this freedom was essential, for they understood that property rights would not be secure without some mechanism to enforce the sanctity of contracts. John Adams's views were typical of the founding generation's: "The moment the idea is admitted into society, that property is not as sacred as the laws of God and that there is not a force of law and public justice to protect it, anarchy and tyranny commence."[13]

In addition, the Commerce Clause outlawed protectionist tariffs in interstate commerce, thereby making the country a free-trade zone, and the Constitution also prohibited export taxes to encourage international commerce. The Fifth Amendment's Due Process Clause ("No person . . . shall be deprived of life, liberty or property, without due process of law") provided a degree of protection for property rights, as well, as it defended private property against arbitrary governmental usurpations.

According to the Constitution, taxes are supposed to be uniform ("all Duties, Imposts and Excises shall be uniform throughout the United States") and devoted only to things that promote "the general welfare"—not the welfare of special-interest groups, as is the case today. Discriminatory taxation was outlawed because, as James Madison wrote in his famous *Federalist* #10 essay, the main purpose of the Constitution was to limit "the violence of faction," by which he meant special-interest groups. If government were to become dominated by special interests (as with mercantilism), legislation would be the result of the power of the majority and would not serve the public interest or justice. As political philosopher Gottfried Dietze has written, "*The Federalist* is a classic treatise on federalism and free government [and] is in a large measure concerned with economic rights."[14] That is, the *Federalist Papers*, which made the case for the Constitution, were largely concerned with establishing a system of government that would protect economic liberties from the encroachments of mercantilism.

This kind of thinking is why the states, which created the federal government as their agent, delegated so precious few powers to it. As delineated in Article I, Section 8, Congress is only given the power to: borrow money; regulate commerce with foreign nations; establish rules for naturalization; coin money and fix standards of weights and measures; punish counterfeiting; establish a post office; promote science with patents; establish the lower courts; punish pirates; declare war; raise and support armies, but only for a term of two years; provide a navy; regulate naval and land forces; call forth the militia to suppress insurrections and invasions; discipline and organize the militia; and administer the nation's capital. While government has certain constitutional functions, they are extremely limited. (Indeed, it would be impossible to construct a logical argument that these powers permit the massive welfare and regulatory state that exists today in America, but how that came about is a story for another time and place.) The reason the founders limited the role of government was that they were aware of the mischief the state could perpetrate if property and contract rights were not reasonably secure. They understood how such a system plagued Europe, and of course they had suffered from it themselves during the end of the colonial era.

Constitutional scholars have long noticed that the Constitution possesses strong property rights protections. Historian Charles Beard went so far as to posit a conspiracy on the part of the founders, arguing that they created the Constitution to protect their own property holdings, which in some cases were substantial. They were supposedly protecting only their own "vested interests," not the general welfare.[15] Beard's argument was strongly challenged—if not debunked—by historian Forrest McDonald,[16] but even if Beard was correct, there is not necessarily any conflict or incongruity here. If the founders were acting in their own self-interest by placing strong property rights protections in the Constitution, so what? By doing so they benefited *all* businesspeople and property owners by making *their* property secure as well. And as discussed in Chapter 1, secure property rights are an essential ingredient to a successful capitalist economy. If the founders were merely acting in their own vested interests in protecting property rights in the Constitution, then that should be considered a blessing to all future generations of Americans.

STATE SOVEREIGNTY VERSUS MERCANTILISM

Not only did the states delegate relatively few powers to the central government while retaining ultimate sovereignty for themselves (repeatedly referring to themselves as "free and sovereign states" in the founding documents), but they explicitly reserved all other powers to the people, or the states, in the Tenth Amendment to the Constitution. The Tenth Amendment was an integral part of what was known as the system of "dual sovereignty." Under this system, the central government was given certain powers to check the tyrannical proclivities of the states (politicians are politicians, no matter what level of government they serve in), and at the same time the states were given equivalent powers to check oppressions by the federal government. As Gottfried Dietze has explained, "Federalism, instituted to enable the federal government to check oppressions by the governments of the states, and vice versa, appears to be a supreme principle of the Constitution."[17]

But not all founders wanted to check the power of the federal government. A group of politically ambitious men wanted a strong central government that could institute the corrupt British mercantilist system in America, knowing that such a system would inevitably provide substantial political power to those who governed it. Alexander Hamilton was the best-known advocate of this viewpoint, as he favored the mercantilist policies of protectionist tariffs, taxpayer subsidies for private road- and canal-building corporations, and a government-run monetary system that could finance such patronage.

Hamilton played a hand in essentially destroying his own Federalist Party by using his influence as secretary of the treasury to have Congress enact several extremely unpopular tax increases. First there was the 25 percent tax on whiskey, which led to the Whiskey Rebellion in Pennsylvania and was considered by many Americans to be a betrayal of the Revolution. Then came a national property tax, which led to the Fries rebellion. Both rebellions had to be put down by a federal army. In an attempt to repulse such antitax protests, the Federalist Party under President John Adams enacted the Alien and Sedition Acts, which made it a criminal act for anyone "to oppose any measure or measures of the government of the United States." Stiff fines and prison sentences awaited anyone who would write or publish "scandalous" or "malicious" articles in opposition to the government. But only members of Thomas Jefferson's Republican Party were ever prosecuted under the Alien and Sedition Acts, which were written so as to expire on the very day that President Adams left office.

The Alien and Sedition Acts have long been recognized as an affront to free speech, but it is important to recognize that one of their main purposes was to serve the Federalist Party's interventionist economic agenda. Jefferson responded to the acts with his Kentucky Resolve of 1798, which said:

> Resolved, that the several States composing the United States of America are not united on the principle of unlimited submission to their General Government; but that by compact under the style and title of a Constitution for the United States and of Amendments thereto, they constituted a General Government for special purposes, delegated to that government definite powers reserving each State to itself, the residuary mass of right to their own self government; and that whensoever the General Government assumes undelegated powers, its acts are unauthoritative, void, and of no force.

Applying the principle of dual sovereignty that was such an important part of the *Federalist Papers,* Jefferson created the principles of state interposition and nullification: the states and the people reserved the right to judge for themselves whether particular acts of the central government were constitutional or not. (James Madison's Virginia Resolve of 1798 served the same purpose.)

In this instance, it was the Alien and Sedition Acts that were at issue. In the future, nullification, interposition, and even the threat of secession would be used to fend off repeated attempts to introduce mercantilism to America and thereby effectively overturn an important part of the American Revolution.

Perhaps no one more clearly stated the link between states' rights and opposition to mercantilism than John Taylor, a contemporary of Jefferson's and a U.S. senator from Virginia. In his book *Tyranny Unmasked,* Taylor articulated his deep mistrust of Hamilton and what historian F. Thornton Miller calls the "advocates of mercantilist economics." As Miller writes in his introduction to the 1992 republication of *Tyranny Unmasked*, Taylor believed that states' rights were an indispensable tool for opposing mercantilist policies.[18] Indeed, Taylor wrote in his book that British mercantilism was "undoubtedly the best [example] which has ever appeared for extracting money from the people; and commercial restrictions, both upon foreign and domestick commerce, are its most effectual means for accomplishing this object. No equal mode of enriching the party of government, and impoverishing the party of the people, has ever been discovered."[19] He denounced "protectionist duties, bounties, exclusive privileges, and heavy taxation"—essentially the Hamiltonian/Federalist agenda—as a recipe for economic depression; argued that taxpayer subsidies to corporations would lead to "an ocean of extravagance" that would impoverish the taxpayers; and stated that a government-run central bank would create "economic gangrene."[20] Taylor "opposed government intervention in the economy and wanted a natural economy, a free market system," writes Miller, and he also believed that "assertive state rights were necessary to preserve liberty," particularly economic liberty.[21]

The principles of states' rights that Taylor and others enunciated were used to protect economic liberty on numerous occasions prior to 1865, when state sovereignty was effectively destroyed as an effective check on the central government.[22] After the War Between the States there would be no more attempts by states to nullify federal laws that were thought to be based on mercantilist exploitation.

In response to British confiscation of American ships and seamen, President Thomas Jefferson imposed a trade embargo on all shipping in 1807. The heavily trade-dependent New England states interposed, citing the Kentucky Resolve, and denounced the embargo as "unjust, oppressive, and unconstitutional" and "not legally binding."[23] The New Englanders defied the embargo law through rampant smuggling, and free trade mostly prevailed.

New Englanders also feared that their political enemies—the Jeffersonians—would do to them what they had attempted to do to Virginia and other southern states when they were in power: use the powers of the federal government to impose disproportionate taxation on other states while directing the lion's share of the benefits of government spending to their own states. Governor Roger Griswold of Connecticut articulated this fear after Jefferson's election in 1800, saying that "the balance of power under the present government is decidedly in favor of the Southern states" and claiming that New England would end up "paying the principal part of the expenses of government" without receiving commensurate benefits.[24] "There can be no safety for the Northern states" from this impending economic plunder, warned Griswold, unless there was "a separation from the confederacy."[25] In fact, New Englanders plotted for more than a decade to secede from the Union, culminating with the Hartford Convention of 1814, where they ultimately decided not to secede.

The citizens of the states also played an important role in defeating another mercantilist institution, central banking. Alexander Hamilton championed the first Bank of the United States, which led immediately to an inflation crisis, suffered from severe mismanagement, and was plagued by corruption.[26] So fearful of how this bank could threaten the economic livelihood of the citizens of the states, a number of states attempted to tax it out of existence. In 1819, for example, the Ohio legislature enacted a $50,000 annual tax on each of the two Ohio branches of the bank. The bank refused to pay, so the Ohio government sent armed marshals to collect two years' worth of taxes, or $100,000.[27] Kentucky, Tennessee, Connecticut, South Carolina, New York, and New Hampshire all enacted similar policies of harassment. Ultimately all of this agitation at the state level was successful, for President Andrew Jackson, an implacable foe of the central bank, vetoed the rechartering of the bank. The bank ceased its operations as a depository of federal funds beginning in 1833.

Perhaps the clearest example of how the founders' system of dual sovereignty was used to defeat mercantilism and preserve a more or less free-market economy was South Carolina's "nullification" of the so-called Tariff of Abominations in 1832. In 1825 the South Carolina legislature condemned the entire Hamiltonian/mercantilist agenda in what historian Chauncey Boucher calls "a set of anti-bank, anti-internal improvement [i.e., anti-corporate subsidy], and anti-tariff resolutions."[28] Three years later, under the leadership of Representative Henry Clay of Kentucky, the U.S. Congress raised the average tariff rate to almost 50 percent, with the tax on some items, such as woolen cloth, approaching 200 percent. Trade-dependent South Carolina, which, like most other southern states at the time, was an agricultural society that manufactured very little for itself, saw this as potentially devastating economically. Not only would imported clothing, shoes, tools, and other items become much more expensive, but also, since South Carolinians exported most of what they produced and had to compete in foreign markets, they would not be able to pass on much, if any, of these higher costs to *their* customers. In other words, they interpreted the tariff as an act of economic exploitation that would benefit only northern manufacturers, who would be protected from competition, mostly at their (South Carolinians') expense. Virginia, Georgia, North Carolina, and Alabama joined South Carolina in condemning the tariff.

In November of 1832 South Carolina adopted an "ordinance of nullification" declaring the Tariff of Abominations to be "null, void, and no law, nor binding upon this State, its officers, or citizens" and refused to collect the increased tariff.[29] The federal government was forced to back down, and a lower compromise tariff rate was adopted. Once again, the citizens of the states were successful in resisting mercantilist exploitation and defending economic freedom and capitalism, in the spirit of the American Revolution. By 1857, the average tariff rate had been reduced to a mere 15 percent.

Yet the tariff issue arose again when the Republican Party gained influence in the late 1850s. In the 1859–1860 session of the House of Representatives, the Republicans fought for the Morrill Tariff, which would more than double the average tariff rate. The debate over the Morrill Tariff was a replay of the Tariff of Abominations episode some thirty years earlier. The main proponents of the tariff were northern manufacturers and unions, whereas the vast majority of the opposition came from the trade-dependent southern states. Eighty-seven percent of northern congressmen voted for the Morrill Tariff, but only 12.5 percent of southern congressmen did.[30] The U.S. Senate passed the Morrill Tariff just days before the inauguration of Abraham Lincoln, a staunch protectionist for his entire political career who supported it.

Although the American Revolution was fought in large part as a revolt against the stifling mercantilist policies of the British government, and although the founders had specifically aimed to guarantee economic liberties to the citizens, it was at this point that effective political opposition to mercantilism in America ended. By the second year of the Lincoln administration the average tariff rate had more than tripled, to over 47 percent, and it remained that high or higher for most of the next fifty years. During the War Between the States, the National Currency Acts cemented central banking into place, and the federal government granted vast subsidies to railroad corporations, which led other industries to lobby feverishly for similar subsidies in the following decades.[31] The revolt against mercantilism that commenced with the Revolutionary generation was ended, and Hamiltonian mercantilism has prevailed, in varying degrees, ever since.

CHAPTER FIVE

Highways of Capitalism

Do public goods and services, such as streets, parks and
dams, have to be provided by government? . . . Collective
goods can be provided by agents in a market process.

—Fred Foldvary, *Public Goods and*
Private Communities (1994)

FOR THE first six decades of the nineteenth century one of the
biggest economic policy debates was over the desirability of
government subsidies for so-called internal improvements, or the
building of roads, canals, and railroads. On the one hand, the followers of Alexander Hamilton, then Henry Clay and his Whig Party, and
finally Abraham Lincoln and the Republican Party advocated a more
centralized government that would actively plan at least part of the
economy. They favored high protectionist tariffs to finance "internal
improvement" subsidies, along with a central bank that could print
money to do the same. On the other hand there were the Jeffersonians,
who feared a more centralized government and were generally
opposed to using tax dollars to subsidize corporations for any reason—
road and canal building or anything else. These opponents of internal improvement subsidies included Jefferson, John C. Calhoun,
James Madison, James Monroe, and Andrew Jackson, among others. Jefferson, Monroe, and Madison believed that taxpayer subsidies
to businesses were unconstitutional; Calhoun led the fight against
using protectionist tariffs to fund the subsidies; and Jackson as presi-

dent defeated the effort to recharter the Bank of the United States and vetoed numerous internal improvement bills.

The basic economic argument in favor of government subsidies for canal or road building was the so-called free-rider problem. According to this argument, individuals are not sufficiently motivated to contribute voluntarily to the provision of "public goods" by which everyone benefits. Thus, the story goes, such projects as road and canal building will be inherently underfunded if we rely totally on private financing. Supposedly taxation is needed to force potential free riders to pay their share for public goods; the government will use the taxpayers' money to subsidize important infrastructure projects that wouldn't be completed otherwise.

But the fact is, most roads and canals were *privately* financed in the nineteenth century. Moreover, in virtually every instance in which state, local, or federal government got involved in building roads and canals, the result was a financial debacle in which little or nothing was actually built and huge sums of taxpayer dollars were squandered or simply stolen. Today we call the concept of tax-funded subsidies to businesses "corporate welfare," and this policy is as economically harmful now as it was in the nineteenth century.

THE LONG FIGHT OVER CORPORATE WELFARE

George Washington's treasury secretary, Alexander Hamilton, first proposed the idea of subsidies for internal improvements in his famous 1791 *Report on Manufactures*. In a fairly clear statement of what modern economists call the free-rider problem, Hamilton wrote, "The public purse must supply the deficiency of private resource. In what can it be so useful, as in prompting and improving the efforts of industry?"[1]

As persuasive as Hamilton might have been, it was Thomas Jefferson's treasury secretary, Albert Gallatin, who presented a detailed proposal for using taxpayer money to fund internal improvements. Presented to Congress in 1806, Gallatin's "Report on Roads and Canals" was "the earliest and most distinguished attempt to formulate a comprehensive national plan of internal improvements," wrote economic historian Carter Goodrich.[2] The so-called Gallatin Plan relied on the free-rider argument; the report declared that "the General Government can alone remove these obstacles" to transportation and that "the early and efficient aid of the Federal government is recommended."[3] Believing in the mythical "efficient government," Gallatin proposed a ten-year plan for government-financed and -supervised canal and road building. He favored a vast system of roads and canals, and he argued that such a system would have to be federally subsidized because, he maintained, there was a "scarcity of private capital" to build in remote areas.[4] Nothing came of Gallatin's proposal, however, because Jefferson and others raised constitutional questions about his plan.

Henry Clay, the leader of the Whig Party, was the great proponent of subsidies to canal, road, and railroad building corporations throughout his long political career. He advocated an economic program he called the "American System," by which he meant the combination of corporate welfare funded with high tariffs and paper money printed by the federal government. As early as 1816 he saw to it that legislation rechartering the Bank of the United States included a $1.5 million appropriation for internal improvement subsidies. Yet Clay, like Albert Gallatin, had his opponents. Chief among them was James Madison, the widely acknowledged "father of the Constitution," who made the most powerful argument against using tax dollars to subsidize private corporations involved in canal or road building. Madison warned that the sort of government expenditures Clay advocated were unconstitutional and said that the Constitution would therefore have to be amended to adopt them.

Madison's very last act as president, in fact, was to veto an internal improvements bill that Clay had sponsored. Clay attempted to sneak the appropriation past the outgoing president in his last days in office, but Madison learned of the tactic in the newspapers and took action on his very last day as president. As historian Robert Allen Rutland recounts, Madison

> decided it was time to teach the nation a lesson in constitutionalism. . . . [Clay's] bill, he said, failed to take into account the fact that Congress had enumerated powers under section eight of the first article of the Constitution, "and it does not appear that the power proposed to be exercised in the bill is among the enumerated powers, or that it falls by any just interpretation within the power to make the laws necessary and proper" for carrying other constitutional powers into execution.[5]

Madison warned Congress that the General Welfare Clause of the Constitution was never intended to become a Pandora's box for special-interest legislation, such as taxpayer subsidies to private businesses.

The president under whom Henry Clay served as secretary of state, John Quincy Adams, was perhaps the second most prominent advocate of taxpayer subsidies for road and canal building. In a private letter written after he left the presidency, Adams opined that "the great effort of my administration was to mature into a permanent and regular system the application of all the superfluous revenge of the Union to internal improvement. . . . With this system . . . the surface of the whole nation would have been checkered over with Rail roads and Canals."[6] In the letter an embittered Adams bemoaned the fact that this gigantic project had been foiled by his predecessor, James Monroe, who had made persuasive constitutional arguments against such expenditures—arguments that Adams blamed on "Jefferson's blighting breath."[7] Another key opponent of Adams's plans had been John C. Calhoun, whom Adams called "the Sable Genius of the South." Because of his opponents' efforts, Adams complained, he had failed to achieve "the great object of my life therefore as applied to the administration of the Government."[8]

The Clay/Adams plans would be thwarted once again under President Andrew Jackson. Throughout his presidency (1829–1837), Jackson vetoed numerous internal improvement subsidy bills, much to the consternation of the tenacious Clay, the principal sponsor of all the bills. Jackson referred to such subsidies as "saddling upon the government the losses of unsuccessful private speculation," and in his Farewell Address he boasted that he had "finally overthrown . . . this plan of unconstitutional expenditure for the purpose of corrupt influence."[9]

Still, Henry Clay continued to fight for his American System until his death in 1852. And after his death, Abraham Lincoln picked up the mantle of the American System. Lincoln, who idolized Clay and looked at him as his political role model, was finally able to implement Clay's American System during his administration. With that, the mercantilist schemes had won out, despite the serious constitutional arguments that had been voiced as far back as Thomas Jefferson—and despite the fact that, as the evidence shows, such schemes were unnecessary.

THE DUBIOUS "FREE-RIDER PROBLEM"

The key argument of the proponents of government-subsidized canal and road building was that pure capitalism would fail to supply adequate capital. This is a plausible theory, but it is contradicted by reality. The fact is, privately funded roads (called "turnpikes") proliferated during the first forty years of the nineteenth century. If government had a role to play, it should have been to reduce or eliminate the taxes and regulations that were imposed on the turnpike-building companies. In other words, it should have encouraged rather than burdened these early American capitalists.

As early as 1800, writes economist Daniel Klein, America had *sixty-nine private road-building companies* chartered by the states.[10] In the next three decades, says Klein,

> the [private road-building] movement built new roads at rates previously unheard of in America. Over $11 million was invested in turnpikes in New York, some $6.5 million in New England, and over $4.5 million in Pennsylvania. . . . Between 1794 and 1840, 238 private New England turnpike companies built and operated about 3,750 miles of road. New York led all other states in turnpike mileage with over 4,000 as of 1821. Pennsylvania was second, reaching a peak of about 2,400 miles in 1832. New Jersey companies operated 500 miles by 1821. . . . Between 1810 and 1845 over 400 [private] turnpikes were chartered and built.[11]

The private turnpike industry was obviously thriving, which makes the "free-rider" argument for government subsidies seem very odd indeed. What was most likely happening was that certain companies wanted simply to reach into the pockets of the taxpayers, and some politicians, like Hamilton, Clay, and Lincoln, understood that a key to political success was to have the country's moneyed corporate elite as financial backers. Hence all the clamoring for government subsidies even when the very existence of this burgeoning industry proved that they weren't necessary.

But why did the private turnpike industry flourish in the first half of the nineteenth century? After all, owning stock in a turnpike company in the early nineteenth century promised a very meager return of 3 percent or less annually. But, as was widely understood at the time, additional economic benefits would accrue to such investments. Local merchants had strong incentives to invest in private turnpikes because they would bring more commerce to their towns. Landowners would see their property values rise, and cities would more generally prosper as improved transportation extended the division of labor and the economic benefits derived from it. It was also understood that the building of roads would encourage settlement and expand the size for markets for merchants' goods. As one Benjamin De Witt wrote in 1807, "Turnpikes encourage settlements, open new channels for the transportation of produce and merchandise, increase the products of agriculture, and facilitate every species of internal commerce."[12]

Shares of stock in the turnpike companies were almost exclusively owned locally, suggesting that merchants, landowners, and citizens in general understood that their investments in these companies did indeed produce benefits aside from the normal rate-of-return calculations. Businessmen in larger cities also invested because they wanted to develop markets for their goods outside of their own cities. At least one state—Connecticut—exempted the income earned from turnpike company stock from taxation.[13]

Also helping the private turnpike industry was the spirit of voluntary association that pervaded early America, before government came to dominate so many areas of life. Alexis de Tocqueville famously remarked in 1840, "Americans . . . constantly form associations. They have not only commercial and manufacturing companies, in which all take part, but associations of a thousand other kinds."[14] Early-nineteenth-century Americans also used social pressure and ostracism to encourage one another to invest in the roads and canals that they would all prosper from. Town meetings were an important vehicle in this regard, as were newspapers. Most adult Americans of the time were avid newspaper readers, and the advocates of privately funded road and canal building often made their case to the entire community in the local newspapers. All of this enabled entrepreneurs to overcome the free-rider problem and build a private transportation network.

Ingenious early American transportation entrepreneurs even invented a kind of privatized "law of eminent domain" whereby rights of way were paid for with shares of stock in the turnpike companies. The value of the property was determined not by government assessors—who would seize private property to build government-owned roads—but by freedom of exchange in the free market.

PRIVATE-SECTOR EFFICIENCY

Overcoming the supposed free-rider problem, Americans in the first half of the nineteenth century constructed a private transportation network that was undoubtedly built smarter, faster, and more efficiently than it would have been if it had been a typical "public works" project. Indeed, private road building is *inherently* more efficient than government-run road building. When private investors financed the roads, the managers of the turnpike companies strove to build the roads in the right places, for one thing, and built them as efficiently as possible, for that would maximize their profit potential. Mistakes were made, of course, as is true of all human endeavors, but the important thing is that the right incentives were in place: efficient road building was rewarded with profits; inefficient road building was penalized with losses. In contrast, with government financing of roads (or anything else), politics inevitably takes the place of economics as the main decision-making criterion. For example, legislators can be counted on to insist that, as a condition for their voting for subsidies, roads be built near where they live or in the vicinity of their major political supporters, even if it would be uneconomical to do so.

Sure enough, in the second half of the nineteenth century, when the federal government began subsidizing internal improvements, noneconomic factors became paramount. During the congressional debates over federal subsidies for transcontinental railroads in 1862, a New Mexico politician complained that "the wrangle of local interests" was such that many congressmen would not support the subsidy bill unless the railroad "starts in the corner of every man's farm and runs through all his neighbors' plantations" in every part of the state.[15] The concerns of the man from New Mexico were not unfounded. Indeed, Congressman Thaddeus Stevens of Pennsylvania "had received a block of . . . stock in exchange for his vote," writes Dee Brown in his popular history of the transcontinental railroads. Stevens also "demanded insertion of a clause [in the railroad bill] requiring that all iron used in the construction and equipment of said road to be American manufacture. In addition to being a congressman, Stevens was an iron manufacturer."[16] At the time, American iron was much more expensive than British iron. The chief lobbyist for subsidies to the transcontinental railroad, Thomas Durant, spent thousands of dollars "distributing Union Pacific stock to congressmen in exchange for their votes."[17]

Thaddeus Stevens was not alone; politicians have a penchant for micromanaging any government-funded project in a way that will benefit *themselves* politically. Thus, government-financed construction projects are inevitably mired in red tape and mostly counterproductive regulations. As Ludwig von Mises wrote, "Bureaucratic conduct of affairs is conduct bound to comply with detailed rules and regulations fixed by authority of a superior body. . . . It is the social apparatus of coercion and compulsion."[18]

In private, competitive markets, investment in businesses is directed by the wishes of consumers. With government-funded projects, however, the whims of politicians tend to replace the desires of consumers, and the result is always economic inefficiency and political corruption. The early-nineteenth-century American transportation entrepreneurs proved that the "market failure" rationale for government transportation subsidies (that is, the free-rider problem) was essentially a myth. In contrast, the real failures in early American transportation came from government-funded projects that were spectacularly wasteful.

GOVERNMENT FAILURES

Starting in the late 1830s, many states subsidized the construction of canals and railroads—and the subsidies invariably turned out to be disastrous. As historian John Bach McMaster wrote, "In *every* state which had gone recklessly into internal improvements the financial situation was alarming. *No* works were finished; little or no income was derived from them; interest on the bonds increased day by day and no means of paying it save by taxation remained [emphasis added]."[19]

Ohio was one of the most active states with regard to granting subsidies for internal improvements. But as Carter Goodrich wrote, "In Ohio, as in other states, revulsion followed the early enthusiasm" for government subsidies to the railroad industry.[20] There was so much waste and corruption that Ohio "stood as one of the chief examples of the revulsion of feeling against governmental promotion of internal improvement."[21] In 1851, in fact, the state *amended its constitution* to prohibit both state and local government subsidies to private companies.

Indiana, Illinois, and Michigan were even less successful with their subsidy programs, which were enacted in 1836 and 1837. In three short years the subsidized canal, road, and railroad projects were all bankrupt and unfinished. By 1850 all three of these states had also amended their constitutions to prohibit state subsidies for internal improvements.[22]

One of the most forceful proponents of state subsidies for canal-

and railroad-building corporations was a young Illinois lawyer named Abraham Lincoln, who would later include among his legal clients the Illinois Central and other large railroad corporations. Lincoln was a leader of the Whig Party in the Illinois legislature and was as influential as anyone in getting the state legislature to allocate more than $11 million for internal improvement subsidies. The subsidy bill, wrote Goodrich,

> had . . . something for everyone: improvements for five rivers; east-west railroads across the state, with various branches; and a great central railroad to extend from the northwestern corner to the southern tip of the state. In addition . . . the act appropriated $200,000 for improvements in counties which did not share in the specific appropriations. The total expenditure authorized was $10,500,000, and the legislature prescribed that work should commence simultaneously on all the projects. . . . The next legislature added . . . $1,000,000.[23]

Abraham Lincoln's law partner, William Herndon, marveled at the spectacular promises that Lincoln and his political compatriots had made to the people of Illinois:

> Every river and stream . . . was to be widened, deepened, and made navigable. A canal to connect the Illinois River and Lake Michigan was to be dug. . . . Cities were to spring up everywhere; capital from abroad was to come pouring in. . . . People were to come swarming in by colonies, until . . . Illinois was to . . . become the Empire State of the Union.[24]

But the project was a colossal disaster because of fraud, mismanagement, corruption, and the recession of 1837. Herndon described the whole project as "reckless and unwise," writing:

The gigantic and stupendous operations of the scheme dazzled the eyes of nearly everybody, but in the end it rolled up a debt so enormous as to impede the otherwise marvelous progress of Illinois. The burdens imposed by this Legislature under the guise of improvements became so monumental in size it is little wonder that at intervals for years after the monster of [debt] repudiation often showed its hideous face above the waves of popular indignation.[25]

In their biography of Lincoln, George Nicolay and John Hay—Lincoln's personal secretaries in the White House—added that "the market was glutted with Illinois bonds; one banker and one broker after another, to whose hands they had been recklessly confided in New York and London, failed, or made away with the proceeds. . . . The internal improvements system had utterly failed."[26]

Michigan's results were almost equally disastrous. The 1837 state-funded project quickly exhibited mismanagement, corruption, and mind-boggling cost overruns. The state was forced to sell the Michigan Central and Michigan Southern Railroads at half the price that it had paid for them. "The state's venture in internal improvements," wrote Carter Goodrich, "was so universally regarded as a failure that prohibitions against both public works and mixed enterprise were voted almost without discussion for inclusion in the [Michigan state] constitution of 1850."[27]

Other states learned valuable lessons from the unmitigated financial disasters that these states experienced. When Wisconsin and Minnesota entered the union in 1848 and 1857, respectively, they adopted constitutions that forbade both state grants and loans to private corporations.[28] In Iowa the state courts also held that *local* aid to private businesses was unconstitutional. Louisiana began subsidizing railroads before Illinois and most other states (in 1833) and consequently was one of the first states to forbid state aid for internal improvements (in 1845).[29] The failures of government-subsidized internal improvements were so pronounced that by 1860 Missouri and Massachusetts were the only two states in the union that had *not* yet amended their constitutions to prohibit internal improvement subsidies. Missouri finally got around to it in 1875.[30]

Opposition to federal subsidies for internal improvements came mostly from southern politicians in the pre–Civil War era, and southerners were so opposed to these subsidies that the Confederate Constitution of 1861 outlawed them. Article I, Section 8, Clause 3 of the Confederate Constitution stipulated:

> The Congress shall have the power to regulate commerce with foreign nations, and among the several States, and with Indian tribes; but neither this, nor any other clause contained in the Constitution, shall ever be construed to delegate power to the Congress to appropriate money for any internal improvement intended to facilitate commerce.[31]

An exception was made for "beacons and buoys" and the dredging of harbors, but that was it. The southern *states* were free to use state tax revenues for internal improvement subsidies, but all of them had also outlawed the subsidies in their own state constitutions.

Of course, as we have seen, the South was not the only region that had forbidden state funding for internal improvements. And in the Northeast and the West, major railroad projects provided further evidence that private financing of internal improvements was most efficient and that the "free-rider problem" and other such claims were bogus. New Hampshire and Vermont gave no subsidies at all to railroads, but a privately funded line was built across the rugged terrain of the two states. There was no government-imposed "right of eminent domain" in New Hampshire, but the private railroad company was not hindered: it simply purchased rights of way.

Similarly, the Mormons built four railroads in Utah without any government subsidies.

And as will be seen in Chapter 7, in the late nineteenth century entrepreneur James J. Hill built a transcontinental railroad that was not subsidized. Hill's privately financed railroad was built better, had a more direct route, and was more profitable than the government-subsidized transcontinental railroads with which he competed, most of which went bankrupt at some point because they were so mired in government regulation and crippled by the inherent inefficiencies of all government-financed or -sponsored "public works" programs.

Despite such successes, however—and despite the failures of government-financed infrastructure development—Abraham Lincoln and the Republican Party remained fierce proponents of internal improvement subsidies, especially for railroads. During the Lincoln, Johnson, and Grant administrations, laws were passed granting railroad corporations millions of acres of land and other subsidies. It is a familiar theme in American history: although capitalism is responsible for the greatest successes, politicians continually overlook or ignore what capitalism has produced and instead shackle the American people with misguided policies.

CHAPTER SIX

How Capitalism Enriched
the Working Class

In the capitalist society there prevails a tendency toward a steady increase in the per capita quota of capital invested. . . . Consequently, the marginal productivity of labor, wage rates, and the wage earners' standard of living tend to rise continually. . . . This improvement in well being . . . is a tendency resulting from the interplay of forces which can freely produce their effects only under capitalism.

—Ludwig von Mises, *Human Action* (1998 ed.)

ONE OF the most pervasive—and pernicious—myths about capitalism is that capitalists have always exploited the working class. To anticapitalist myth makers, the industrial revolution was a horror that subjected the American working class to nightmarish working conditions while a relative few capitalists became wealthy on the backs of the working poor, and that subjugation has only continued.

But the historical record of capitalism in America—and in every other country where it has been practiced—reveals something quite different: capitalism has continually improved the lot of the working class.

To be sure, the advent of capitalism—and factory production—created working conditions that seem unpleasant or even deplorable by today's standards, but it is important to understand that they were a significant improvement over the conditions the working class had previously endured. In the early days of capitalism no one forced laborers to leave the farms, poorhouses, or the streets. People *voluntarily* went into the factories because they knew they could improve their standards of living by doing so. It was the precapitalist era that was utterly miserable for the average working person; capitalism saved the working class from an impoverished existence that had remained stagnant for generations prior to the advent of capitalism. Ludwig von Mises put the early days of capitalism into perspective when he wrote:

> The factory owners did not have the power to compel anybody to take a factory job. They could only hire people who were ready to work for the wages offered to them. Low as these wage rates were, they were nonetheless much more than these paupers could earn in any other field open to them. It is a distortion of facts to say that the factories carried off the housewives from the nurseries and the kitchens and the children from their play. These women had nothing to cook with and to feed their children. These children were destitute and starving. Their only refuge was the factory. It saved them, in the strict sense of the term, from death by starvation.[1]

The same can be said of the conditions in some of the world's less-developed countries today. Those who deplore "child labor" and "sweatshops" fail to recognize or acknowledge that as deplorable as these conditions may seem by the standards of modern-day America, these people are *much better off* for having the opportunity to work in a higher-paying factory. In many parts of today's world starvation is still the alternative to budding capitalism. To child laborers in parts of the world, the alternatives to "sweatshop labor" are malnutrition and starvation, child prostitution, and begging and stealing.

In the early days of industrialization in America, as capitalism grew and there was more capital investment (that is, investment in machinery and equipment), workers became progressively more productive and therefore better paid. This is no surprise, for in a capitalist society the only way the standard of living can increase is through increased productivity (output per worker), and the most important ingredient in increased productivity is capital investment. Skill, education, and on-the-job training ("human capital investment," in the language of economics) do improve productivity, but only very slowly. In contrast, when a capitalist invests in newer or better machinery or equipment, this can increase the output per employee *immediately*. At once the very same employees—without a shred of additional training, education, or experience—are producing more goods and services per hour worked and, most important from the capitalist's perspective, are contributing more to profits. And when the laborer becomes more productive, his value to the employer increases—that is, the laborer's wages go up. Skilled, reliable workers are always in demand, which means that employers must pay more to keep their more productive employees or else risk losing them to competing employers. In this sense labor is indeed a commodity in that its price—wages or compensation—is determined in the marketplace by the forces of supply and demand.

And wages in manufacturing industries did in fact rise steadily in the nineteenth century. From 1820 to 1860 wages grew at about a 1.6 annual rate, and during this period the purchasing power of an average worker's paycheck increased between 60 and 90 percent, depending on what region of the country the worker resided in.[2] Between 1860 and 1890, during what economists call the "second industrial revolution," real wages—that is, wages adjusted for inflation—increased by 50 percent in America. The average work-week was shortened as well, meaning that the real earnings of the average American worker probably increased more like 60 percent during that time.[3]

Capitalism improves the quality of life for the working class not just because it leads to improved wages but also because it produces new, better, and cheaper goods. In the second half of the nineteenth century, at the same time that American workers' wages were shooting upward, more and more consumer products were being invented that made life more comfortable for the working class, including kerosene lamps, which made it possible to light one's house inexpensively. Although the products of capitalism almost invariably benefit the "wealthy" first, these goods become common-place as capitalism enriches the working class and mass production allows for lower and lower costs of production. For example, when Henry Ford first started selling automobiles only the relatively wealthy could afford them, but soon enough working-class families were buying his cars. The same was true even in the earliest days of American capitalism: in the late eighteenth century, textile mills in New England quickly adopted the policy of producing cheap cotton apparel for the masses.

Indeed, with capitalism, the emphasis shifted to producing goods as cheaply as possible for the masses—the working class— whereas artisans had previously produced their goods and wares mostly for the aristocracy. Under capitalism *every* business wants to cater to the masses, for that is where the money is. There is no better way to become wealthy than to produce and sell a valued product cheaply enough so that almost anyone can afford to buy it. Thus, American capitalism from the very beginning produced a dual benefit for the working class: it provided new, better-paying jobs, and it supplied cheaper goods—clothing, shoes, and much else that the working class could hardly have afforded before the advent of mass factory production. Higher pay and cheaper goods translate into a rising standard of living.

To put into perspective the almost miraculous benefits that capitalism has created for the American working class, consider this: the average middle-class family today lives better than millionaires did a hundred years ago, and better than kings and queens did two hundred years ago. Federal Reserve Board economists Michael Cox and Richard Alm explain:

> A nineteenth-century millionaire couldn't grab a cold drink from the refrigerator. He couldn't hop into a smooth-riding automobile for a 70-mile-an-hour trip down an interstate highway to the mountains or seashore. He couldn't call up news, movies, music, and sporting events by simply touching the remote control's buttons. He couldn't jet north to Toronto, south to Cancun, east to Boston, or west to San Francisco in just a few hours. He couldn't transmit documents to Europe, Asia, or anyplace else in seconds. He couldn't run over to the mall to buy auto-focus cameras, computer games, mountain bikes, or movies on videotape. He couldn't escape the summer heat in air conditioned comfort. He couldn't check into a hospital for a coronary bypass to cure a failing heart, get a shot of penicillin to ward off infection, or even take an aspirin to relieve a headache.[4]

None of these things was available a century ago at any price. Then, at first, every one of them was available only to the "rich." But over time each became available to virtually everyone. Refrigeration was invented at the turn of the century and was only for the affluent, but after about twenty years refrigerators were commonplace in American homes. Commercial air travel began in the 1920s—again, only for the wealthy. Today, just about everyone flies.

To illustrate how capitalism has benefited the average working family over the past century, Cox and Alm computed how many hours the typical laborer had to work to purchase various consumer

TABLE 6.1: WORK TIME (IN MINUTES) REQUIRED
TO PURCHASE VARIOUS FOODS AND SERVICES, 1900–1999

PRODUCT	1900	1950	1999
Half gallon of milk	56	16	7.0
Loaf of bread	na*	6	3.5
Dozen oranges	na	21	9.0
Chocolate bar	20	2	2.1
Gallon of gas	na	11	5.7
Movie ticket	na	18	19.0
Pair of jeans	9 hrs.	4 hrs.	3 hrs.
3-lb. chicken	2 hrs. 40 min.	1 hr. 11 min.	24 min.
100 kw of electricity	107 hrs. 17 min.	2 hrs.	14 min.
3-minute coast-to-coast phone call	na	1 hr. 44 min.	2 min.

*na = data not available
Source: Michael Cox and Richard Alm, *Myths of Rich and Poor* (New York: Basic Books, 1999), 43.

goods in 1900 and then again in 1999 (see Table 6.1). In addition, Cox and Alm found that a pound of ground beef cost 30 minutes of labor time in 1919 but only about 5 minutes today. And a sample of a dozen food items that would comprise three square meals a day cost 9.5 hours of labor in 1919 compared with 1.5 hours today. When portable radios first appeared in American stores, the average American worker had to labor 13 hours to buy one; today he or she toils for only about 1 hour. In the 1920s it took 79 hours of work to buy a nice men's suit; today it takes less than half that. At the beginning of the twentieth century the average American family spent three-quarters of its income on food, clothing, and shelter; today it spends about one-third on those items, and spends an even greater proportion on taxes.[5]

In 1908 the typical American worker had to work *two years* to earn enough money to buy an average-quality car. Today a Ford Taurus costs an American worker about eight months of labor, but the car is a technological miracle compared with the cars of yesteryear, with standard air conditioning, power seats, safety devices of all kinds, cruise control, a sunroof, tinted glass, a CD player, and so on. In 1970 an IBM mainframe computer sold for around $4.7 million; today, a personal computer that operates thirteen times faster goes for under $1,000.

Capitalism has also allowed the average worker to take more and more leisure time. The average workweek has declined from sixty-one hours in 1870, to forty-eight hours in 1929, to about thirty-four hours today.[6] How did this happen? "Decade by decade," write Cox and Alm, "American workers have become more efficient, applying technology, better tools, and improved skills to produce more goods and services on the job."[7] Being more productive, in other words, allows workers to produce more with the same work effort, or even to produce more while spending less time on the job. In 1870, in the early days of the "second industrial revolution," the average American began working full-time for a living at age 13; today it's at 19.4 years. The average American today works about half the number of hours as the 1870 worker did, spends much less time at home doing chores (thanks to such capitalist inventions as microwave ovens, refrigeration, frozen food, vacuum cleaners, etc.), and enjoys many more hours of leisure activity each year.[8]

The shorter workweek was entirely a capitalist invention and not the result of government policy or labor union pressure. As labor productivity increased—thanks largely to capital investment by entrepreneurs—and wages rose, more and more workers could afford to work fewer hours and still support themselves and their families. As capitalism grew, and as more and more new markets were created, the competition between employers for workers became more and more intense. One way in which employers competed—and compete today—is to offer workers shorter hours. Once a few employers started recruiting the best employees in this way, others followed suit. Those who did not were left at a competitive disadvantage. With rivals offering fewer hours of work per week, those employers who did not do so were compelled by competition to offer a wage premium to get employees to work longer hours. Either way—longer hours or higher pay—they put themselves at a competitive disadvantage. This is how America has gone from an average eighty-hour workweek to one of less than forty hours.

Competition in labor markets is also the reason why child labor has essentially been eliminated. Young people originally worked in the harsh setting of factories because they had to as a matter of their and their families' survival. But as workers became more and more productive and better paid—thanks to the investments of capitalists—they could afford to keep their children at home and in school instead of sending them to work. Legislation banning child labor only codified what the free market had already created.

Child labor in agriculture followed much the same path. More than a century ago, one of the advantages of large farm families was that all the children could pitch in with the farm work. But mechanized agriculture—that is, increasing doses of capitalism—made agricultural workers more productive. Consequently, fewer workers were required, which reduced the need to have children work in the fields. Capitalism saved many children from backbreaking agricultural work.

Interestingly, there was never an organized propaganda campaign against child labor in agriculture, even though the work performed on a farm could be every bit as hard and grueling as in any factory. The most likely reason for this is that labor unions were the driving force behind the anti-child labor crusades, and unions were concerned about child labor in large part because it represented competition for union labor. In other words, the unions' first concern was their own membership rolls and dues revenues, not necessarily the welfare of children.

The workplace has also become progressively safer over the past century and a half, not because of the Occupational Safety and Health Administration (OSHA), which was created in the 1970s, but because of the economics of capitalism. A dangerous workplace is costly to employers because, if they have a reputation of having a dangerous workplace, then in a competitive labor market they must pay a wage premium to entice workers to take the extra risk. More dangerous or unpleasant jobs, from working in an oil field to riding on the back of a garbage truck in the winter in New England, always require a wage premium if they are to be filled. Thus, capitalists do strive to make their own workplaces safer as a way of reducing their wage bill and consequently increasing their *profits*. An added incentive for safety is that a worker who is off the job because of an injury is not producing anything that the employer can sell, and it is costly to hire and train replacements.

Human beings will always make mistakes and cause accidents, and some employers are smarter than others in terms of going about the task of improving job safety. But overall, the profit incentive embedded in capitalism is the strongest driving force leading to a safer work environment. And the workplace is indeed safer now. On-the-job deaths have declined in America from 428 per million workers in 1930, to 214 per million in 1960, to 38 per million today.[9] Occupational injuries are at an all-time low of 59 per 1,000 employees. Interestingly, they have not gone down since the creation of OSHA.

Of course, the way in which American capitalism has evolved also makes the workplace much safer. Mechanization made work easier and safer for farmers and everyone else, and now the "information age" has created millions of jobs that are inherently safer than machine-age jobs or backbreaking, unmechanized agricultural labor. And as competition for labor has become more and more intense, employers have tailored their compensation to meet the changing desires of their employees. Better working conditions, better pay, and a mix of pay and fringe benefits that is to the employees' liking are all the products of capitalism and not any kind of government program or labor union demands.

WHAT ABOUT INEQUALITY?

It is undeniable that American capitalism has been the great engine of economic advancement for the working class. But the critics of capitalism have always complained of "inequality." On the face of it, such complaints are usually nonsensical, since they do not acknowledge the plain fact that every human being is unique—has a unique level of motivation, experience, education, interests, desires, and education. We all pursue different life courses and develop different skills and knowledge. This is the beauty of the division of labor: we can specialize in what we do best and/or interests us the most, earn money doing it, and then trade the dollars we earn for products and services that others produce in very different ways and in very different settings. All of our wages are determined primarily by the supply of and demand for the goods and services we participate in producing, which naturally leads to wage inequality. Older, more experienced workers will always be paid more than the less experienced in the same trade in a capitalist economy, but so what? It is nothing to fret about.

Nevertheless, the anticapitalist mentality is stuck on a mindless egalitarianism that insists that "equality" must be pursued even though no two people were ever equal in terms of talent, productivity, interests, and so forth. (Making everyone equal *under the law* is an entirely different matter.) The quixotic pursuit of economic equality is essentially a revolt against human nature.

Statistics on "income inequality" can be very misleading, providing a totally inaccurate picture of American capitalism. For example, critics of capitalism are fond of pointing to U.S. Census Bureau data that seem to indicate that "the rich are getting richer and the poor are getting poorer." From 1967 to 1997, for example, census data show that the share of total national income going to the top 20 percent of income earners in America increased from 43.2 percent to 49.4 percent, whereas the share going to the bottom 20 percent fell from 4.4 percent to 3.6 percent in that period.[10] But such statistics are deceiving because they are a snapshot at a single point in time and say nothing about how actual individuals progress over time. That is, they tell us nothing about the degree of economic opportunity and advancement in the U.S. economy. The critics suggest that there is little or no room for the "poor" to advance, that a class of people is essentially stuck in the bottom 20 percent. But this is unequivocally false. In reality, the bottom 20 percent (like all other quintiles) is constantly made up of *different people*. A family in the lowest income quintile today, as recorded by the census data gatherers, will typically move up into a higher income category over the next five or ten years and be replaced in the lower category by a different family, perhaps immigrants to America who, like so many immigrants throughout history, come with very little money in their pockets. They come with little money but great ambition, and they typically move up the economic ladder, as has been the American story for generations.

Cox and Alm have demonstrated the upward mobility of the American labor force—and the uselessness of static income distribution statistics—as clearly as anyone has. To look at a representative socioeconomic sample of American society, the two Federal Reserve Board researchers used a University of Michigan tracking study of more than fifty thousand Americans that has been going on since 1968. Tracking the incomes of *specific, individual families over time* (in this case, from 1975 to 1991) provided an entirely different understanding of the degree of "inequality" in the American labor market from what static government statistics do. And the results were very revealing:

- Only 5 percent of families in the bottom fifth of the income distribution in 1975 were still there in 1991. More than three-fourths of them had made their way up to the two highest income quintiles.
- The poorest families made the largest gains. Those who started in the bottom 20 percent in 1975 had an inflation-adjusted *gain in annual income* of $27,745 by 1991; those who started in the top 20 percent in 1975 also improved, but only by $4,354. The "rich" *are* getting richer, the researchers concluded, but the "poor" are getting richer even faster.
- Less than 1 percent of the sample population remained in

the bottom 20 percent during the entire time period under study.

• Among the second poorest quintile in 1975, more than 70 percent had moved to a higher quintile by 1991, and one-fourth reached the top 20 percent bracket.

• With education and training the rise up the income brackets can be very swift: more than half of the families who were in the bottom 20 percent in 1975 made it to a higher bracket within four years.[11]

A U.S. Treasury Department study yielded similar results about income mobility in America: 86 percent of those in the lowest 20 percent of income earners in 1979 had moved to a higher income category by 1988; 66 percent reached the middle range or above, while 15 percent ascended to the top fifth of income earners.[12]

America has always enabled this kind of upward mobility, as the stories of wave after wave of immigrants attest. Indeed, America still draws immigrants from all over the globe who want to enjoy the benefits of American capitalism and freedom; many come to America to escape socialist hellholes (which supposedly champion "equality"), whether they be in Cuba, Africa, China, or elsewhere.

The anticapitalists rail against income inequality, and there will always be income inequality in a vibrant, capitalist economy. But the same is true of a socialist economy, where wages are often determined by political rather than economic considerations. Indeed, *any* type of economy will produce income inequality. More important, when listening to the critics of capitalism, one must put American income inequality into proper perspective, as Cox and Alm do so effectively:

America isn't an egalitarian society. It wasn't designed to be. Socialism, a failed and receding system, sought to impose an artificial equality. Capitalism, a successful and expanding system, doesn't fight a fundamental fact of human nature—we vary greatly in capabilities, motivation, interests, and preferences. Some of us are driven to get ahead. Some of us are just plain lazy. Some of us are willing to work hard so we can afford a lifestyle rich in material goods. Some of us work just hard enough to provide a roof overhead, food, clothes, and a few amenities. It shouldn't come as a surprise that our incomes vary greatly.[13]

WHAT ABOUT LABOR UNIONS?

Despite all their immodest boasts, labor unions are not responsible for the long-term rise in wages and living standards in America. Historically, real wages (wages adjusted for the effects of inflation) rose at about 2 percent per year *before* the advent of unions, and at a similar rate afterward.[14] If labor unions were responsible for the historical rise in wages in the United States, then the solution to world poverty would be self-evident: unionize all the poorest nations on earth.

Private-sector unions reached their peak in terms of membership in the 1950s, when they accounted for about a third of the workforce. Today, they represent barely 10 percent of the private-sector workforce. All during this time of *declining* union membership, influence, and power, wages and living standards have *risen* quite substantially. All of the "declining industries" in America from the 1970s on tended to be the highly unionized ones, whereas the growing industries, especially in the high-technology fields, are almost exclusively nonunion.

At best, unions can improve the living standards of *some* of their members, but only at the expense of other, nonunion workers, consumers, and others. When unions use their power to go on strike, or threaten to strike, and succeed in increasing their members' wages above what they could earn on the free market, they inevitably cause some union members to lose their jobs. This is because of a variant of the economic law of demand: when wages rise, making labor more costly, it becomes less profitable (or unprofitable) for employers to employ as many workers. Typically it is the younger, less experienced union members who lose their jobs because of this phenomenon. For example, if a unionized carpenter's apprentice can contribute, say, $10 an hour to the profitability of a home-building business, the home builder will find it profitable to pay him up to that price. Older, more experienced carpenters will be paid more in a free market because they have higher productivity levels and hence are more valuable to employers. But if their union negotiates a wage of, say, $15 an hour, even for the apprentice, then it is clearly no longer profitable for the employer to employ the younger and less experienced worker.

This is how unionization causes what economists call a "disemployment effect." The newly unemployed workers seek work elsewhere, including in the nonunionized workforce. The increased supply of workers in the nonunion workforce creates more of a "buyers' market" for labor, as employers are able to offer lower wages than they could if labor were more scarce. Thus, union gains always come at the expense of nonunion labor. That is why unions refer to their competition—nonunion labor—as "scabs" or worse. It is why the long history of union violence has been directed mostly at the persons and property of nonunion workers, not at corporate executives. Nonunion workers, not corporate executives, have been shot or shot at, been beaten, and had their automobiles and other property vandalized or destroyed by "union activists." Union rhetoric has it that "the company is the enemy," but unions' own actions belie this rhetoric. To unions, competing nonunion workers are the real enemy.

Increased productivity is the chief cause of increased wages and standards of living, and the principal components of increased productivity are, as noted, capital investment and "human capital" investment—education, experience, and training. Unions focus on *redistributing* wealth from nonunion to unionized workers, but apart from apprenticeship programs and the like, they do not focus on increasing worker productivity. Indeed, unions are notorious for *harming* worker productivity—with their "featherbedding rules" (requiring more people than necessary to do the job); with rules allowing only certain kinds of workers to perform various mundane tasks in the workplace (for example, when only electricians can change lightbulbs); with their opposition to labor-saving equipment and technology; and of course with their strikes and walkouts, which shut down plants and factories altogether. By harming productivity, unions *hamper* the rise in wages over time.

The productivity-harming actions of unions are in essence a tax on productivity on certain industries, which makes investment in those industries less profitable. And since capital investment is the primary source of productivity improvements—and therefore of rising wages—over the long run unions are a drag on productivity and on higher wages in such industries. Indeed, if unions were good for productivity, as some have claimed, then businesses would be inviting them in rather than spending large sums to avoid unionization.

THE ANTICAPITALIST CRUSADE

Looking carefully at the historical record reveals that capitalism has produced tremendous benefits in this country—not only for wealthy entrepreneurs but also for the working class. But myths persist that capitalists only exploit workers, that capitalism is an unfair system because it produces income inequality, and that the only thing protecting the working class is the labor unions and government bureaucrats. All this is what the anticapitalists would have us believe. Among the leaders of the anticapitalist crusade are the labor unions, the supposed champions of the American worker who have actually done more harm than good to the working class. One reason that unions spread anticapitalist propaganda is self-preservation: they need workers to see the company as the enemy so that they do not begin to question why they must pay dues year in and year out to labor unions that, in many instances, don't seem to be doing much for them.

The antibusiness climate fostered by labor unions and others makes it easier for myths about capitalism to persist. Anticapitalist sentiment can also allow ambitious politicians to impose productivity-harming regulations and taxes on businesses. For example, in the late summer of 2003 the lieutenant governor of California, who was running for governor at the time, announced an endorsement by the state AFL-CIO on the same day that he proposed imposing price controls on gasoline. The AFL-CIO had been at the forefront of efforts to publicly demonize the oil companies in California, and the lieutenant governor took advantage of these efforts to advocate price controls—even though such controls always cause shortages and other misallocations. In the long run these anticapitalist crusades deter capital investment and therefore *harm* American workers by leading to a situation in which there are fewer jobs and lower pay levels. The truth is, so many of those who claim to speak for the "oppressed" working class stand in the way of the true source of higher living standards in America and elsewhere: free-market capitalism.

CHAPTER SEVEN

The Truth About
the "Robber Barons"

Free-market capitalism is a network of free and voluntary
exchanges in which producers work, produce, and exchange
their products for the products of others through prices vol-
untarily arrived at. State capitalism consists of one or more
groups making use of the coercive apparatus of the govern-
ment . . . for themselves by expropriating the production of
others by force and violence.

—Murray N. Rothbard, *The Logic of Action* (1997)

T HE LATE nineteenth and early twentieth centuries are often referred to as the time of the "robber barons." It is a staple of
history books to attach this derogatory phrase to such figures as
John D. Rockefeller, Cornelius Vanderbilt, and the great nineteenth-
century railroad operators—Grenville Dodge, Leland Stanford,
Henry Villard, James J. Hill, and others. To most historians writing
on this period, these entrepreneurs committed thinly veiled acts of
larceny to enrich themselves at the expense of their customers.

Once again we see the image of the greedy, exploitative capitalist, but in many cases this is a distortion of the truth. As common as
it is to speak of "robber barons," most who use that term are confused about the role of capitalism in the American economy and fail
to make an important distinction—the distinction between what

might be called a market entrepreneur and a political entrepreneur. A pure *market entrepreneur*, or capitalist, succeeds financially by selling a newer, better, or less expensive product on the free market without any government subsidies, direct or indirect. The key to his success as a capitalist is his ability to please the consumer, for in a capitalist society the consumer ultimately calls the economic shots. By contrast, a *political entrepreneur* succeeds primarily by influencing government to subsidize his business or industry, or to enact legislation or regulation that harms his competitors. In the mousetrap industry, for instance, you can be a market entrepreneur by making better mousetraps and thereby convincing consumers to buy more of your mousetraps and less of your competitors', or you can lobby Congress to prohibit the importation of all foreign-made mousetraps. In the former situation the consumer voluntarily hands over his money for the superior mousetrap; in the latter case the consumer, not given anything (better) in return, pays more for existing mousetraps just because the import quota has reduced supply and therefore driven up prices.

The American economy has always included a mix of market and political entrepreneurs—self-made men and women as well as political connivers and manipulators. And sometimes, people who have achieved success as market entrepreneurs in one period of their lives later become political entrepreneurs. But the distinction between the two is critical to make, for market entrepreneurship is a hallmark of genuine capitalism, whereas political entrepreneurship is not—it is neomercantilism.

In some cases, of course, the entrepreneurs commonly labeled "robber barons" did indeed profit by exploiting American customers, but these were *not market* entrepreneurs. For example, Leland Stanford, a former governor and U.S. senator from California, used his political connections to have the state pass laws prohibiting competition for his Central Pacific railroad,[1] and he and his business partners profited from this monopoly scheme. Unfortunately, the resentment that this naturally generated among the public was unfairly directed at other entrepreneurs who succeeded in the railroad industry without political interference that tilted the playing field in their direction. Thanks to historians who fail to (or refuse to) make this crucial distinction, many Americans have an inaccurate view of American capitalism.

HOW TO BUILD A RAILROAD

Most business historians have assumed that the transcontinental railroads would never have been built without government subsidies. The free market would have failed to provide the adequate capital, or so the theory asserts. The evidence for this theory is that the Union Pacific and Central Pacific railroads, which were completed in the years after the War Between the States, received per-mile subsidies from the federal government in the form of low-interest loans as well as massive land grants. But there need not be cause and effect here: the subsidies were not needed to *cause* the transcontinental railroads to be built. We know this because, just as many roads and canals were privately financed in the early nineteenth century, a market entrepreneur built his own transcontinental railroad. James J. Hill built the Great Northern Railroad "without any government aid, even the right of way, through hundreds of miles of public lands, being paid for in cash," as Hill himself stated.[2]

Quite naturally, Hill strongly opposed government favors to his competitors: "The government should not furnish capital to these companies, in addition to their enormous land subsidies, to enable them to conduct their business in competition with enterprises that have received no aid from the public treasury," he wrote.[3] This may sound quaint by today's standards, but it was still a hotly debated issue in the late nineteenth century.

James J. Hill was hardly a "baron" or aristocrat. His father died when he was fourteen, so he dropped out of school to work in a grocery store for four dollars a month to help support his widowed mother. As a young adult he worked in the farming, shipping, steamship, fur-trading, and railroad industries. He learned the ways of business in these settings, saved his money, and eventually became an investor and manager of his own enterprises.[4] (It was much easier to accomplish such things in the days before income taxation).

Hill got his start in the railroad business when he and several partners purchased a bankrupted Minnesota railroad that had been run into the ground by the government-subsidized Northern Pacific (NP). The NP had been a patronage "reward" to financier Jay Cooke, who in the War Between the States had been one of the Union's leading financiers.[5] But Cooke and his NP associates built recklessly; the government's subsidies and land grants were issued on a per-mile-of-track basis, so Cooke and his cohorts had strong incentives to build as quickly as possible, which only encouraged shoddy work. Consequently, by 1873 the NP developers had fallen into bankruptcy.[6] The people of Minnesota and the Dakotas, where the railroad was being built, considered Cooke and his business associates to be "derelicts at best and thieves at worst," writes Hill biographer Michael P. Malone.[7]

It took Hill and his business partners five years to complete the purchase of the railroad (the St. Paul, Minneapolis, and Manitoba), which would form the nucleus of a road that he would eventually build all the way to the Pacific (the Great Northern). He had nothing but contempt for Cooke and the NP for their shady practices and corruption, and he quickly demonstrated a genius for railroad construction. Under his direction, the workers began laying rails twice as quickly as the NP crews had, and even at that speed he built what everyone at the time considered to be the highest-quality line. Hill micromanaged every aspect of the work, even going so far as to spell workers so they could take much-needed coffee breaks.[8] His efficiency extended into meticulous cost cutting. He passed his cost reductions on to his customers in the form of lower rates because he knew that the farmers, miners, timber interests, and others who used his rail services would succeed or fail along with him. His motto was: "We have got to prosper with you or we have got to be poor with you."[9]

In keeping with his philosophy of encouraging the prosperity of the people residing in the vicinity of his railroad, Hill publicized his views on the importance of crop diversification to the farmers of the region. He didn't want them to become dependent on a single crop and therefore subject to the uncertainties of price fluctuation, as the southern cotton farmers were.[10] Hill also provided free seed grain—and even cattle—to farmers who had suffered from drought and depression; stockpiled wood and other fuel near his train depots so farmers could stock up when returning from a delivery to his trains; and donated land to towns for parks, schools, and churches.[11] He transported immigrants to the Great Plains for a mere ten dollars if they promised to farm near his railroad, and he sponsored contests for the beefiest livestock or the most abundant wheat. His "model farms" educated farmers on the latest developments in agricultural science. All of this generated goodwill with the local communities and was also good for business.

Hill's rates fell steadily, and when farmers began complaining about the lack of grain storage space, he instructed his company managers to build larger storage facilities near his rail depots. He refused to join in attempts at cartel price fixing and in fact "gloried in the role of rate-slasher and disrupter of [price-fixing] pooling agreements," writes historian Burton Folsom.[12] After all, he knew that monopolistic pricing would have been an act of killing the goose that lays the golden egg.

In building his transcontinental railroad, from 1886 to 1893, Hill applied the same strategy that he had in building the St. Paul, Minneapolis, and Manitoba: careful building of the road combined with the economic cultivation of the nearby communities. He always built for durability and efficiency, not scenery, as was sometimes the case with the government-subsidized railroads. He did not skimp on building materials, having witnessed what harsh Midwest winters could do to his facilities and how foolish it was for the NP to have ignored this lesson. (The solid granite arch bridge that Hill built across the Mississippi River was a Minneapolis landmark for many years.)[13] Burton Folsom describes Hill's compulsion for excellence:

Hill's quest for short routes, low grades, and few curvatures was an obsession. In 1889, Hill conquered the Rocky Mountains by finding the legendary Marias Pass. Lewis and Clark had described a low pass through the Rockies back in 1805; but later no one seemed to know whether it really existed or, if it did, where it was. Hill wanted the best gradient so much that he hired a man to spend months searching western Montana for this legendary pass. He did in fact find it, and the ecstatic Hill shortened his route by almost one hundred miles.[14]

Hill's Great Northern was, consequently, the "best constructed and most profitable of all the world's major railroads," as Michael P. Malone points out.[15] The Great Northern's efficiency and profitability were legendary, whereas the government-subsidized railroads, managed by a group of political entrepreneurs who focused more on acquiring subsidies than on building sound railroads, were inefficiently built and operated. Jay Cooke was not the only one whose government-subsidized railroad ended up in bankruptcy. In fact, Hill's Great Northern was the only transcontinental railroad that never went bankrupt.

JAMES J. HILL VERSUS THE *REAL* ROBBER BARONS

By the summer of 1861, after the Battle of First Manassas, it was apparent to all that the War Between the States was going to be a long, drawn-out campaign. Nevertheless, in 1862 Congress, with the southern Democrats gone, diverted millions of dollars from the war effort to begin building a subsidized railroad. The Pacific Railroad Act of 1862 created the Union Pacific (UP) and the Central Pacific (CP) railroads, the latter to commence building in Sacramento, California, and the former in Omaha, Nebraska. For each mile of track built Congress gave these companies a section of land—most of which would be sold—as well as a sizable loan: $16,000 per mile for track built on flat prairie land; $32,000 for hilly terrain; and $48,000 in the mountains.[16] As was the case with Jay Cooke's Northern Pacific, these railroads tried to build as quickly and as cheaply as possible in order to take advantage of the governmental largesse. Where James J. Hill would be obsessed with finding the shortest route for his railroad, these government-subsidized companies, knowing they were paid by the mile, "sometimes built winding, circuitous roads to collect for more mileage," as Burton Folsom recounts.[17] Union Pacific vice president and general manager Thomas Durant "stressed speed, not workmanship," writes Folsom, which meant that he and his chief engineer, former Union Army general Grenville Dodge, often used whatever kind of wood was available for railroad ties, including fragile cottonwood. This, of course, is in stark contrast to James J. Hill's insistence on using only the best-quality materials, even if they were more expensive. Durant paid so many lumberjacks to cut trees for rails that farmers were forced to use rifles to defend their land from the subsidized railroad builders; not for him was the Hill motto, "We have got to prosper with you or we have got to be poor with you." Folsom continues:

> Since Dodge was in a hurry, he laid track on the ice and snow. . . . Naturally, the line had to be rebuilt in the spring. What was worse, unanticipated spring flooding along the Lower fork of the Platte River washed out rails, bridges, and telephone poles, doing at least $50,000 damage the first year. No wonder some observers estimated the actual building cost at almost three times what it should have been.[18]

In 1869, after seven years of construction, the two subsidized railroads managed to meet up at Promontory Point, Utah, amidst much hoopla and celebration. What is not often mentioned, however, is that after the big celebration both of the lines had to be rebuilt and even relocated in places, a task that took five more years (into 1874).

The wasteful costs of construction were astonishing. The subsidized railroads routinely used more gunpowder blasting their way through mountains and forests on a single day than was used during the entire Battle of Gettysburg.

With so much tax money floating around, the executives of the CP and UP stole funds from their own companies in order to profit personally, something that would have been irrational for James J. Hill or any other private, market entrepreneur to do. For example, the UP managers created their own coal company, mining coal for two dollars per ton and selling it to themselves for six dollars per ton, pocketing the profits. This crooked scam was repeated in dozens of instances and would be exposed as the Crédit Mobilier scandal. (Crédit Mobilier was the name of one of the companies run by UP executives.)

With virtually everything riding on political connections, as opposed to creating the best-quality railroad for consumers, the UP and CP executives naturally spent an inordinate amount of time on politics as opposed to business management. While James J. Hill detested politicians and politics and paid little attention to them, things were very different with the UP. Folsom explains:

> In 1866 Thomas Durant wined and dined 150 "prominent citizens" (including senators, an ambassador, and government bureaucrats) along a completed section of the railroad. He hired an orchestra, a caterer, six cooks, a magician (to pull subsidies out of a hat?), and a photographer. For those with ecumenical palates, he served Chinese duck and Roman goose; the more adventurous were offered roast ox and antelope. All could have expensive wine and, for dessert, strawberries, peaches, and cherries. After dinner some of the men hunted buffalo from their coaches. Durant hoped that all would go back to Washington inclined to repay the UP for its hospitality.[19]

In addition, free railroad passes and Crédit Mobilier stock were routinely handed out to members of Congress and state legislators, and General William Tecumseh Sherman was sold land near Omaha, Nebraska, for $2.50 an acre when the going rate was $8.00.

Congress responded to the 1874 Crédit Mobilier scandal by enacting a blizzard of regulations on the UP and CP that would in the future make it impossible for them to operate with any semblance of efficiency. Because of the regulations, managers could not make quick decisions regarding leasing, borrowing money, building extensions of the rail lines, or any other day-to-day business decision. Each such decision literally required an act of Congress. Political interference also meant that separate rail lines were required to be built to serve communities represented by influential members of Congress even if those lines were uneconomical. No business could possibly survive and earn a profit under such a scenario. The UP went bankrupt in 1893; the Great Northern, on the other hand, was still going strong. Not having accepted any government subsidies, James J. Hill was free to build and operate his railroad in a way that he deemed was most efficient and most profitable. He prospered while most of his subsidized competitors went bankrupt at one point or another. Hill continued to show how effective market entrepreneurs could be. Having completed the Great Northern, he then got into the steamship business in order to facilitate American exports to the Orient. As usual, he succeeded, increasing American exports to Japan sevenfold from 1896 to 1905. He continued to reduce his rail rates in order to make American exports profitable. Being an ardent free trader, Hill was a Democrat for most of his life, because the Republican Party since the time of Lincoln had been the main political force behind high protectionist tariffs. (He switched parties late in life when the Democratic Party abandoned its laissez-faire roots and became interventionist, but he considered the Republican Party to be merely the lesser of two evils.)

Recognizing a market in the American Midwest for timber from the Northwest, Hill convinced his next-door neighbor, Frederick Weyerhauser, to get into the timber business with him. He cut his freight charges from ninety to forty cents per hundred pounds, and he and Weyerhauser prospered by selling Northwest timber to other parts of the country.[20]

Despite the quality services and reduced costs that Hill brought to Americans, he would be unfairly lumped in with the political entrepreneurs who were fleecing the taxpayers and consumers. The public eventually began complaining of the monopoly pricing and corruption that were *inherent* features of the government-created and -subsidized railroads. The federal government responded to the complaints with the Interstate Commerce Act of 1887, which was supposed to ban rail rate discrimination, and later with the Hepburn Act of 1906, which made it illegal to charge different rates to different customers. What these two federal laws did was to outlaw Hill's price cutting by forcing railroads to charge *everyone* the same high rates.[21] This was all done in the name of consumer protection, giving it an Orwellian aura.

This new round of government regulation benefited the government-subsidized railroads at Hill's expense, for he was the most vigorous price cutter. His trade to the Orient was severely damaged since he could no longer legally offer discounts on exports in order to induce American exporters to join with him in entering foreign markets. He eventually got out of the steamship business altogether, and as a result untold opportunities to export American products abroad were lost forever.

The Interstate Commerce Commission soon created a bureaucratic monstrosity that attempted to micromanage all aspects of the railroad business, hampering its efficiency even further. This was a classic example of economist Ludwig von Mises's theory of government interventionism: one intervention (such as subsidies for railroads) leads to market distortions, which create problems for which the public "demands" solutions. Government responds with even more interventions, usually in the form of more regulation of business activities, which cause even more problems, which lead to more intervention, and on and on. The end result is that free-market capitalism is more and more heavily stifled by regulation.

And on top of that, usually the free market, not government intervention, gets the blame. Thus, all of the railroad men of the late nineteenth century have gone down in history as "robber barons," although this designation definitely does not apply to James J. Hill. It does apply to his subsidized competitors, who deserve all the condemnation that history has provided them. (Also deserving of condemnation are the politicians who subsidized them, enabling their monopoly and corruption.)

Another prime example of a market entrepreneur whom generations of writers and historians have inaccurately portrayed—indeed, demonized—is John D. Rockefeller. Like James J. Hill, Rockefeller came from very modest beginnings; his father was a peddler who barely made ends meet. Born in 1839, he was one of six children, and his first job upon graduating from high school at age sixteen was as an assistant bookkeeper for fifteen cents a day (under ten dollars a day today, even accounting for nearly 150 years of inflation).[22]

Rockefeller was religious about working and saving his money. After working several sales jobs, by age twenty-three he had saved up enough to invest four thousand dollars in an oil refinery in Cleveland, Ohio, with a business partner and fellow church member, Samuel Andrews.[23] Like James J. Hill, Rockefeller paid meticulous attention to every detail of his business, constantly striving to cut his costs, improve his product, and expand his line of products. He also sometimes joined in with the manual laborers as a means of developing an even more thorough understanding of his business. His business partners and managers emulated him, which drove the company to great success. As economist Dominick Armentano writes, the firm of Rockefeller, Andrews, and Flagler, which would become Standard Oil,

> prospered quickly in the intensely competitive industry due to the economic excellence of its entire operations. Instead of buying oil from jobbers, they made the jobbers' profit by sending their own purchasing men into the oil region. They also made their own sulfuric acid, barrels, lumber, wagons, and

glue. They kept minute and accurate records of every item from rivets to barrel bungs. They built elaborate storage facilities near their refineries. Rockefeller bargained as shrewdly for crude as anyone has before or since; and Sam Andrews coaxed more kerosene from a barrel of crude than the competition could. In addition, the Rockefeller firm put out the cleanest burning kerosene and managed to profitably dispose of most of the residues, in the form of lubricating oil, paraffin wax, and Vaseline.[24]

Rockefeller pioneered the practice known as "vertical integration," or in-house provision of various inputs into the production process; that is, he made his own barrels, wagons, and so on. This is not always advantageous—sometimes it pays to purchase certain items from specialists who can produce those items at very low cost. But vertical integration has the advantage of allowing one to monitor the quality of one's own inputs. It has the further advantage of avoiding what modern economists call the "hold-up problem." If, say, an electric power plant contracted with a nearby coal mine for coal to fuel its generating plant, the coal mine might effectively break its contract at one point by demanding more money for its coal. In such instances the power plant has the choice of paying up, engaging in costly litigation, or going without the coal and closing down. None of these options is attractive. But if the power plant simply buys the coal mine, all of these problems disappear. That is what Rockefeller, the compulsive micromanager, did with many aspects of the oil-refining business. He reduced his costs and avoided hold-up problems through vertical integration.

Rockefeller also devised means of eliminating much of the incredible waste that had plagued the oil industry. His chemists figured out how to produce such oil byproducts as lubricating oil, gasoline, paraffin wax, Vaseline, paint, varnish, and about three hundred other substances. In each instance he profited by eliminating waste.

Just as James J. Hill spent the extra money to build the highest quality railroad lines possible, Rockefeller did not skimp in building his refineries. So confident was he of the safety of his operations that he did not even purchase insurance.

Rockefeller also made the oil-refining industry much more efficient. There had been vast overinvestment in the oil industry in its first decades, as everyone had wanted to get rich quick in the business. Northwestern Pennsylvania, where the first oil well had been drilled, was littered with oil derricks and refineries of all sizes, many of which were operated by men who really should have been in another line of work. Rockefeller purchased many of these poorly managed operations and put their assets to far better use. There was never any threat that these "horizontal mergers"—the combination of two firms that are in the same business—would create a monopoly, for Standard Oil had literally hundreds of competitors, including such oil giants as Sun Oil, not to mention its many large competitors in international markets.

One of Rockefeller's harshest critics was journalist Ida Tarbell, whose brother was the treasurer of the Pure Oil Company, which could not compete with Standard Oil's low prices. She published a series of hypercritical articles in *McClure's* magazine in 1902 and 1903, which were turned into a book entitled *The History of the Standard Oil Company,* a classic of antibusiness propaganda.[25] Tarbell's writings are emotional, often illogical, and lacking in any serious attempt at economic analysis. But even she was compelled to praise what she called the "marvelous" economy of the entire Standard Oil operation. In a passage describing one aspect of Standard Oil's vertical integration she wrote:

Not far away from the canning works, on Newtown Creek, is an oil refinery. This oil runs to the canning works, and, as the newmade cans come down by a chute from the works above, where they have just been finished, they are filled, twelve at a time, with the oil made a few miles away. The filling apparatus is admirable. As the newmade cans come down the chute they are distributed, twelve in a row, along one side of a turn-table. The turn-table is revolved, and the cans come directly under twelve measures, each holding five gallons of oil—a turn of a valve, and the cans are full. The table is turned a quarter, and while twelve more cans are filled and twelve fresh ones are distributed, four men with soldering cappers put the caps on the first set. . . . The cans are placed at once in wooden boxes standing ready, and, after a twenty-four-hour wait for discovering leaks, are nailed up and carted to a nearby door. This door opens on the river, and there at anchor by the side of the factory is a vessel chartered for South America or China . . . waiting to receive the cans. . . . *It is a marvelous example of economy, not only in materials, but in time and footsteps* [emphasis added].[26]

Because of Standard Oil's superior efficiency (and lower prices), the company's share of the refined petroleum market rose from 4 percent in 1870 to 25 percent in 1874 and to about 85 percent in 1880.[27] As Standard Oil garnered more and more business, it became even more efficient through "economies of scale"—the tendency of per-unit costs to decline as the volume of output increases. This is typical of industries in which there is a large initial "fixed cost"—such as the expense involved in building an oil refinery. Once the refinery is built, the costs of maintaining the refinery are more or less fixed, so as more and more customers are added, the cost per customer declines. As a result, the company cut its cost of refining a gallon of oil from 3 cents in 1869 to less than half a cent by 1885. Significantly, Rockefeller passed these savings along to the consumer, as the price of refined oil plummeted from more than 30 cents per gallon in 1869 to 10 cents in 1874 and 8 cents in 1885.[28] Because he could refine kerosene far more cheaply than anyone else could, which was reflected in his low prices, the railroads offered Rockefeller special low prices, or volume discounts. This is a common, ordinary business practice—offering volume discounts to one's largest customers in order to keep them—but Rockefeller's less efficient competitors complained bitterly. Nothing was stopping them from cutting their costs and prices and winning similar railroad rebates other than their own inabilities or laziness, but they apparently decided that it was easier to complain about Rockefeller's "unfair advantage" instead. Cornelius Vanderbilt publicly offered railroad rebates to any oil refiner who could give him the same volume of business that Rockefeller did, but since no one was as efficient as Rockefeller, no one could take him up on his offer.[29]

All of Rockefeller's savings benefited the consumer, as his low prices made kerosene readily available to Americans. Indeed, in the 1870s kerosene replaced whale oil as the primary source of fuel for light in America. It might seem trivial today, but this revolutionized the American way of life; as Burton Folsom writes, "Working and reading became after-dark activities new to most Americans in the 1870s."[30] In addition, by stimulating the demand for kerosene and other products, Rockefeller also created thousands upon thousands of new jobs in the oil and related industries.

Rockefeller was extremely generous with his employees, usually paying them significantly more than the competition did. Consequently, he was rarely slowed down by strikes or labor disputes. He also believed in rewarding his most innovative managers with bonuses and paid time off if they came up with good ideas for productivity improvements, a simple lesson that many modern corporations seem to have never learned.

Of course, in every industry the less efficient competitors can be expected to snipe at their superior rivals, and in many instances sniping turns into an organized *political* crusade to get the government to enact laws or regulations that harm the superior competitor. Economists call this process "rent seeking"; in the language of economics, "rent" means a financial return on an investment or activity in excess of what the activity would normally bring in a competitive market. This sort of political crusade by less successful rivals is precisely what crippled the great Rockefeller organization.

The governmental vehicle that was chosen to cripple Standard Oil was antitrust regulation. Standard Oil's competitors succeeded in getting the federal government to bring an antitrust or anti-monopoly suit against the company in 1906, after they had persuaded a number of states to file similar suits in the previous two or three years.

The ostensible purpose of antitrust regulation is to protect consumers, so on the face of it the government's case against Standard Oil seems ludicrous. Because of Standard Oil's tremendous efficiencies, the price of refined petroleum had been plummeting for several decades, generating great benefits for consumers and forcing all other competitors to find ways to cut *their* costs and prices in order to survive. Product quality had improved, innovation was encouraged by the fierce competition, production had expanded dramatically, and there were hundreds of competitors. None of these facts constitutes in any way a sign of monopoly.

As happens in so many federal antitrust lawsuits, a number of novel theories were invented to rationalize the lawsuit. One of them was so-called predatory pricing. According to this theory, a "predatory firm" that possesses a "war chest" of profits will cut its prices so low as to drive all competitors from the market. Then, when it faces no competition, it will charge monopolistic prices. It is *assumed* that at that point no other competition will emerge, despite the large profits being made in the industry. Journalist Ida Tarbell did as much as anyone to popularize this theory in her book on Standard Oil, in a chapter entitled "Cutting to Kill." To economists, however, predatory pricing is theoretical nonsense and has no empirical validity, either. It has never been demonstrated that a monopoly has ever been created in this way. Certainly predatory pricing was not a tactic used by Standard Oil, which was never a monopoly anyway. In a now-classic article on the topic in the prestigious *Journal of Law and Economics,* John S. McGee studied the Standard Oil antitrust case and concluded not only that the company did not practice predatory pricing but also that it would have been irrational and foolish to have attempted such a scheme.[31] And whatever else may be said about John D. Rockefeller, he was no one's fool.

McGee was quite right about the irrationality of predatory pricing. As an investment strategy, predatory pricing is all cost and risk and no potential reward. The would-be "predator" stands to lose the most from pricing below its average cost, since, presumably, it already does the most business. If the company is the market leader with the highest sales and is losing money on each sale, then that company will be the biggest loser in the industry.

There is also great uncertainty about how long such a tactic could take: ten years? twenty years? No business would intentionally lose money on every sale for years on end with the pie-in-the-sky hope of someday becoming a monopoly. Besides, even if that were to occur, nothing would stop new competitors from all over the world from entering the industry and driving the price back down, thereby eliminating any benefits of the predatory pricing strategy.

Finally, there is a logical contradiction in the theory. The theory assumes a "war chest" of profits that is used to subsidize the money-losing strategy of predatory pricing. But where did this war chest come from? The theory posits that predatory pricing is what creates a war chest of "monopoly profits," but at the same time it simply assumes that these profits already exist!

After examining some eleven thousand pages of the Standard Oil case's trial record, McGee concluded that there was no evidence at all presented at trial that Standard Oil had even attempted to practice predatory pricing. What it did practice was good old competitive price cutting, driven by its quest for efficiency and customer service.

The antitrust case against Standard Oil also seems absurd because its share of the petroleum products market had actually dropped significantly over the years. From a high of 88 percent in 1890, Standard Oil's market share had fallen to 64 percent by 1911, the year in which the U.S. Supreme Court reaffirmed the lower court finding that Standard Oil was guilty of monopolizing the petroleum products industry.[32] The court argued, in essence, that Standard Oil was a "large" company with many divisions, and if those divisions were in reality separate companies, there would be more competition. The court made no mention at all of the industry's economic performance; of supposed predatory pricing; of whether industry output had been restrained, as monopoly theory holds; or of any other economic factors relevant to determining harm to consumers. The mere fact that Standard Oil had organized some thirty separate divisions under one consolidated management structure (a trust) was sufficient reason to label it a monopoly and force the company to break up into a number of smaller units.

In other words, the organizational structure that was responsible for the company's great efficiencies and decades-long price cutting and product improving was seriously damaged. Standard Oil became much *less* efficient as a result, to the benefit of its less efficient rivals and to the detriment of consumers. Standard Oil's competitors, who with their behind-the-scenes lobbying were the main instigators of the federal prosecution, are (along with "muckracking" journalists like Ida Tarbell) the real villains in this story. They succeeded in using political entrepreneurship to hamstring a superior market entrepreneur, which in the end rendered the American petroleum industry *less* competitive.

The prosecution of Standard Oil was a watershed event for the American petroleum industry. It emboldened many in the industry to pay less and less attention to market entrepreneurship (capitalism) and more to political entrepreneurship (mercantilism) to profit.

During World War I the oil industry became "partners" with the federal government ostensibly to assure the flow of oil for the war effort. (Of course, in such arrangements the government is always the "senior partner.") As Dominick Armentano writes:

> The Oil Division of the U.S. Fuel Administration in cooperation with the War Services Committee, was responsible for determining oil production and for allocating crude supplies among various refiners. In short, these governmental organizations, with the coordinating services of leading business interests, had the legal power to operate the oil industry as a cartel, eliminating what was described as "unnecessary waste" (competition), and making centralized pricing and allocative decisions for the industry [i.e., price fixing] as a whole. Thus, the wartime experiment in "planning" (i.e., planning by political agents to satisfy political interests rather than by consumers, investors, and entrepreneurs to meet consumer demand) crea-

ted what had previously been unobtainable: a government sanctioned cartel in oil.[33]

After the war, oil industry executives favored extending this government-sanctioned and -supervised cartel. President Calvin Coolidge created a Federal Oil Conservation Board that enforced the "compulsory withholding of oil resources and state prorationing of oil," a convoluted way of saying "monopoly."[34] The newly formed American Petroleum Institute, an industry trade association, lobbied for various regulatory schemes to restrict competition and prop up prices; it did not even pretend to be in favor of capitalism or free enterprise. The institute even endorsed the use of National Guard troops to enforce state government production quotas in Texas and Oklahoma in the early 1930s.

During the 1930s even more teeth were put into government/ oil industry cartel schemes. The National Recovery Act empowered the federal government to support state oil production quotas to assure output reductions and higher prices. Interstate and foreign shipments of oil were strictly regulated so as to create regional monopolies, and import duties on foreign oil were raised to protect the higher-priced American oil from foreign competition.[35]

In 1935 Congress passed the Connally Hot Oil Act, which made it illegal to transport oil across state lines "in violation of state proration requirements."[36] In the 1950s the government placed import quotas on oil, creating an even greater monopoly power. All of this, you will recall, came on the heels of the government's antitrust crusade against the Standard Oil "monopoly." Clearly, the purpose of the political persecution of Standard Oil had been to begin stamping out competition in the oil industry. That process was continued with a vengeance with forty years of squalid political entrepreneurship. By the middle of the twentieth century, real capitalism had all but disappeared from the oil industry.

VANDERBILT TAKES ON THE MONOPOLISTS

The battle between market and political entrepreneurs was not confined to the railroad and oil industries. Indeed, from the midnineteenth century onward, this sort of battle marked the development of much of American industry—the steamship industry, the steel industry, and the auto industry, to name just a few. For example, the great steamship entrepreneur Cornelius Vanderbilt competed with government-subsidized political entrepreneurs for much of his career. In fact, he got his start in business by competing—illegally—against a state-sanctioned steamship monopoly operated by Robert Fulton. In 1807, the New York state legislature had granted Fulton a legal, thirty-year monopoly on steamboat traffic in New York—a classic example of mercantilism.[37] In 1817, however, a young Cornelius Vanderbilt was hired by New Jersey businessman Thomas Gibbons to defy the monopoly and run steamboats in New York. Vanderbilt worked in direct competition with Fulton, charging lower rates as his boats raced from Elizabeth, New Jersey, to New York City; to underscore the challenge to Fulton's monopoly, Vanderbilt flew a flag on his boats that read NEW JERSEY MUST BE FREE. Slowly he was breaking down the Fulton monopoly, which the U.S. Supreme Court finally ended in 1824, ruling in *Gibbons* v. *Ogden* that only the federal government, not the states, could regulate interstate trade under the Commerce Clause of the Constitution.[38]

As the cost of steamboat traffic plummeted because of deregulation, the volume of traffic increased significantly and the industry took off. Vanderbilt became the leading market entrepreneur in the industry, but he would continue to face government-subsidized competitors. For example, steamship operator Edward K. Collins convinced Congress that it needed to subsidize the transatlantic steamship business to compete with the Europeans and to create a military fleet in case of war. In 1847 Congress awarded Collins

$3 million, plus $385,000 per year. Sitting on these fat subsidies, Collins had little incentive to build his ships efficiently or to watch his costs once they were built. Instead of focusing on making his business more efficient, Collins spent lavishly on lobbying, including wining and dining President Millard Fillmore, his entire cabinet, and many congressmen.[39]

Like James J. Hill in the railroad industry, Vanderbilt did not shy away from competing against his heavily subsidized rivals. Not surprisingly, these government-supported rivals ultimately could not keep up with Vanderbilt, in large part because the stifling regulations that were inevitably attached to the government subsidies made these steamship lines remarkably inefficient. By 1858, Collins's line had become so inefficient that Congress ended his subsidy, and he promptly went bankrupt. He could not compete with Vanderbilt on an equal basis.

THE REAL HISTORY

The lesson here is that most historians are hopelessly confused about the rise of capitalism in America. They usually fail to adequately appreciate the entrepreneurial genius of men like James J. Hill, John D. Rockefeller, and Cornelius Vanderbilt, and more often than not they lump these men (and other market entrepreneurs) in with genuine "robber barons" or political entrepreneurs.

Most historians also uncritically repeat the claim that that government subsidies were necessary to building America's transcontinental railroad industry, steamship industry, steel industry, and other industries. But while clinging to this "market failure" argument, they ignore (or at least are unaware of) the fact that market entrepreneurs performed quite well without government subsidies. They also ignore the fact that the subsidies themselves were a great source of inefficiency and business failure, even though they enriched the direct recipients of the subsidies and advanced the political careers of those politicians who dished them out.

Political entrepreneurs and their governmental patrons are the real villains of American business history and should be portrayed as such. They are the real robber barons.

At the same time, the market entrepreneurs who practiced genuine capitalism, whose genius and energy fueled extraordinary economic achievement and also brought tremendous benefits to Americans, should be recognized for their achievements rather than demonized, as they so often are. Men like James J. Hill, John D. Rockefeller, and Cornelius Vanderbilt were heroes who improved the lives of millions of consumers; employed thousands and enabled them to support their families and educate their children; created entire cities because of the success of their enterprises (for example, Scranton, Pennsylvania); pioneered efficient management techniques that are still employed today; and donated hundreds of millions of dollars to charities and nonprofit organizations of all kinds, from libraries to hospitals to symphonies, public parks, and zoos. It is absolutely perverse that historians usually look at these men as crooks or cheaters while praising and advocating "business/government partnerships," which can only lead to corruption and economic decline.

CHAPTER EIGHT

Antitrust Myths

The world of antitrust is reminiscent of Alice's Wonderland: everything seemingly is, yet apparently isn't, simultaneously. It is a world in which competition is lauded as the basic axiom and guiding principle, yet "too much" competition is condemned as "cutthroat." It is a world in which actions designed to limit competition are branded as criminal when taken by businessmen, yet praised as "enlightened" when initiated by the government. It is a world in which the law is so vague that businessmen have no way of knowing whether specific actions will be declared illegal until they hear the judge's verdict—after the fact.

—Alan Greenspan, "Antitrust" (1962)

A NYONE WHO has studied American business history is probably aware of the following story: in the late nineteenth century, with the birth of big business, corporations merged or formed "trusts" that served the same purpose—combining several corporations to act as one. Soon enough, these trusts evolved into monopolies, to the point that a small number of cartels dominated the American economy and gouged consumers while in some cases delivering inferior or dangerous products. To rein in the newly formed cartels, state governments passed antitrust laws in the mid- and late 1880s, and then, in 1890, the U.S. Congress passed the Sherman

Antitrust Act (named after Senator John Sherman, Republican of Ohio).

This story can be found in the scholarly literature in the field of economics. Indeed, one of the severest critics of government regulation and a champion of free markets, Judge Richard Posner, formerly of the University of Chicago Law School, wrote in his textbook on antitrust law that "the Sherman Act was passed in 1890 against a background of rampant cartelization and monopolization of the American economy."[1] The late George Stigler, another University of Chicago free-market economist (and a Nobel laureate), once declared that the Sherman Act was "a public interest law" in the same sense that laws enforcing private property and contracts or suppressing crime are public-interest (as opposed to special-interest) laws.[2] Another textbook author, Marshall Howard, described the Sherman Act as "the Magna Carta of free enterprise."[3]

Thus, the story of how capitalism supposedly became monopolistic in the late nineteenth century, and how it was brought under control by antitrust regulation, is an important chapter in the folklore of American capitalism. And folklore it is. For there was never any *evidence* that the trusts and "combinations" of the late nineteenth century actually harmed consumers in the way that monopolies are supposed to harm consumers—by colluding to restrict production to drive up prices.

At least a little skepticism should have been in order for those who advocated antitrust laws. To begin, from the end of the War Between the States to the end of the nineteenth century America experienced steady *deflation*, meaning that the average price level— the consumer price index—was continually declining. If industry was becoming more and more monopolistic, how is it that prices across the board went down for some *four decades* after the war?

So why would John Sherman and the Republican Party have

fought for the Sherman Act? After all, Sherman was as staunch a protectionist as anyone, and the GOP had since its inception been the party of high, protectionist tariffs—which, as was widely known at the time, tended to *nurture monopoly.*[4] In other words, the same political party that championed the Sherman Act as a proconsumer law had for decades stood for policies that *hurt* consumers and *helped* big business. Would the Republican Party have suddenly decided to wage a suicidal political war on its base constituency, big business? Probably not.

No, the real explanation for this seeming about-face is that antitrust regulation wasn't so proconsumer after all. More important, American capitalism *wasn't* monopolistic in the late nineteenth century; the whole story of antitrust is a myth.

THE SHERMAN ACT AND THE "MONOPOLIES"

As noted in Chapter 7, journalist Ida Tarbell relentlessly attacked John D. Rockefeller's Standard Oil in print. But she was just one of many "yellow journalists"—some with axes to grind, like Tarbell, and others with reputations to enhance—to launch broadsides against trusts in the late nineteenth century. This journalistic vitriol certainly fueled the movement for antitrust laws. Historian William Letwin summarized the standard condemnation of the trusts:

> Trusts, it was said, threatened liberty, because they corrupted civil servants and bribed legislators; they enjoyed privileges such as protection by tariffs; they drove out competitors by lowering prices, victimized consumers by raising prices, defrauded investors by watering stocks, and somehow or other abused everyone. The kind of remedy that the public desired was also clear enough: it wanted a law to destroy the power of the trusts.[5]

Consider each one of these indictments. First, it is true that some businesses "bribed legislators"—that would be the political entrepreneur class discussed in Chapter 7. But bribery was not a consequence of the existence of the trust, which was merely a form of business management. Nor is it safe to assume that the trusts wielded tremendous political power simply because of their size. If the trusts had been as politically powerful as the yellow journalists portrayed them as being, in fact, there never would have been an antitrust law; they would have easily defeated it. Small businesses, farmers, labor unions, and others can be as politically powerful as, if not more powerful than, larger businesses. Indeed, at that time the most potent political lobbying organizations in the United States were groups such as the Grangers, which were coalitions of relatively *small* farmers.

Second, if the trusts benefited from protectionist tariffs, as some obviously did, then that was the fault of Senator Sherman's high tariff policy. In any case, enterprises such as Standard Oil grew large and had millions of customers not because of protectionist tariffs but because they were so successful at cutting costs and prices and at developing newer and better products and services.

Third, driving out competitors with low prices is the essence of *competition* and something that government policy should approve of rather than condemn. A successful free market is one that rewards those businesses (with profits) that can best satisfy consumers and penalizes those businesses that fail to do so. The resources of the failed businesses (land, labor, capital, natural resources, and so forth) can then be purchased by more successful businesses, which will make better use of those resources in serving consumers.

Fourth, the charge that the trusts "victimized consumers by raising prices" is sheer nonsense. The trusts' efficiencies and economies of scales enabled them to *lower* prices for consumers. Even if the charge is that the trusts practiced predatory pricing—

first cutting prices below costs to drive out all the rivals and then raising prices once the competition is eliminated—that is still nonsense. As discussed in Chapter 7, so-called predatory pricing is illogical and foolish as a business practice; moreover, it has never been established that a real-life monopoly has *ever* been formed in this way.

Finally, if any businesses defrauded investors then they deserved to be prosecuted under *criminal law*. In no way should that have led to a law regulating or breaking up all trusts. Fraud is fraud, regardless of the kind of enterprise it emanates from—corporations, government, churches, nonprofit organizations, or wherever.

Another indictment of the trusts was that, even if they weren't monopolies, they were supposedly creating a "dangerous concentration of wealth" in the hands of the top capitalists of the day. The conspicuous wealth of the Rockefellers, Vanderbilts, Stanfords, and others seemed to support this charge. But in reality the nation's wealth was *not* being concentrated in the hands of the leading capitalists. As economic historians Robert Gray and James Peterson pointed out, from 1840 to 1900 the division of all income in America remained the same: labor received 70 percent and property owners ("capital and natural resource suppliers") received 30 percent. In fact, said Gray and Peterson, "Over the same time span, both capital and developed natural resources increased faster than the labor force. This means that labor incomes per unit of labor *rose* compared with profits and interest per unit of property input [emphasis added]."[6] Or, in plain English, it was a competitive labor market, so as workers grew more productive—thanks in part to the trusts' investment in machinery, equipment, and resources—they were more handsomely rewarded. It is always this way in competitive labor markets, for employers have to offer higher wages to compete for increasingly skilled labor.

Nevertheless, perceptions are often more important than reality when it comes to political crusades, and the crusade to regulate the trusts had much more to do with (contrived) perception than with reality. Self-interest was also important, as it always is when one evaluates a law or regulation. Many less competitive businesses supported the Sherman Act because they wanted the government to break up their *more efficient, lower-priced competitors.* Historian Sanford Gordon surveyed public attitudes toward the trusts prior to the 1890 Sherman Act and concluded that special-interest groups did indeed lobby for the law out of their own self-interest. Gordon wrote:

> Perhaps the most violent reaction against [industrial combinations] of any single special interest group came from farmers. . . . They singled out the jute bagging and alleged binder twine trust, and sent petitions to both their state legislators and to Congress demanding some relief. Cotton was suggested as a good substitute for jute to cover their cotton bales. In Georgia, Mississippi, and Tennessee the [farmers'] Alliances passed resolutions condemning the jute bagging trust and recommended the use of cotton cloth.[7]

So cotton farmers were upset that jute, rather than cotton, was being used to cover cotton bales for shipping. As a result, they petitioned the government to prohibit competition by jute farmers. That would have only increased the price of cotton, meaning that cotton farmers would have profited at the expense of *consumers.* This is the kind of special-interest lobbying that preceded the passage of the Sherman Act. It was not a "public interest" law, as George Stigler so naively proclaimed.

Looking closely at the "monopolies" the Sherman Act was intended to break up reveals how much perception overwhelmed reality. Standard economic theory holds that to be a monopoly, a business must restrict output in order to push up prices. Although this definition of monopoly was not well developed in 1890, some scholars believe that it was nevertheless what Senator Sherman and his colleagues had in mind in promoting antitrust legislation. Robert Bork, who taught antitrust law at Yale Law School for more than fifteen years and is a frequent critic of antitrust regulation, stated in the *Journal of Law and Economics* that "Sherman demonstrated more than once that he understood that higher prices were brought about by a restriction of output. . . . Sherman and his colleagues identified the phrase 'restraint of commerce' or 'restraint of trade' with 'restriction of output.' "[8] Senator Sherman may have said this, but the facts contradict the contention that the trusts were reducing output and raising prices. Quite the contrary: the late-nineteenth-century trusts that were accused of "rampant cartelization" were *expanding* production and *dropping* prices faster than the economy as a whole during this time of general industrial expansion and price deflation.

I surveyed the *Congressional Record* for 1889 and 1890 to compile a list of industries that were accused during the Sherman Act debates of being monopolies. Data that go that far back are sketchy and incomplete, but I acquired price and output data for seventeen such industries. The results were startling: while real (inflation-adjusted) gross national product (GNP) increased by approximately 24 percent from 1880 to 1890, those industries that were allegedly restricting output actually *increased* production in that period—by *175 percent*, on average. (For example, steel production rose 258 percent; zinc, 156 percent; coal, 153 percent; steel rails, 142 percent; petroleum, 79 percent; and sugar, 75 percent.)[9] In other words, in the decade preceding passage of the Sherman Act, those industries targeted as "monopolies" grew at *seven times* the rate of the economy as a whole.

In the same period, prices charged by the trusts also fell faster than the general price level did. The consumer price index fell by

7 percent from 1880 to 1890, but on average the trusts' prices fell more dramatically: steel rail prices fell 53 percent; refined sugar was 22 percent cheaper; the price of lead declined 12 percent; the price of zinc was reduced by 20 percent; and the price of bituminous coal remained steady.

So much for a key justification for antitrust legislation. In fact, evidence indicates that members of Congress *knew* that the trusts were benefiting consumers by making products cheaper. A Congressman Mason stated during the U.S. House of Representatives debates on the Sherman Act that "trusts have made products cheaper, have reduced prices." In the same statement, however, the congressman exposed the real rationale for the Sherman Act: "But if the price of oil, for instance, were reduced to one cent a barrel, it would not right the wrong done to the people of this country by the 'trusts' which have destroyed legitimate competition and driven honest men from legitimate business enterprises."[10] In other words, it didn't matter that the trusts were marvels of efficiency that were expanding production, employing thousands, and dropping consumer prices. The problem was that they were driving less efficient, higher-priced competitors from the market. These competitors chose not to compete but to lobby Congress to pass a law that would hobble their more efficient rivals. Thus the Sherman Antitrust Act was protectionist at its root; it was always designed to protect incompetent businesses from superior competition, not to protect consumers from monopoly. In short, political chicanery (mercantilism again) triumphed over free enterprise.

If the trusts really had raised prices, as monopolies are supposed to do, there would have been no complaints whatsoever from the "honest men" in "legitimate business enterprises." Higher prices from the trusts would have been a tremendous *benefit* to their competitors, enabling these other businesses to raise their own prices (and profit levels as well) or to maintain lower prices and outsell the trusts. The fact that the competition *did* complain about the trusts is further proof that the trusts were not harming consumers. In reality, the supporters of the Sherman Act, not the trusts, were the enemies of the American consumer.

Then there is the old predatory pricing canard. True, one might say, the trusts were dropping prices. But weren't they just doing this temporarily in hopes of driving all the competition from the market? This, of course, would have been the height of economic folly—to drop your price below cost *for several decades* in hopes of someday making a monopoly profit. And remember, even John D. Rockefeller's Standard Oil faced hundreds of competitors, so it would have been rather difficult to drive out all competition.

Interestingly, the *New York Times,* which at the turn of the century had already established itself as perhaps the leading paper in the United States, strongly opposed the Sherman Act after initially being in favor of it. The reason it gave for this reversal was the blatantly hypocritical behavior of Senator Sherman and the Republican Party. Just four months after passage of the Sherman Act, Congress passed the McKinley Tariff, one of the biggest tariff increases up to that point. This was a continuation of the hyperprotectionist trade policy that the Republican Party had championed since the Lincoln administration. In light of these developments, the *New York Times* editorialized on October 1, 1890:

> That so-called Anti-Trust law was passed to deceive the people and to clear the way for the enactment of this . . . law relating to the tariff. It was projected in order that the party organs might say to the opponents of tariff extortion and protected combinations, "Behold! We have attacked the Trusts. The Republican party is the enemy of all such rings." And now the

author of it [Sherman] can only "hope" that the rings will dissolve of their own accord.[11]

The *Times* obviously believed that the Sherman Act had been designed to divert the public's attention away from the real source of monopoly power in the U.S. economy, the protectionist tariff—and it was right. In the same editorial the *Times* noted that the tariff rates were "affixed" by lobbyists for the very same corporations that would benefit from the newly enhanced tariff protection. The newspaper also pointed out that Sherman himself had condemned the trusts because they "subverted the tariff system" with their low prices, quite an odd statement from the author of the "Magna Carta of free enterprise."[12]

The *Times* referred to the McKinley Tariff as the "Campaign Contributors Tariff Bill," since corporate contributors to the Republican Party were the main designers and beneficiaries of the bill. The newspaper considered Sherman's speeches on the bill in the U.S. Senate to be a "confession" that he was not at all interested in protecting consumers but cared only about providing benefits to the Republican Party's corporate supporters *at the expense of consumers.*

ANTITRUST BEFORE SHERMAN

Even before Congress passed the Sherman Act, the enactment of state antitrust laws made clear that special interests could push government to thwart competition. The agitation for antitrust laws seems to have started in the Midwest among farm groups, not industrialists. In response to the formation of large corporate farms that were taking advantage of economies of scale to reduce their prices, Missouri farmers began to organize politically. An 1889 Farmers' Alliance meeting in St. Louis called for legislation "to suppress . . . all unhealthy rivalry."[13] This of course is a telling statement: despite the common folklore about antitrust, state antitrust regulation had its origins in a movement to *suppress* competition.

The farmers at the forefront of the antitrust movement claimed to be victims of "monopolies," but in reality they were merely bitter about the success of their more efficient competitors. The hallmarks of monopoly according to standard economic theory—restrictions in output and increased prices—were nowhere to be found in the farm belts during this period. Indeed, *falling* prices were prompting the calls for antitrust legislation. In the South, for example, farmers pushed for antitrust laws to halt the decline in cotton prices. The Missouri farmers who formed the Farmers' Alliance in 1889 were responding to the declining prices of their staples—cattle, hogs, and wheat. Consumers, of course, were benefiting immensely: beef prices were 38 percent lower than they had been in 1884; the price of hogs had fallen 19 percent since 1883; and the price of wheat was about 35 percent lower than it had been a decade earlier.[14] But that is precisely why these agricultural political entrepreneurs began clamoring for an antitrust law—so they could, in effect, legally pick consumers' pockets. It didn't seem to matter that the farmers themselves were benefiting from reduced costs during this period. Rail rates and interest rates had declined—farm mortgage rates fell from 11.41 percent in 1880 to 7.84 percent in 1889, a 31 percent reduction—and farm machinery was becoming less and less expensive as well.

At the state level, a major impetus for antitrust legislation came from the meatpacking industry, of all places. The "Big Four" meatpackers—Swift, Armour, Morris, and Hammond—had all created marvelously efficient operations that were vertically integrated into wholesaling and retailing and were shipping inexpensive, dressed beef by train all across the country from their centralized facilities in Chicago. Consequently, the price of beef fell throughout the 1880s.

Suddenly there was ominous talk of a "beef trust." Cattlemen combined with local butchers to begin an organized political campaign against declining beef prices. They succeeded in persuading Senator George Vest of Missouri to convene a commission to investigate the cause of lower beef prices. The Vest Commission concluded that "the principal cause of the *depression* in the prices paid to the cattle raiser and of the remarkable fact that the cost of beef has not fallen in proportion, comes from the artificial and abnormal centralization of markets, and the absolute control by a few operators thereby made possible [emphasis added]."[15]

So the Vest Commission admitted that its principal concern was lower prices. It did not dispute the fact that the "beef trust" was benefiting consumers immensely with lower-priced beef. Instead, it made the uneconomic and nonsensical argument that all cost reductions must be met proportionally with price reductions. The argument is nonsensical because it assumes that only supply and cost, and not consumer demand, determine prices. But in a free market both supply and demand determine prices, and each is constantly fluctuating. There is therefore no reason to believe that, say, a 20 percent cost reduction will always lead to a 20 percent price reduction; strong consumer demand may give sellers enough latitude to cut prices by only, say, 10 or 15 percent, depending on competitive conditions.

Nevertheless, the Missouri legislature passed a state antitrust law in 1889 that prohibited any actions designed "to limit" prices.[16] It is reasonable to assume that the phrase "to limit" meant "to keep from rising." Thus, the law explicitly made it illegal to do what the Big Four had been doing—limiting price increases or, more accurately, *dropping* beef prices. This law provided even more impetus for the federal antitrust law that would be passed a year later.

THE ANTITRUST RECORD

For more than a century, legal scholars and economists have studied antitrust regulation in practice and have concluded that there have been hundreds, perhaps thousands, of instances in which antitrust enforcement was harmful to competition—exactly the opposite of what the public has been led to believe is the purpose of antitrust. Much of this criticism came from scholars associated with the University of Chicago during the 1960s and 1970s. Economist Yale Brozen summarized much of it in his 1982 treatise *Concentration, Mergers, and Public Policy,* in which he concluded that antitrust laws were "restraining output and growth in productivity" and contributing to "a deterioration of the competitive position of the United States in competitive markets."[17] This research, clearly indicating that, in practice, antitrust is almost always anticompetitive, constituted a "revolution" in economics, Brozen remarked. Most Americans are almost completely unaware of this research, however, since it is found almost entirely in esoteric economics journals and scholarly treatises. But a review of some of the more famous (or notorious) historical cases reveals how misguided antitrust laws are. Indeed, in conducting a review of the fifty-five best-known antitrust cases in American legal history, former University of Hartford economics professor Dominick Armentano made a devastating case against antitrust. Armentano's landmark book *Antitrust and Monopoly: Anatomy of a Policy Failure* concludes that *in every single case* either there was no hard evidence that a monopoly had been created or the evidence pointed in the opposite direction—that the prosecuted business was in fact operating competitively, usually more competitively than most other businesses in the same industry.[18] It is clear, then, that "the entire antitrust system—allegedly created to protect competition and increase consumer welfare—has worked, instead, to lessen business competition and lessen the efficiency and productivity associated with the free-market process."[19]

In 1908 a circuit court found the American Tobacco Company guilty of violating the Sherman Antitrust Act, a decision that the U.S. Supreme Court upheld in 1911.[20] The circuit court held that the simple act of merging a number of companies to form the American Tobacco Company was illegal, despite the fact that there was no evidence at all that the company had harmed consumers and that evidence abounded that the mergers had benefited consumers by expanding production and reducing prices.

The circuit court admitted, for example, that "the record in this case does not indicate that there has been any increases in the price of tobacco products to the consumer" and that there was no evidence of "unfair competition" or "improper practices" with regard to competitors.[21] The court noted, in fact, that the volume of output of tobacco products had "enormously increased." As Armentano concluded, "Three of the four [circuit court] judges admitted that there was solid evidence to indicate that American tobacco was efficient, had not raised prices, had expanded outputs, and not depressed leaf prices, and had not 'dragooned' competitors."[22] Nevertheless, the formation of a trust was ruled illegal.

What, exactly, had American Tobacco done that was detrimental to society, according to the government? The five leading tobacco companies had merged in January of 1890 to form the American Tobacco Company. After the merger, however, there were still literally thousands of firms in the industry; the cigar industry alone had some twenty thousand manufacturing plants in 1910.[23] Moreover, as economists have long understood, in a marketplace where there is entry and potential entry of new competitors, such mergers are almost always caused by a desire to use economies of scale to reduce costs and prices. In the case of American Tobacco, for instance, there was a tremendous advantage in spreading advertising costs over five previously separate firms. The merger had also enabled American Tobacco to build state-of-the-art manufacturing facilities, whereas other brand-name cigarettes were being manufactured at old, outdated factories. The new facilities allowed American Tobacco to reduce its manufacturing costs. The company also cut its costs through vertical integration, just as Standard Oil was doing at the time; by avoiding unionization; and by employing "some of the industry's keenest managerial talent," as Armentano observes.[24] These efficiency-enhancing moves had quite an effect on the price to the consumer: despite a 40 percent increase in the cost of raw materials (raw tobacco) from 1895 to 1907, the price of most tobacco products actually fell. For example, the price of cigarettes fell from $2.77 in 1895 to $2.20 in 1907, the year before the circuit court found the company guilty of "monopolizing" the tobacco products industry. Cigars sold for $4.60 (per thousand, less tax) in 1895 and $3.60 in 1907.[25]

THE ALCOA CASE: CONDEMNING ECONOMIC EFFICIENCY

In 1937 the federal government brought an antitrust case against the Aluminum Company of America (Alcoa), seeking dissolution of the company and "relief" for the petitioners (that is, Alcoa's competitors). Federal district court judge Francis G. Caffey issued an extraordinary nine-day oral decision that carefully exonerated Alcoa of all 140 charges that the government had made. The government appealed, however, and the U.S. Circuit Court of Appeals found Alcoa guilty of one count of "illegally monopolizing" virgin ingot aluminum. Judge Learned Hand's majority opinion was one of the most absurd, Orwellian statements in all antitrust history.

It is true that Alcoa faced no competitors in the primary ingot aluminum market, but that doesn't mean that it was able to behave like a monopolist. Numerous other companies attempted to enter the business, including companies associated with the Ford family of Detroit and J. B. Duke, the president of the American Tobacco Company. These were people with ample financial resources, but they could not compete with Alcoa in this market because, as Armentano points out, "no competitor could expect to match, much less excel, [Alcoa's] economic performance during this period. In 1937, Alcoa was producing slightly under one-half billion tons of metal and selling it for 22 cents a pound; its average rate of return on capital investment was 10 percent in the period 1912–1936."[26] In short, because of the company's excellence and low prices, it was unprofitable for even the Ford and Duke families to enter the business (with inevitably lower-quality and higher-priced products).

Judge Hand also overlooked a key point that the federal district court had made in exonerating Alcoa. Although Alcoa was the only virgin ingot producer, one can and should consider scrap aluminum to be a substitute for virgin aluminum; if one takes those two markets (virgin and scrap) together, Alcoa had only about one-third of the total market.

Judge Hand revealed a mastery of doubletalk when he wrote about how Alcoa had achieved this supposed monopoly of the virgin ingot market. Hand condemned Alcoa for its "superior skill, foresight, and industry."[27] This was "exclusionary," he said, for not all companies in the industry shared this skill, foresight, and industry. He further condemned Alcoa for advertising its business, thereby stimulating sales, and then "efficiently supplying a demand" that it had "evolved."[28] Worse yet, Hand said, Alcoa had correctly anticipated increases in customer demand and then "doubled and re-doubled" its capacity to fill the demand and "embraced every new opportunity" with "a great organization manned with elite business personnel."[29]

Thus, Alcoa was prosecuted for having an elite management team that was a marvel of efficiency and cost cutting. No evidence was ever presented that consumers were harmed. Only less efficient competitors were harmed, as they should be in a competitive free-enterprise system where the customer has the ultimate say in which businesses will thrive and which ones will not.

ANTITRUST REGULATORS NEVER LEARN

More than forty years after the wrongly decided Alcoa case, the Federal Trade Commission (FTC) initiated a very similar case, making many of the same illogical arguments, against the ready-to-eat cereal industry.[30] By the late 1970s the four largest ready-to-eat cereal companies had some 90 percent of sales in the industry. The FTC accused them of "brand proliferation"—of maintaining that high market share by constantly introducing new brands of cereal (only some of which were successful), which "foreclosed" competition by other cereal companies. The government proposed forcing the companies to create three new companies, and then granting licenses to their trademarked cereal brands, free of charge, to any competitor who wanted them.

Echoing the arguments of Judge Hand in the Alcoa case, the government made the following case against the cereal companies: it was very costly and risky to introduce new cereal brands; the existing companies had nevertheless introduced scores of new brands to fill consumer demand "niches" very quickly; and all of this investment and entrepreneurial activity excluded competitors.

It did exclude competitors, to the great benefit of consumers.

These companies, in a fiercely competitive business, made extraordinary efforts to provide better products to consumers. All of the experimentation was a mark of competition, not monopoly; indeed, the companies took great risks with their investments, since many of the new brands did not sell.

Besides, the government defined the market in an inappropriately narrow way: There are many substitutes for dry cereal—bagels, muffins, ham and eggs, fruit, waffles, cooked cereal, and more. If the cereal manufacturers had begun charging monopolistic prices, consumers could have easily shifted to any or all of these readily available substitutes, thereby negating any attempt at monopoly pricing.

The cereal companies eventually won the case, but only after spending millions of dollars and thousands of hours defending themselves against these baseless charges. They were forced, in other words, to divert an enormous amount of time, money, and energy away from their primary business. At least some of these costs were inevitably passed on to consumers in the form of higher cereal prices. This, of course, is exactly what the smaller and less successful cereal manufacturers had hoped that the government would achieve—making the cereal industry *less* competitive.

GIVING COMPETITION THE BOOT (AND THE SHOE)

In 1956 the Brown Shoe Company, the nation's largest shoe manufacturer, merged with the G. R. Kinney company, the largest shoe retailer. A district court found against the merger, arguing that it would lessen competition. In keeping with standard antitrust practice, the court admitted that the merger would actually enhance efficiency, mentioning that company-owned retail outlets had cost advantages in advertising, insurance, inventory and price control, and so on, and that these advantages would likely be reflected "in *lower* prices or in higher quality at the same prices [emphasis added]."[31] In 1962 the U.S. Supreme Court reaffirmed the district court's decision, with similar convoluted reasoning. Chief Justice Earl Warren argued that the cost reductions and product improvements caused by the merger would enable these combined companies to "market their own brands at prices below those of competing independent retailers."[32] Thus, economic efficiency and lower prices are to be outlawed in the name of consumer protection!

The doubletalk in Warren's opinion rivaled that in Judge Learned Hand's Alcoa ruling. In one sentence Warren stated (correctly) that "it is competition, not competitors, that the [Sherman] Act protects," but in the next sentence he claimed that Congress also wanted "to promote competition through protection of viable, small, locally owned businesses."[33] According to Warren, then, the Sherman Act protects competition, not competitors, by protecting competitors!

The Brown Shoe decision, like so many other antitrust decisions, revealed how the federal government uses the antitrust laws to protect competitors from competition, to the detriment of American consumers.

ANTITRUST MYTHS, ALIVE AND WELL

It has been decades since Dominick Armentano originally published his landmark book on antitrust, but unfortunately the government has continued with its misguided, anticonsumer attacks on supposed monopolies. The highest-profile antitrust case in the 1990s was the Justice Department's case against the Microsoft Corporation, which was as wrongheaded as any of the above-mentioned cases (as will be discussed in more detail in the concluding chapter). In a 1998 *Forbes* magazine article entitled "Read Your History, Janet," business historian John Steele Gordon chided Attorney General Janet Reno for prosecuting Microsoft.[34] Microsoft was the victim of a political persecution, said Gordon, and he faulted the government for its ignorance of history (and economics). Gordon ran through a series of key antitrust cases to show how fears of monopoly had been misplaced, since market forces usually toppled the economic juggernaut about which the government had been so concerned. Moreover, in at least some cases the government had critically wounded industry leaders in the name of fostering "competition."

For example, beginning in 1969 the federal government spent thirteen years prosecuting IBM for allegedly monopolizing the computer market. The government finally abandoned the case after causing IBM to spend many millions of dollars and untold hours responding to its requests. Meanwhile, IBM's competitive position had been eclipsed by such companies as Microsoft and Wang Computer.

In 1962 the government forced the Schwinn Bicycle Company to divorce itself from its network of dealers, which the government claimed gave Schwinn an advantage over its competition (though of course the essence of competition is trying to gain advantages over competitors). Foreign competitors eventually drove Schwinn into bankruptcy.

During the 1950s federal antitrust regulators decided to prohibit RCA from charging royalties to American licensees, which was allegedly a monopolistic practice. So RCA licensed many of its products to Japanese companies, which gave rise to the existence of the Japanese electronics industry, which eventually outcompeted the American electronics industry.

Antitrust regulation literally destroyed Pan American World Airways by forbidding it to acquire domestic routes. That supposedly would have been unfair competition for other domestic airlines. Deprived of "feeder traffic" for its international flights, Pan Am went bankrupt in 1990.

General Motors (GM) was never prosecuted under antitrust

laws, but the company so feared prosecution that its official policy from 1937 until 1956 was never to let its market share top 45 percent. To that end, division managers were instructed to make sure that GM cars were not too high quality or too low priced. This fear of antitrust prosecution made GM a less competitive company, and it therefore was incapable of effectively competing when Japanese and German automakers began dominating the U.S. auto market in the 1970s.

Gordon's point was an important one: antitrust regulation almost never serves the purpose it is intended to serve, and it invariably causes great harm. So why does the federal government continue to prosecute alleged monopolists, even when the record shows that this only leads to *less* competition, *less* efficiency, *less* productivity, and *higher* prices? Dominick Armentano has the answer:

> Antitrust policy in America is a misleading myth that has served to draw public attention away from the actual process of monopolization that has been occurring throughout the economy. The general public has been deluded into believing that monopoly is a free-market problem, and that the government, through antitrust enforcement, is on the side of the "angels." The facts are exactly the opposite. Antitrust . . . served as a convenient cover for an insidious process of monopolization in the marketplace.[35]

That is, government generates tremendous publicity for itself by prosecuting high-profile firms primarily for engaging in *competitive* behavior. Meanwhile, government itself is the main cause of real monopoly—with its protectionist tariffs; with its regulation of certain industries (from cable television to taxi services) that creates franchise monopolies; with its occupational licensing regulation, which makes it difficult or impossible to enter hundreds of occupations; and with antitrust regulation itself, which is often used as a political weapon against the most successful businesses. Political weapons are often wielded at the request of a company's less successful but politically well-connected rivals, as legal scholar (and later federal judge) Richard Posner pointed out when he said that FTC investigations are seldom in the public interest. If Posner's claim seems difficult to believe, consider that three scholars writing in the prestigious *Journal of Law and Economics* provided detailed statistical evidence in support of the argument that antitrust regulation is effectively another form of "pork barrel politics."[36]

Unfortunately, it seems that our government leaders are unwilling to examine the historical record closely. If they did, perhaps we would avoid the costly antitrust regulation that has plagued the American economy for more than a century. But for now, the myth persists that monopoly is an intrinsic feature of capitalism that must be controlled and regulated by enlightened antitrust regulation.

CHAPTER NINE

Did Capitalism Cause the Great Depression?

The Great Depression was a failure not of capitalism but of the hyperactive state.

—Paul Johnson, introduction to Murray N. Rothbard's
America's Great Depression (2000)

The ideas embodied in the New Deal legislation were a compilation of those which had come to maturity under [President Herbert] Hoover's aegis. . . . We all of us owed much to Hoover.

—Rexford Tugwell, economic adviser to President
Franklin D. Roosevelt (1946)

G ENERATIONS OF American schoolchildren have been taught that the Great Depression of the 1930s was caused by a "breakdown" of capitalism, which supposedly suffers from certain inherent weaknesses. Every once in a while, the official story goes, the economy will go into a recession or, worse, a depression, because capitalism is by its very nature unstable. The most infamous example of this, of course, is the Great Depression, during which unemployment in the United States was as high as *25 percent*.

A corollary to the breakdown-of-capitalism theory is that the solution to the Great Depression was—and should be for all future economic downturns—government intervention to "save" capitalism from itself. Tax increases, debt, inflation, wage and price supports, gigantic government spending programs, and pervasive regulation of business were allegedly necessary to "tame capitalism."

But in fact, as will be discussed in this and the next chapter, this commonly accepted story is precisely the *opposite* of the truth. The tales of capitalism's natural breakdowns and the necessity of government intervention are *one big myth*.

THE AMERICAN WAY OF DEALING WITH RECESSIONS

The Great Depression was not America's first encounter with economic decline. The Panic of 1819 was quite severe, as was the depression of 1837. In these and other instances of economic downturn prior to the Great Depression, the government's "response" was largely restricted to a policy of laissez-faire. The occasional attempts at government intervention to "do something" about an economic crisis were generally trivial. That was a good thing, for the economic crises themselves were mostly *caused by* misguided government banking and debt policies.

Why did the government not intervene to "solve" economic crises? Because American political leaders understood one of the first lessons of economics: the lesson of opportunity cost. The "opportunity cost" of government spending is, simply, the value placed on whatever the same funds would have been spent on (or would have generated in savings) had they remained in private hands. Government can never spend a single cent unless it taxes, borrows, or prints money. In each case, money and resources are diverted from the private sector (the capitalist economy) to government.

Thus, in any economic downturn, what is needed is more capitalism, the sole engine of wealth creation and job creation. Cutting *back* on government frees up more resources for the private sector. The best recipe is to cut taxes, cut government spending, quit engaging in inflationary finance through monetary creation, put an end to governmental borrowing, and deregulate or free up private enterprise so that it can do what it does best: create products, wealth, and jobs.

The U.S. government followed this laissez-faire model almost religiously during the depression of 1837. That was the deepest economic recession prior to the Great Depression, but because President Martin Van Buren's administration took the appropriate steps (or, more appropriately, *didn't* take the *wrong* steps), the downturn was also short-lived. Van Buren had made clear in his Inaugural Address that he advocated the laissez-faire approach, for the speech was "essentially a charter for inaction," as Van Buren biographer Major L. Wilson writes.[1] And he did not waver from this position when the country experienced a major banking crisis just two months into his term. All but six of the nation's eight hundred or so banks had ceased redeeming their bank notes in gold or silver, but in his first message to Congress the president proclaimed that his policy would be one of governmental retrenchment. "All communities are apt to look to government for too much," Van Buren warned, "especially at periods of sudden embarrassment and distress."[2] Moreover, "all former attempts on the part of Government" to "assume the management of domestic or foreign exchange" had "proved injurious."[3] What was needed was "a system founded on private interest, enterprise and competition [i.e., pure capitalism], without the aid of legislative grants or regulations by law."[4]

President Van Buren, a strong believer in Jefferson's dictum that "that government is best which governs least," refused to suggest to Congress any specific plan for government intervention to attempt to alleviate the effects of the depression. The big-government interventionists of the day—Daniel Webster, Henry Clay, and other

Whigs—denounced him, but he stuck to his principles. Rather than intervening, Van Buren fought for financial deregulation, ushering in the Independent Treasury System, a new national banking system under which all bank notes were redeemable in gold and silver. This financial deregulation produced what was arguably the most stable monetary system the United States has ever had.[5] What bank losses there were stemmed from remaining state-level regulations, such as prohibitions on branch banking and requirements that banks purchase extremely risky and sometimes worthless state government bonds.

In addition to financial deregulation, notes historian Jeffrey Hummel, Van Buren "thwarted all attempts to use economic depression as an excuse for expanding government's role."[6] Henry Clay and the Whigs (including a young Abraham Lincoln) viewed the depression as a political opportunity to get the federal government to enact their favorite pork-barrel schemes for "internal improvements," which amount to corporate welfare for companies that built roads, railroads, and canals. Van Buren thwarted them every step along the way. He also defeated the Whigs' attempts to get the federal government to bail out the states, many of which had unwisely pursued Clay's policy of issuing massive amounts of debt for "internal improvements." In fact, total federal government expenditures *fell* in absolute dollar terms during Van Buren's term, from $30.9 million in 1836 to $24.3 million in 1840, a 21 percent reduction.[7] The level of federal debt also remained steady, and prices of goods, services, and labor were left free to fluctuate according to free-market forces. In addition, President Van Buren championed free trade and lower tariffs while keeping the United States out of foreign wars and other entanglements.

Thanks to Van Buren's laissez-faire policies, the depression of 1837 ended very quickly. Had the U.S. government adopted the hyperinterventionist schemes of Henry Clay and the Whigs (more taxes, more spending, more debt, etc.), the depression of 1837 would have been much more severe.

According to the popular mythology, the 1920s was a decade of laissez-faire, and the "excesses" of all that economic freedom were the main cause of the Great Depression. President Herbert Hoover has caught the lion's share of the blame for his supposedly "do-nothing" policies. Hoover deserves a share of the blame for the Great Depression, but not because he did nothing; rather, he did *too much*. In reality, Hoover was a hyperinterventionist who expanded government interference in the American economy, and these interventionist policies were the cause of the Great Depression. Worse, these policies continued into Franklin Roosevelt's administrations, as FDR's own top economic adviser, Rexford Tugwell, acknowledged when he said that the New Dealers "owed much to Hoover." As we will see in the next chapter, Roosevelt's continuation of these interventionist policies made the Depression longer and more severe than it otherwise would have been.

Hoover may have become somewhat of a advocate of laissez-faire in his retirement, but in the 1920s, first as secretary of commerce and then as president, he was an FDR-style interventionist. Historian Joan Hoff Wilson accurately describes Hoover as a "forgotten progressive." In the first two decades of the twentieth century the so-called progressives—quasi-socialists—advocated pervasive government regulation and control of business, "progressive" income taxation, pro-union labor legislation, and generally a more activist state.[8] The progressive movement was on the wane by the 1920s, but Hoover took up the task of reengineering American society as soon as he was appointed secretary of commerce in 1921. According to Wilson, his immediate objective was "the elimination of poverty in the United States," and his ultimate goal was even more ambitious—"the transformation of American society."[9] There is nothing laissez-faire about that kind of attitude.

At the time, Russian central planners were deluding themselves with talk of "scientific socialism," and many prominent Americans had the same kinds of delusions about centralized economic planning, even if they had no desire to establish a dictatorial regime like Russia's. Hoover was one of these; a highly successful mining engineer before entering government, he believed that society could be engineered just as a mining operation could be. Like the Russian central planners, Hoover "believed that human manipulation could triumph over any alleged 'laws' of economics," as historian William J. Barber has written.[10]

To that end, Hoover as secretary of commerce increased his department's budget by more than 50 percent, expanded the Commerce Department into thirty divisions, and hired more than three thousand additional government bureaucrats. He intended to centrally plan American industry into prosperity, but his efforts as secretary of commerce provide a case study of the futility of such "planning."

Hoover may have been a world-class mining engineer, but he had a dangerously poor grasp of economics, which fed his desire to remake American society. Joan Hoff Wilson describes Hoover's basic economic beliefs as follows:

There was too much lawlessness, destructive competition, and economic waste, too much unemployment and repetitiveness in factory work; the twelve-hour day was too long; labor lacked the guarantee of collective bargaining; child labor still existed despite prewar progressive legislation; education was inadequate in most states; some people were making too much money—"far beyond the needs of stimulation to initiative."[11]

Each of these statements reflected Hoover's fundamental misunderstanding of economics. While Hoover complained of the "lawlessness" bred by capitalism, it seems to have been lost on him that most of the lawlessness of the 1920s was a direct effect of federal regulation—Prohibition. He also seems not to have considered that there was no shortage of federal law enforcement authority in the age of Prohibition.

An even more important misconception was that there was too much "destructive competition," which supposedly led to "economic waste." This old, socialist criticism of capitalism is based on a misunderstanding of competition in the capitalist process. Competition, as Nobel Prize–winning economist Friedrich Hayek said, is a "dynamic discovery process."[12] The struggle for the consumer's dollar leads businesses to constantly experiment with and invest in new products, better production methods, different approaches to labor relations, and more—all in an attempt to provide the best quality products and services at the lowest prices in order to maximize profits. Hoover and others who condemned "destructive competition" believed that central planning was the answer—that rather than have various independent, unconnected groups trying to figure how best to serve consumers, install a planner to oversee all companies and all industries to determine how best to run the economy. This, of course, is what Hayek called the "fatal conceit"—the notion that a planner or group of planners could ever acquire and process all the information necessary to make the economy operate smoothly and efficiently.[13] History has proven Hayek right: it is the *process of competition* that reveals to us the best ways to do business. Competition seems "wasteful" only to those who do not understand this fundamental fact. Unfortunately, Hoover was one of those people.

As for the twelve-hour day being "too long," it is not too long to the more ambitious and energetic workers who aspire to get ahead by working longer and harder. To these workers, legislation to mandate shorter workdays—which Hoover favored—would interfere with their career and life goals. Indeed, once the government mandated time-and-a-half pay for overtime, employers had an incentive to keep employees from working long hours; some employers simply cannot justify the cost of having an overtime workforce. Thus, the law limits opportunities for the more ambitious.

Hoover condemned "child labor," but many of the "children" (mostly teenagers) who worked in the 1920s often did so because, as unpleasant as factory conditions might have been, the alternative—unemployment and poverty—was worse. The same is certainly true today in many parts of the Third World, where going to work can mean the difference between eating and starving—between life and death—for a child and his or her family.

Hoover's belief that certain people made "too much money" was a crudely socialistic idea. It ignored the fact that much of the wealth of "the rich" goes into savings and fuels business investment; that the lure of great wealth is what so often spurs hard work and innovation, which benefits all of society; and that wealthy entrepreneurs create jobs, invest millions of dollars in the economy, and are often the very source of economic survival for many communities. The denigration of "the rich" would of course become one of Franklin D. Roosevelt's themes throughout his presidency.

Even beyond these misconceptions, Hoover believed in what economists call the purchasing power fallacy. He said that a key to prosperity was "to maintain the purchasing power of labor through high wages."[14] Consequently, as commerce secretary he was the main initiator of labor legislation in the Harding and Coolidge administrations, all of which was aimed at artificially propping up wages. The fallacy here is the belief that "high" wages can be sustained without increased production or productivity. Whenever government passes laws that artificially push wages up above what is justified by labor productivity, the end result is higher unemployment.

Other policies Hoover championed were equally misguided. He was the chief supporter of the Railway Labor Act, which was the first federal law to interfere with private labor relations and a precursor of New Deal labor legislation. The Railway Labor Act, like New Deal labor legislation, artificially empowered labor unions at the expense of employers and, ultimately, of consumers.

In addition, Hoover advocated "easy credit," mistakenly believing that if the Federal Reserve Board created money it would lead to prosperity. He espoused what he termed the "scientific management of the money supply."[15] As we shall shortly see, however, the Fed's easy money policy of the late 1920s was a major cause of the Great Depression.

To try to eliminate "destructive competition," as commerce secretary he advocated "associationalism" or "cooperative competition"— that is, government-supervised competition that would allow social engineers such as himself to ensure that there was not "too much" wasteful competition. This was the basis of the New Deal's National Industrial Recovery Act, which will be discussed in the next chapter and which the U.S. Supreme Court eventually ruled unconstitutional. The National Recovery Administration took Hoover's ideas to their logical conclusion, using governmental coercion to attempt to create a cartel in almost every industry in America. Even during Hoover's time as commerce secretary, his tinkering with "associationalism" ended up fostering "oligopoly," or government-supervised monopoly power.[16]

Hoover also preached the Republican Party gospel with regard to high protectionist tariffs, which benefited the manufacturers who financially supported the party. As president he initiated the ill-fated Smoot-Hawley tariff, which precipitated an international trade war that greatly exacerbated the Great Depression.

Did Capitalism Cause the Great Depression?

As commerce secretary, Hoover was a frenetic regulator. He attempted to interfere in dozens of industries, including broadcasting and airlines. Believing that radio featured too much advertising, he initiated a policy whereby the government granted broadcast licenses mostly to larger radio broadcasters, creating essentially a government-approved cartel in that industry. To oversee the airlines he created the Bureau of Aeronautics within the Commerce Department. This was the predecessor of the Civil Aeronautics Board, which was deregulated in the late 1970s because it was so obviously another cartel scheme whereby government bureaucrats would see to it that there was not too much competition in the airline industry.

Throughout his political career as commerce secretary and later as president, Hoover held literally hundreds of conferences to promote legislation related to conservation, the oil industry, the electric power industry, flood control, farming, labor arbitration, foreign debt, child hygiene, ocean shipping, exports, and much else. He championed public works spending to stimulate the economy, failing to understand that government can "stimulate" one sector of the economy only by *depressing* other sectors, since it must tax, borrow, or inflate the money supply to finance the spending. Nevertheless, government spending designed to stimulate the economy would be a hallmark of New Deal legislation; as William J. Barber has written, "The general design of a fiscal strategy to counter fluctuations in aggregate economic activity was ... shaped during Hoover's years at the Commerce secretariat."[17]

Joan Hoff Wilson writes that Hoover's pervasive interventionism and his "unceasing activities as secretary of commerce were so farflung, so impressive in their own right, and so well publicized, that his fame was inevitable."[18] William J. Barber notes that Americans "of Hoover's persuasion" believed in the federal government as "a catalyst, as a coordinator, as a regulator and as a stabilizer of economic activity" and called for "a degree of governmental intervention without peacetime precedent in the American economy."[19] Indeed, during the presidential campaign of 1932 Hoover described his own activities in two Republican administrations as "the most gigantic program of economic defense and counterattack ever evolved in the history of the Republic."[20]

It is truly stunning, and reflects a remarkable feat of propaganda, that so many Americans consider Herbert Hoover to have been an advocate of laissez-faire.

THE HOOVER ADMINISTRATION VERSUS LAISSEZ-FAIRE

Once elected president, Hoover continued with his frenetic interventionism and unbounded optimism in his ability to centrally plan the U.S. economy. One of his first items of business was to convene one of dozens of conferences, this one to promote the idea that businesses must not, in a slow economy, reduce wages, even in the face of shrinking profits. But artificially propping up wages was even more harmful in the depressed economy than it had been when he was commerce secretary. In a recession, of course, inflexible wages cause unemployment to be *higher* than it otherwise would be. The demand for labor by employers is what economists call a "derived demand." That is, it is derived from the demand for the product or service that the labor produces. When business slows down there is less consumer demand for the product and, consequently, less derived demand for the labor to produce that product. When Americans purchase fewer new automobiles, for example, there is less of a need for autoworkers. So Hoover's high-wage policy blocked one of the free market's key means of minimizing the dislocations of unemployment: wage adjustment. In periods of weak consumer demand it may no longer be profitable to employ as many workers *at the existing wage rate*, but if wages can fall it remains profitable to keep at least some of the workers employed—especially since there are usually training costs involved in rehiring new employees once the economy recovers.

Still, Hoover got a number of large American corporations to agree not to cut wages; Henry Ford actually increased wages. Of course, in such a scenario agreements are not completely voluntary; businesses always recognize the threat of governmental coercion. If they do not cooperate, legislation or regulation will probably be passed to force them to "cooperate." Whenever government and businesses pose as "partners" in such endeavors, government is always the senior and dominating partner.

Hoover also advocated "work sharing," or pressuring businesses to reduce the number of hours per worker so that more workers could remain on the job. This just spread unemployment around, however. The only thing that reduces unemployment is increased production (which increases the derived demand for labor).

As economist Murray Rothbard explained, Hoover was pursuing the agenda of organized labor. "The point is that unions did not have the power to enforce wage *floors* [i.e., above-market wages] throughout industry . . . and so the federal government was proposing to do it for them."[21] Satisfied that his strong-arm tactics had worked, Hoover announced to Congress on December 3, 1929, "I have instituted . . . systematic . . . cooperation with business . . . that wages and therefore earning power shall not be reduced."[22] Indeed, all of the leading industrialists had agreed to maintain wages, expand production, and adopt Hoover's socialistic "work sharing" programs. Though all of this was a recipe for higher unemployment, labor unions enthusiastically supported Hoover's labor market interventionism—interventionism that would be radically expanded under President Roosevelt, as will be seen in the next chapter.

President Hoover, supposedly a champion of laissez-faire, also took resources out of the increasingly sluggish private economy to finance an expanded public works program. In 1929 Hoover devoted a sizable chunk of the federal budget—half a billion dollars, or 13 percent of the total budget—to public works spending. At the same time he pressured state governments to increase their own public works spending. By 1931, total government public works spending would be as high as at any other point in the decade—this despite the fact that FDR employed some ten million bureaucrats in government public works jobs with his Public Works Administration, Works Progress Administration, Civilian Conservation Corps, and the rest.[23]

The negative effects of Hoover's public works spending were almost immediately apparent. All this government spending took money out of the private sector, extracted through taxes. (Hoover even rescinded a minuscule 1 percent temporary tax relief program.) As a result, private-sector spending, which could have reinvigorated the economy, declined. For example, private construction spending dropped drastically in 1930.[24]

Hoover did not pay attention to the failures of his public works programs, however. In 1932 he signed the Emergency and Relief Construction Act, which poured an additional $2.3 billion into public works programs, further impairing the private sector. He eventually did come to believe that these programs had failed, but by then it was too late; the economic damage had been done and Franklin Roosevelt was about to be elected.

By 1931 Hoover's uncontrolled government spending had created a $2 billion deficit, which induced him to sign the calamitous Revenue Act of 1932, one of the largest tax increases in American history up to that point. Rothbard explained:

> The range of tax increases was enormous. Many wartime excise taxes were revived, sales taxes were imposed on gasoline, tires, autos, electric energy, malt, toiletries, furs, jewelry, and

other articles; admission and stock transfer taxes were increased; new taxes were levied on bank checks, bond transfers, telephone, telegraph, and radio messages; and the personal income tax was raised drastically as follows: the normal rate was increased from a range of 1½ percent–5 percent, to 4 percent–8 percent; personal exemptions were sharply reduced, and an earned credit of 25 percent eliminated; and surtaxes were raised enormously, from a maximum of 25 percent to 63 percent on the highest incomes. Furthermore, the corporate income tax was increased from 12 percent to 13¾ percent, and an exemption for small corporations eliminated; the estate tax was doubled, and the exemption floor halved; and the gift tax, which had been eliminated, was restored, and graduated up to 33⅓ percent.[25]

Of course, all this came during a depression, when tax *reduction* is necessary. But Hoover just could not understand the true workings of free-market capitalism. Indeed, he praised the estate tax, which the Revenue Act doubled, as a tool for eliminating the evils of "economic power." Hoover was essentially a socialist when it came to the issue of inheritance, and he failed to recognize how the hefty tax harmed ordinary Americans. For example, many small business owners and family farmers who inherited property from their deceased parents simply could not pay the tax, and a significant number of those who managed to pay the tax were nonetheless crippled economically.

DEPRESSING THE FARM ECONOMY

Hoover's farm programs were another attack on free-market capitalism in that they established government-sponsored farm cartels that reduced agricultural output and raised prices—exactly the opposite of what was needed in a depression. Hoover had subsidized farmers during his term as commerce secretary, and the 1929 Agricultural Marketing Act was a continuation of those policies. The act created a Federal Farm Board (FFB) that in turn established "stabilization corporations" to "control farm surpluses and bolster farm prices," as Rothbard explained.[26] In other words, since antitrust laws made it illegal for farm corporations—or any other corporations—to collude to restrict farm production in order to drive up farm prices and incomes, the government stepped in and organized a *legal* cartel for them. The FFB consisted of the chief executives of large agricultural corporations, who were given governmental powers to stifle competition and raise prices. Among them were James C. Stone of the Tobacco Growers Association, Carl Williams of the Cotton Farmers Cooperative Association, C. B. Denman of the National Livestock Producers' Association, C. C. Teague of the Fruit Growers' Exchange, William F. Schilling of the National Dairy Association, and Samuel McKelvie, a lobbyist for grain farmers. What a sweetheart deal: the board set up ostensibly to regulate agriculture was administered by the very people who were supposed to be regulated. Naturally, they worked diligently to create a huge agricultural cartel.

Farmers were paid for *not* growing crops or raising livestock in order to create a cartel (monopoly) pricing structure. Eventually the FFB even purchased "surplus" wheat and other commodities to take them off the market and prop up prices. Wheat prices increased for a time, but that gave wheat farmers incentive to plant more wheat. The increased wheat supply ruined the cartel scheme by imposing downward pressure on prices. Hoover condemned wheat farmers for their alleged "profiteering" and harshly criticized "the evils of overproduction."[27] He then redoubled his "stabilization" efforts by putting even more money behind the programs to pay farmers for not farming. Of course, less agricultural production meant less demand for farm labor and, consequently, more unemployment in the farm sector. By June of 1930 the federal government had purchased 65 million bushels of wheat that it was keeping off the market.

Similar cartel schemes were attempted in cotton, wool, livestock, beans, pecans, citrus, figs, grapes, potatoes, apples, sugar beets, honey, nuts, maple syrup, tobacco, poultry, eggs, and rice, with equally dismal results. The economic laws of supply and demand that Hoover had scoffed at as commerce secretary were not so easy to repeal after all. As Rothbard concluded:

> The grandiose stabilization effort of the FFB failed ignominiously. Its loans encouraged greater production, adding to its farm surpluses, which overhung the market, driving prices down. . . . The FFB thus aggravated the very farm depression that it was supposed to solve. With the FFB a generally acknowledged failure, President Hoover began to pursue the inexorable logic of government intervention to the next step: recommending that productive land be withdrawn from cultivation, that crops be plowed under, and that immature farm animals be slaughtered—all to reduce the very surpluses that government's prior intervention had brought into being.[28]

THE SMOOT-HAWLEY-HOOVER TARIFF

One of Herbert Hoover's first acts as president was to begin the process of raising tariffs, which had always been the hallmark of Republican Party economic policy. In April of 1929 he asked Congress to raise the average tariff rate; Congress took his advice and haggled over the shape of tariff legislation for the next nine months. In March of 1930 Congress sent Hoover a tariff bill to sign, sponsored by Representatives Willis Hawley of Oregon and Reed Smoot of Utah. Hoover signed the bill despite a protest letter signed by more than a thousand economists—a majority of the membership of the American Economic Association. The stock market plummeted sharply on the day Hoover signed the Smoot-Hawley tariff bill, which should more appropriately be labeled the Smoot-Hawley-Hoover tariff.

On the eve of the Great Depression the Smoot-Hawley tariff increased tariff rates on about 800 separate items, from sugar beets and wool to shoes, textiles, and chemicals. The average tariff rate soared to 59.1 percent, the highest in American history up to that point.[29] Many of the tariff rates were so high that they cut off imports altogether. World leaders who had hoped to aid their own economies through increased trade with the United States were shocked. Twelve countries retaliated immediately, with Spain placing a prohibitive tariff on American-made automobiles, Switzerland boycotting American products altogether, and Canada imposing higher tariffs on 125 American export items.[30]

As a result, world trade shrank dramatically, and the Depression deepened. At the beginning of 1929 the seventy-five most active trading countries had accounted for some three billion dollars per month in trade, but by March of 1933 their trade had shrunk to less than half a billion dollars per month—an 83 percent reduction. The United States suffered the most: the volume of exports was 53 percent lower in 1932 than it had been in 1929.[31]

The Smoot-Hawley tariff had another unintended consequence: the 23 percent increase in tariffs on Japanese imports strengthened the political hand of the fascists vis-à-vis the liberals in that country and helped lead to Japan's militaristic nationalism.

"The major lesson from Smoot-Hawley," conclude international trade economists Wilson Brown and Jan Hogendorn, "is that trade wars provoked by protection can cause a meltdown of world trade, that reductions in trade can make depressions much worse, and that the political results can be doleful."[32]

Did Capitalism Cause the Great Depression?

MISALLOCATING CAPITAL

Perhaps the most important element of capitalism is capital markets. These markets provide the financial wherewithal for resources in declining industries to be transferred to more highly valued uses by consumers. When the personal computer was invented, for example, there was a reallocation of capital from the typewriter industry to the personal computer industry as consumer demand disappeared in the former and blossomed in the latter. The more quickly these capital transfers take place, the more efficient are markets.

Government intervention into capital markets always slows down or blocks the efficient reallocation of capital that is constantly occurring in a dynamic economy. It also tends to foster the inefficient use of capital by indirectly subsidizing declining industries. This is exactly what Herbert Hoover did with yet another unprecedented government intervention: the creation of the Reconstruction Finance Corporation (RFC).

Originally capitalized in January of 1931 with $500 million, the RFC would exist until the mid-1950s and would allocate some $50 billion in capital. The purpose of the RFC was economically perverse: to subsidize failing or uncreditworthy businesses with cheap credit. Capital markets succeed precisely because they do not lend money to such failing enterprises; by turning down borrowing requests from weak, unprofitable enterprises, capital markets can divert capital to those businesses and industries where consumer demand and the prospect for profit are stronger. But with the RFC, the government was causing the capital markets to fail.

In its first five months of operation the RFC made more than $1 billion in subsidized or low-interest loans, mostly to banks and railroad corporations—the two most important constituent groups of the Republican Party since its inception. Much of the RFC money was thinly veiled corporate welfare for banks. Many banks had made unwise loans to railroads, which could not pay off the loans. The RFC subsidies to the railroads enabled them to pay off the loans to the banks, *at the expense of American taxpayers.*

The recipients of RFC subsidies, by definition, had to be uncreditworthy. Thus, the program introduced inefficiency into capital markets that made economic recovery that much more difficult and unlikely. What was needed was a liquidation of unprofitable businesses so that the resources (land, labor, capital and machinery, natural resources, etc.) could be put to better, more profitable uses elsewhere. The RFC's intervention into the capital markets interfered with these necessary economic adjustments.

RFC loans were also politicized, as is everything government does. That is, they tended to go to businesses that were the most politically connected, not necessarily to ones that were the most economically promising. The subsidies were, in other words, a way of using taxpayers' funds to buy votes and campaign contributions. (FDR would master this dark art during his years in office.) In a number of cases, as a result of the corruption that plagued the organization from the very beginning, government money went directly to the companies of RFC officials. For example, the head of the RFC, Atlee Pomerene, promptly authorized a $12.3 million loan to the Guardian Trust Company of Cleveland, of which he was a director.[33]

Another reason why the RFC hindered rather than helped economic recovery was that federal credit allocation crowded out private-sector credit allocation, just as tax-financed government spending crowded out private spending. The billions of dollars in government-approved credit allocation to politically favored banks and railroads necessarily had to be diverted from alternative, private-sector uses. Private credit allocation is driven by economics, government credit allocation by politics.

In addition to interfering in capital markets with the RFC,

Hoover waged a propaganda campaign against the stock market—the last thing the market needed. He railed against "speculators," seemingly oblivious to the fact that speculation tends to smooth out fluctuations in prices. (For example, a speculator in coffee futures purchases coffee when it is in plentiful supply, putting upward pressure on prices when they are low, and holds it in order to sell when it is in shorter supply, thereby causing prices to decline. Overall, the effect is to moderate price volatility.)

Hoover launched numerous "investigations" of the New York Stock Exchange, which could not have helped investor confidence. He also made the absurd public statement that investments in the stock market should not be based on earnings prospects of the stocks being traded, but on "the future of the United States," which of course is always extremely nebulous and unpredictable.[34]

SO WHAT CAUSED THE BUST?

In 1913 the U.S. government created the Federal Reserve Board at least in part to facilitate bank credit expansion. And it worked: while the price level, as measured by the Consumer Price Index, was about the same in 1913 as it had been in 1789, since the Fed's creation it has gone up by at least a multiple of fifteen.

But bank credit expansion is what causes the so-called boom-and-bust cycle in an economy, as Austrian School economist Ludwig von Mises—the only economist of the 1920s to predict the Great Depression—first explained. Mises's theory of the business cycle was advanced by his student, Nobel laureate Friedrich Hayek, and later by another one of his students, Murray Rothbard, in his book *America's Great Depression*. According to the so-called Austrian theory, the money in circulation is either spent on consumption items (such as food and clothing) or saved and ultimately invested in capital goods (machinery, tools, equipment, and so on), which are used by businesses. How much is saved and how much is spent on consumption depend on people's rate of time preference—that is, their preference for present versus future consumption spending. When people have a low time preference, for example, they want to save more for the future and consume less. The higher level of savings will result in lower interest rates.

Interest rates can also drop when the government creates new money and injects it into the economic system, for the more plentiful supply of credit lowers the price of credit—that is, the interest rate. Since borrowing costs are now cheaper, businesses believe that there is an increased pool of savings available from which to borrow. Consequently, many businesses do borrow more, which provides them with new funds that are used to invest more, start up new enterprises, expand existing businesses, and much more. The economy now has more capital goods than consumption goods. But the businesses have been fooled. Savings have not really increased; the central bank's money creation has caused the interest rate to decline. Businesses will eventually find that there is not sufficient consumer demand for the products produced with their additional capital investments; that is, businesses have made wasteful investments during the "boom" phase of the business cycle. Some businesses, therefore, will have to be liquidated. This is the "bust" phase—recession or depression, which occurs as the economy adjusts to the waste caused by the central bank's expansion of credit. Recessions, unfortunately, are a necessary process of returning an economy to "normal" in terms of the pattern of present versus future consumption.

The Austrian theory, in fact, explains precisely what happened in the 1920s, in the years leading up to the Great Depression. The "Roaring Twenties" began to roar economically in mid-1921, after a sharp recession. The boom continued until mid-1929, three months before the infamous stock market crash. As Rothbard determined,

"Over the entire period of the boom [1921–1929], we find that the money supply increased by $28.0 billion, a 61.8 percent increase over the eight-year period. This is an average annual increase of 7.7 percent, a very sizable degree of inflation [of the money supply]."[35] Thus, an inflationary monetary policy was a feature of the Harding and Coolidge administrations. Indeed, the Fed itself announced that one of its chief aims was to provide cheap credit for American industry. And as the Austrian theory explains, cheap credit causes the boom-and-bust cycle—it does, for a while, stimulate the economy, but in that stimulation are the seeds of recession.

Another impetus for the high rate of monetary expansion during the 1920s—a period of Republican Party domination in Washington—was protectionism. The idea was to keep interest rates artificially low in the United States; that would, among other things, stimulate foreign lending, which allowed more American exports to be sold. As economist Frank Fetter explained, "Foreign loans were glorified by the same political leaders who wanted bigger and better trade restrictions, entirely oblivious to the problems involved in the repayment of such loans. . . . A tremendous volume of foreign loans made possible exports far in excess of imports."[36]

But the Fed's burst of money creation was pretty much over by the end of 1929. "From that time onward," Rothbard writes, "the money supply remained level. . . . And therefore, from that time onward, a depression to adjust the economy was inevitable."[37] The bust was caused by government, not capitalism.

Ludwig von Mises understood that the booming stock market and the strong economy reflected the inflation in the price of capital assets, and he foresaw what was about to happen. But few others did. Worse, when the economy did begin to adjust—that is, when the bust came— the Hoover administration did not recognize that its best policy would be laissez-faire: let the market participants adjust to their previous errors as quickly as possible. Whereas Martin Van Buren and other

American political leaders of the nineteenth century recognized that recession was a necessary, if regrettable, adjustment process, Herbert Hoover orchestrated massive interventions—high-wage policies, tax and spending increases, protectionism, government credit rationing, and much else. In short, Hoover did just about everything wrong that could have been done, for his hyperinterventionism destroyed the economy's prospects for the kinds of adjustments that needed to take place. He turned a recession into the Great Depression.

Herbert Hoover's successor, Franklin D. Roosevelt, was an even bigger interventionist. Indeed, his policies made the Great Depression longer and more severe than was necessary, as will be explained in the next chapter.

CHAPTER TEN

How the New Deal Crippled Capitalism

We shall tax and tax, spend and spend, and elect and elect.

—Harry Hopkins, adviser to President
Franklin D. Roosevelt (1933)

THE BIGGEST economic myth of the twentieth century is the notion that President Franklin D. Roosevelt's unprecedented peacetime economic interventions "got us out of the Great Depression" and thereby "saved capitalism" from itself.[1] Even Republicans accept this tale: in the 1990s, for example, Speaker of the House Newt Gingrich often praised Roosevelt's economic interventionism, saying that FDR "did bring us out of the Depression" and was therefore "the greatest figure of the 20th century."[2] Virtually every U.S. history book repeats this notion, despite readily available evidence to the contrary.

In reality, FDR's economic policies made the Great Depression much worse; caused it to last much longer than it otherwise would have; and established interventionist precedents that have been a drag on economic prosperity and a threat to liberty to this day.

WHAT RECOVERY?

Despite a doubling of federal government expenditures from 1933 (Roosevelt's first year in office) to 1940, the creation of dozens of new federal programs, and the direct employment of some ten million Americans in government "relief" jobs, the economy was basically no better off in 1938 than it was in 1933. Indeed, it was precisely *because* of all these programs and expenditures that the Great Depression dragged on until after World War II.

One measure of how FDR's interventionism failed to effect an economic recovery was the unemployment rate, which remained extraordinarily high throughout Roosevelt's first two terms, as Table 10.1 reveals. The average rate of unemployment from 1933 to

TABLE 10.1: U.S. UNEMPLOYMENT RATE (PERCENT OF CIVILIAN LABOR FORCE), 1929–1940

YEAR	UNEMPLOYMENT RATE
1929	3.2%
1930	8.7
1931	15.9
1932	23.6
1933	24.9
1934	21.7
1935	20.1
1936	16.9

How the New Deal Crippled Capitalism

YEAR	UNEMPLOYMENT RATE
1937	14.3
1938	19.0
1939	17.2
1940	14.6

Source: U.S. Department of Commerce, *Historical Statistics of the United States* (Washington, D.C.: U.S. Government Printing Office, 1961), 73.

1940 was 17.7 percent—more than five times the 1929 level. Unemployment was extremely high in Roosevelt's first three years in office, and after a short and shallow recovery in the mid-1930s, the unemployment rate shot back up from 14.3 percent to 19.0 percent in a single year, during the "Roosevelt recession" of 1938. This spike in unemployment was a result of what economist Benjamin Anderson described as a "sudden, extraordinarily severe and precipitous break both in the volume of business and in stock market prices running through autumn 1937 and into spring 1938."[3] More than ten million Americans were unemployed in 1938, compared with eight million in 1931, the year before Roosevelt's election. Unemployment levels would come down only after FDR conscripted millions of men and sent them to an overseas war (a fate much worse than temporary unemployment).

Per capita GNP statistics also reveal that, in terms of aggregate production, there was no recovery until after World War II ended and a massive *reduction* in government expenditures and employment occurred. As seen in Table 10.2, per capita gross national product (GNP) did not recover to its 1929 level until 1940, and even then, just barely so.

TABLE 10.2: PER CAPITA GNP, 1929–1940

YEAR	PER CAPITA GNP
1929	$857
1930	772
1931	721
1932	611
1933	590
1934	639
1935	718
1936	787
1937	846
1938	794
1939	847
1940	916

Source: U.S. Department of Commerce, *Historical Statistics of the United States* (Washington, D.C.: U.S. Government Printing Office, 1961), 139.

Data on personal consumption expenditures tell the same story—there was no economic recovery. Table 10.3 shows that personal consumption expenditures were approximately 8 percent lower in 1940 than they were in 1929.

There was also a massive reduction in private capital invest-

TABLE 10.3: PERSONAL CONSUMPTION
EXPENDITURES, 1929–1940 ($BILLIONS)

YEAR	TOTAL CONSUMPTION EXPENDITURES
1929	$78.9
1930	70.9
1931	61.3
1932	49.3
1933	46.4
1934	51.9
1935	56.3
1936	62.6
1937	67.3
1938	64.6
1939	67.6
1940	71.9

Source: U.S. Department of Commerce, *Historical Statistics of the United States* (Washington, D.C.: U.S. Government Printing Office, 1961), 179.

ment. From 1930 to 1940 net private investment was *minus* $3.1 billion, as Americans failed to add anything to their capital stock.[4] No economy can grow without capital accumulation. American manufacturing equipment had grown so obsolete by 1940 that 70 percent of all metal-working equipment was more than ten years old, a 50 percent increase over the 1930 level of obsolescence.[5]

Further evidence that President Roosevelt's massive interventions actually hindered recovery is the fact that most European nations pulled out of the Great Depression more quickly than the United States did. By 1937, for example, Great Britain's unemployment rate had declined to 10.3 percent—four percentage points below the U.S. rate.[6]

As of 1940 the economy had not recovered from the Great Depression, and in fact the economic recovery would not be complete until *after* World War II. It is foolish to argue, as many economists and historians do, that the Second World War ended the Depression. Sure, unemployment was virtually eliminated when more than twelve million men went off to war, but this cannot be interpreted as a return to prosperity. Consumer goods production was replaced by the production of military goods; price controls were pervasive; and rationing was imposed for consumer goods. All of this meant that the economic well-being of consumers continued to *decline* during the war years. The wartime price controls also skewed economic data on GNP and inflation so much that such data were virtually useless as barometers of economic health.

It was not until 1947, when the wartime economic controls were ended and government spending and employment levels fell dramatically, that prosperity was restored.[7] Federal government expenditures fell from $98.4 billion in 1945 to $33 billion by 1948, the first full year of genuine recovery.[8] Keynesian economists expected a two-thirds reduction in government spending to lead to another depression, but they were dead wrong. With the price controls and rationing schemes of the war years mostly out of the way, and the dramatic reduction in government spending, the private economy quickly recovered. Private-sector production increased by almost one-third in 1946 alone, as private investment boomed for the first time in eighteen years. Corporate share prices also soared.[9] It was capitalism that finally ended the Depression, once some of FDR's massive interventions were scaled back and the federal budget was reduced by about two-thirds.

FDR'S MISTAKES IN THE FIRST NEW DEAL

In *The Roosevelt Myth,* John T. Flynn devotes a chapter to "The Dance of the Crackpots"—that is, to the crackpot economic ideas that were widely discussed in Washington in the early 1930s. Unfortunately, some of these ideas actually became policy under Herbert Hoover. Worse, Franklin Roosevelt adopted one of these crackpot ideas as the *primary basis* of his economic policy.[10] Roosevelt's great mistake—which led to all of his misguided interventions in the economy—was that he fundamentally misinterpreted what had caused the Depression; indeed, he had cause and effect exactly backwards. The main cause of the Depression, FDR and his advisers believed, was low prices. But low prices and wages did not cause the Depression; low prices and wages were *caused by* the Depression. Having confused cause and effect, however, Roosevelt and his advisers concluded that the "obvious solution" to the Depression was government-mandated price and wage increases. In other words, FDR accepted the Hoover "purchasing power" theory of economic recovery, and his programs greatly expanded on what Hoover had begun.

Price and wage increases were precisely what Roosevelt set out to achieve when he came into office, in the so-called First New Deal (1933–1934). (The Second New Deal would last from 1935 to 1938.) Of the dozens of new federal laws and programs FDR initiated during his first two years in office—the Civilian Conservation Corps, the Federal Emergency Relief Administration, the Tennessee Valley

Authority, and much more—the supposed crowning achievements were the National Industrial Relations Act (NIRA) and the Agricultural Adjustment Act. The NIRA (June 16, 1933) sought to cartelize virtually every industry in America under the auspices of the federal government (while suspending antitrust laws), and the Agricultural Adjustment Act (May 12, 1933) sought to do the same for agriculture.

The First New Deal was essentially a scheme to turn the U.S. economy into one massive, government-run system of industrial and agricultural cartels. At a time when underemployment or unemployment of resources (including labor resources) was of tragic proportions, the focus of the government was to *restrict* output and employment even further with supply-reducing cartel schemes and limitations on hours worked.

The scheme was destined to fail. First, if wages are forced up by government fiat, the effect is to reduce the demand for labor, which creates *more* unemployment. It is well known that the minimum-wage law causes unemployment, especially among lower-skilled workers. But at least the minimum-wage law applies primarily to entry-level employees and is therefore limited in the amount of harm it can do. The NIRA was an *economy-wide* minimum-wage (and maximum-hour) program, which rendered the job-destroying effect of the minimum-wage law universal.

Second, higher prices caused by a government-run cartel scheme may increase the incomes of sellers, but only by reducing the incomes of buyers by an equivalent amount. On net, the economy is not "stimulated." The NIRA was the public policy equivalent of a Rube Goldberg machine.

The NIRA created the National Recovery Administration (NRA), which was a bureaucratic monstrosity. The NRA organized each industry into a federally supervised trade association called a Code Authority, which had the authority to regulate production, prices, and distribution methods. Every businessperson was required to sign a pledge to observe the government's minimum wage, maximum hours, prohibitions on "child labor," and other regulations. Signers of the pledge were given a Blue Eagle badge, which they were to wear to show their compliance.

Under administrator Hugh Johnson, a former army general, the NRA adopted more than seven hundred industry codes and employed thousands of code-enforcement police. The NRA was empowered to enforce *minimum* prices, but not maximum prices. Prices were not legally permitted to fall below "costs of production," even if weak consumer demand would necessitate such pricing (temporarily) on the free market. Moreover, what counted as allowable "costs of production" for pricing purposes was determined arbitrarily by government bureaucrats in an unholy collaboration with industry executives. In the lumber industry, for example, prices were prohibited from falling below a "weighted average cost of production," which included thirteen different cost categories. "When all of these items are thrown in," Henry Hazlitt wrote, "the lumber industry should be able to present a very impressive figure for cost of production. In other words, it can fix a very substantial minimum price."[11] Once again the corporate world proved true to Adam Smith's dictum that businessmen can seldom meet, even for "merriment," without eventually turning the discussion to some conspiracy against the public. (As always, *effective* price-fixing conspiracies must use the coercive powers of the state to enforce compliance.)

In the New York garment industry, writes John T. Flynn, the code-enforcement police

> roamed through the garment district like storm troopers. They could enter a man's factory, send him out, line up his employees, subject them to minute interrogation, take over his books on the instant. Night work was forbidden. Flying squadrons of these private coat-and-suit police went through

the district at night, battering down doors with axes looking for men who were committing the crime of sewing together a pair of pants at night.[12]

A New Jersey tailor named Jack Magid was arrested, convicted, fined, and imprisoned for the "crime" of pressing a suit of clothes for thirty-five cents when the Tailors' Code fixed the price at forty cents.[13] Every town in America, writes Flynn, could offer a similar example.

More than six thousand patronage jobs were ladled out to "statisticians" who prepared reports regarding the "appropriate" prices that ought to be charged in each and every industry, a sort of Soviet-style central planning bureaucracy. Henry Hazlitt explained the work of some of these statistical wizards in a December 1933 article in *The American Mercury:*

> The corset and brassiere industry, while permitting manufacturers or wholesalers to contribute up to 50% of the net cost of a retailer's advertising space, prohibits them from paying *any* of the cost of advertising on "corsets, combinations, girdle-corsets, or step-in corsets" which are advertised for retail sale at less than $2, or on brassieres which are advertised for retail sales at less than $1.[14]

Of course, the codes were in reality nothing but a monopoly scheme. Government-enforced high prices were said to constitute "fair competition," much to the delight of the industries that believed they would benefit from the scheme—and that would likely make hefty campaign contributions to FDR in return.

The NIRA also cartelized the oil industry with a provision that created state "control boards" to restrict the amount of oil sold in interstate and international commerce.[15]

The government launched a massive propaganda campaign,

complete with a mammoth New York City parade, to promote public acceptance of the NRA. The government campaign championed the NRA codes while smearing and denigrating capitalists and capitalist institutions. Competition was called "economic cannibalism"; rugged individualists were "industrial pirates"; competitive price cutting was denounced as "cutthroat and monopolistic price slashing"; price cutters were branded "chiselers"; and government-enforced cartels were praised as "cooperative arrangements."[16] As so often happens when government enters into policy debates, it was able to drown out other voices; that is, the NRA propaganda worked.

One dissenting voice was journalist Henry Hazlitt, who in a December 1933 *American Mercury* article perfectly summarized the NRA as a government program under which

> the American consumer is to become the victim of a series of trades and industries which, in the name of "fair competition," will be in effect monopolies, consisting of units that agree not to make too serious an effort to undersell each other; restricting production, fixing prices—doing everything, in fact, that monopolies are formed to do. . . . Instead of a relatively flexible system with some power of adjustment to fluid world economic conditions we shall have an inadjustable structure constantly attempting—at the cost of stagnant business and employment—to resist these conditions.[17]

The First New Deal's other supposed achievement, the Agricultural Adjustment Act, created the Agricultural Adjustment Administration (AAA) within the Department of Agriculture in order to cartelize agricultural markets. FDR adopted a program of paying farmers millions of dollars annually for literally burning their crops and slaughtering their livestock while many Americans were going hungry. One corporation alone that was in the business of refining sugar was paid $1 million for *not* producing sugar.[18] This policy of reducing food production when many Americans were going hungry created a public relations disaster for Roosevelt, who then wised up and began paying farmers and ranchers *for not raising livestock and planting crops in the first place.* The AAA initiated acreage allotments, restrictive marketing agreements, the licensing of food processors and dealers to "eliminate unfair pricing," and numerous other agricultural cartel schemes. The agency was an awful burden on poor sharecroppers, thousands of whom were evicted so that the landowners could collect their governmental bounties for not producing.[19] Who needs sharecroppers when being paid not to grow crops?

The First New Deal involved a number of other bizarre and harmful schemes. Perhaps the most sinister of FDR's price-fixing schemes had to do with his handling of the gold stock. Roosevelt abandoned the gold standard, the only certain restraint on federal government growth and inflation. He nationalized the gold stock by making the private ownership of gold illegal (except for jewelry, scientific or industrial uses, and foreign payments) and nullifying all contractual promises to pay for anything in gold. This was effectively an act of outright theft, and it didn't even inflate prices, as FDR had hoped it would. Because of the severity of the Depression, the price level remained fairly steady for the entire decade of the 1930s.

One of Roosevelt's first acts as president was to order the closing of the banks. This bank holiday was intended to halt the run on banks—that is, FDR hoped the closing would calm down panicking depositors and prevent them from demanding all their savings. And some would claim that this is precisely what Roosevelt achieved: later, one of FDR's advisers, Raymond Moley, publicly proclaimed that because of his boss's bank closings, "capitalism was saved in eight days."[20] But in fact the bank holiday only heightened the state of panic and did nothing to improve the banking system or alleviate the Depression.

Moreover, the 1917 Trading with the Enemy Act that Roosevelt invoked to justify the bank closings had been designed specifically as a wartime measure. The act stipulated that "during the time of war" the president may "regulate, or prohibit, any transactions in foreign exchange, transfers of credit or payments between, by, through, or to any banking institution" with respect to transactions involving "any property in which any foreign country or a national thereof has any interest."[21] Since the United States was not at war at this point, FDR obviously stretched the purpose of the act far beyond what its legislative sponsors could have intended it for. Roosevelt used the crisis mentality to ignore the law and grant himself powers that he was not intended to have.

ECONOMIC FASCISM

Franklin Roosevelt's First New Deal was such a debacle that in early 1935 the U.S. Supreme Court ruled both the NRA and AAA unconstitutional. Even before that, the NRA had created such protest over its storm-trooper tactics that the U.S. Senate in 1934 had forced FDR to appoint a commission to evaluate the agency. The commission, headed by renowned attorney Clarence Darrow, described the NRA as "harmful, monopolistic, oppressive, grotesque, invasive, fictitious, ghastly, anomalous, preposterous, irresponsible, savage, wolfish."[22] Given these stunning repudiations of Roosevelt's First New Deal, it is difficult to fathom how FDR can be regarded as a great hero for "rescuing" America from the Great Depression. It is even more difficult to understand the Roosevelt mythology when one considers that his economic interventionism—especially the NRA and AAA—was essentially modeled after the Italian fascist system.

John T. Flynn noted the striking similarities between Benito Mussolini's economic system and the First New Deal:

[Mussolini] organized each trade or industrial group or professional group into a state-supervised trade association. He called it a cooperative. These cooperatives operated under state supervision and could plan production, quality, prices, distribution, labor standards, etc. The NRA provided that in American industry each industry should be organized into a federally supervised trade association. It was not called a cooperative. It was called a Code Authority. But it was essentially the same thing. . . . this was fascism.[23]

Flynn is quite right. Just as Roosevelt wanted to use government cartels to artificially prop up prices and wages, Mussolini's "legally recognized syndicates"—essentially regional trade associations, with names like the National Fascist Confederation of Commerce and the National Fascist Confederation of Credit and Insurance— were meant to counter (if not eliminate) free-market competition.[24] As one of Mussolini's economic advisers put it, by making sure the "various categories of producers" collaborated, the government could ensure that "the principle of private initiative" would not serve the purposes of private citizens (such as consumers) but would be "useful in the service of the national interest" (the "national interest" as Mussolini defined it, of course).[25] Another Mussolini adviser said that these central planning agencies fostered "a spirit of collaboration which would not be possible under any other system."[26]

Like FDR and his NRA appointees, the Italian fascists waged a fierce propaganda campaign against the principles of free markets and individual liberty. In numerous speeches Mussolini bemoaned the "selfish pursuit of material prosperity," explained that fascism was "a reaction against the flaccid materialistic positivism of the nineteenth century," and urged Italians to abandon the ideas of Adam Smith and "the economistic literature of the eighteenth century."[27] "If the nineteenth century was the century of the individual (liberalism implies individualism)," Mussolini wrote, then "this [the twentieth century] is the 'collective' century, and therefore the century of the State. . . . Fascism spells government."[28] As Flynn has observed, Mussolini and his "corporative system" had many admirers among American intellectuals, politicians, and businessmen, which is how these ideas came to have such influence on Franklin Roosevelt's administration. Many of America's political and business elites offered glowing tributes to Mussolini in the 1920s and 1930s. Typical was this paean from former U.S. ambassador to Italy Richard Washburn Child, found in the foreword to Mussolini's 1928 autobiography: "In our time it may be shrewdly forecast that no man will exhibit dimensions of permanent greatness equal to those of Mussolini. . . . The Duce is now the greatest figure of this sphere and time."[29]

American businessmen were the primary promoters of economic fascism. In 1932 Henry I. Harriman, the president of the U.S. Chamber of Commerce, was impressed at how businessmen had been "conspicuously zealous in promoting the effort to carry into practical effect the philosophy of the planned economy."[30] Among those conspicuous efforts was a popular plan presented in the 1920s by Gerard Swope, General Electric's chief executive officer. As historians Martin Fausold and George T. Mazuzan described it, Swope proposed a system that would "operate through compulsory trade associations, made up of all major firms and empowered by law to regulate production, prices, and trade practices."[31]

In fact, Mussolini was not the only noncapitalist model for America's business and political leaders in the 1930s. Many of these elites admired something even more totalitarian than Italian fascism—Soviet central planning. Economist Stuart Chase considered central planning to be such an important aspect of any economic system that he actually scoffed at the Soviets for believing that *they,* and not Americans, had invented the planned economy. Presenting a "Ten Year Plan for America" in the June 1931 issue of

Harper's magazine (a plan that was extremely popular among businessmen), Chase wrote, "These Slavs seem to think that they discovered national planning" when in reality the "credit" for it should go to Woodrow Wilson and his War Industries Board. Said Chase, these "fifteen hundred businessmen, economists, engineers, statisticians, [and] map makers [were] running the country" during World War I.[32]

The idea that war planning could be a model for peacetime planning of the economy, and that the Soviet system was to be admired, permeated the Roosevelt administration. Before becoming FDR's most influential economic adviser, Rexford G. Tugwell of Columbia University wrote a book in which he praised Soviet communism, which he believed would be more prosperous and more egalitarian than capitalism. In *American Economic Life* (1930), Tugwell wrote that the Soviet Union's "worst enemies are being forced to admit that the system appears to be able to produce goods in greater quantities than the old one and to spread such prosperity as there is over wider areas of the population."[33] Soviet central planning enabled the Soviets to plan and to "carry out their industrial operations in accordance with a completely thought-out program," Tugwell commented admiringly.[34] "The available evidence as to the success of the scheme seems to indicate clearly enough that it works."[35] There were admittedly "those who suffer under it," but according to Tugwell "the major advantages . . . outweigh the disadvantages of the supposed loss of incentive, red tape, unimaginative centralized authority."[36] Or as Stalin reportedly said, one must break a few eggs to make an omelet. Tugwell also acknowledged a certain "ruthlessness" and "disregard for liberties and rights" in the Soviet Union, as well as "repression, spying, and violence," but socialism did not cause any of this, he said.[37] Anyone interested "in peace, prosperity, and progress must, in the coming years, devote much study and thought to Russia and the Russians," according to Tugwell.[38]

How the New Deal Crippled Capitalism

Writing in the *American Economic Review* in 1932, the year of FDR's election, Tugwell denounced capitalistic profits for producing "insecurity" by creating "overcapacity" and "inflation"; essentially he was echoing Karl Marx's theory of surplus value.[39] Profits, he said, "create unemployment and hardship," "persuade us to speculate" in "dangerous endeavors," and, most harmfully, "hinder measurably the advance of [centralized] planning."[40] To Tugwell the NRA, as onerous and unconstitutional as it was, did not nearly go far enough in regulating and regimenting the U.S. economy.

Others in the Roosevelt administration agreed. Despite repudiations of the First New Deal by the Supreme Court and the Senate, the wily and irrepressible Roosevelt resurrected many of the programs in the Second New Deal. The AAA programs, for instance, were continued under the subterfuge of a "soil conservation program." Many other programs that the Supreme Court had previously ruled unconstitutional were continued but in a different form; many of them are in place even today, in fact. And it is important to remember that, as economist Charlotte Twight observes in *America's Emerging Fascist Economy*, many (perhaps most) of the governmental institutions that Americans take for granted today were introduced during the New Deal—and were explicitly modeled after the European fascist economies of the 1930s. Economic fascism, says Twight, seeks to "empower an elite to determine the specific purposes that other individuals in the society are compelled to serve"; it "is the antithesis of limited government and individualism," as it "uncompromisingly seeks to obliterate individual rights"; its view of capitalism is "regulated capitalism" and "government intervention in the economy on a massive scale"; it "supplants ... market considerations with political considerations" with only "perfunctory regard for economic costs or consumers' wishes"; it uses the language of "the national interest" to justify myriad government interventions; and it "attempts to fuse management and labor, molding them into a monolithic instrument for achieving whatever government officials decree to be the national interest."[41]

MAKING MATTERS WORSE: THE SECOND NEW DEAL

On January 4, 1935—only a few months before the U.S. Supreme Court ruled most of the First New Deal unconstitutional—FDR announced his Second New Deal. The principal additions were the Social Security Act, the National Labor Relations Act, the Fair Labor Standards Act (the minimum-wage law), the Works Progress Administration, and punitive taxes imposed ostensibly to punish "economic royalists" and other entrepreneurs whom Roosevelt wanted to blame for the country's troubles. Every one of these programs was a drain on the private sector and/or an impediment to employment. As such, they all made the Great Depression even worse.

The Social Security payroll tax and the two labor laws increased the cost to employers of hiring workers, which led to higher unemployment. The payroll tax was a straightforward increase in the cost of labor, as was the minimum-wage law. The National Labor Relations Act (or Wagner Act) created a system of government-sanctioned legal privileges for labor unions that greatly enhanced their bargaining powers and, in many ways, enabled them to become more or less outlaw organizations. The Norris-LaGuardia Act, signed by President Hoover in 1932 and vigorously enforced during the Roosevelt administration, made it extremely costly and difficult to obtain an injunction against union violence. Laws against extortion exempted unions as long as the extortion involved "the payment of wages by a bona fide employer to a bona fide employee."[42]

We feel the effects of many of these laws even today. Thanks primarily to FDR's Depression-era labor legislation, labor unions can compel workers to pay dues as a condition of keeping their jobs, with the dues often being used for political purposes unrelated to collective bargaining; are immune from most federal court injunctions; are legally empowered to "represent" all workers in a bargaining unit, regardless of whether they are union members; can compel employers to make their private property available to union officials; are all but immune from paying damages for personal and property injury that they inflict; and can force employers to open up their books to them.[43] As Friedrich Hayek wrote in *The Constitution of Liberty* (1960), "We have now reached a state where they [unions] have become uniquely privileged institutions to which the general rules of law do not apply. They have become the only important instance in which governments fail in their prime function—the prevention of coercion and violence."[44]

These new laws granting special privileges to unions (and at the same time expanding state control over labor relations) were virtually identical to the kind of arrangements that had been adopted in Italy and Germany in the 1920s and 1930s. In each instance, the objective was to put the state in control of regulating labor relations in such a way as to achieve *the state's* objectives—higher wages to "enhance purchasing power," in FDR's case. In each instance *individual* bargaining with employers was all but outlawed and was replaced by state-supervised and -controlled *collective* bargaining, with unions as the state-sponsored bargaining agents for all workers within a unionized workplace. According to labor historian Howard Dickman, New Deal labor legislation was "the beginning of a fascistic regulation of our quasi-syndicalist system of industrial democracy."[45]

These labor laws made the Great Depression worse. The virtual exemption from the rule of law allowed unions to force up wages during the Great Depression at a much faster pace than labor productivity was increasing, thereby causing higher unemployment. Wages rose by a phenomenal 13.7 percent during the first three quarters of 1937 alone.[46] The union/nonunion wage differential increased from 5 percent in 1933 to 23 percent by 1940.[47] On top of this, the Social Security payroll and unemployment insurance taxes contributed to a rapid rise in government-mandated fringe benefits, from 2.4 percent of payrolls in 1936 to 5.1 percent just two years later.

Economists Richard Vedder and Lowell Gallaway have determined the costs of all this misguided legislation, showing how most of the abnormal unemployment of the 1930s would have been avoided had it not been for the New Deal. Using a statistical model, Vedder and Gallaway concluded that by 1940 the unemployment rate was more than 8 percentage points higher than it would have been without the legislation-induced growth in unionism and government-mandated fringe-benefit costs imposed on employers.[48] Their conclusion: "The Great Depression was very significantly prolonged in both its duration and its magnitude by the impact of New Deal programs."[49]

In addition to fascistic labor policies and government-mandated wage and fringe-benefit increases that destroyed millions of jobs, the Second New Deal was responsible for economy-destroying tax increases and massive government spending on myriad government make-work programs. "I've got four million at work [in federal jobs]," FDR adviser Harry Hopkins told the president in 1935, "but for God's sake, don't ask me what they are doing."[50] Even before the military mobilization for World War II was under way, federal spending had more than doubled, from $4.6 billion in 1932 to $9.1 billion in 1940, while approximately $24 billion in deficits were accumulated. Annual deficits during this time averaged 42 percent of the federal budget.[51] Prior to Roosevelt's terms in office, budget deficits were universally denounced—even by FDR himself during the 1932 election campaign.

How the New Deal Crippled Capitalism

FDR thought the government could get the country out of the Great Depression by spending, but of course that could never work. There is no free lunch: every dollar the government spends on some kind of make-work program must necessarily depress genuine, market-driven economic growth because resources are diverted from the private to the governmental sector. That is why, despite the fact that the federal budget more than doubled in eight years, the Depression did not end and, indeed, unemployment was higher in 1938 than it was in 1931.

FDR's vaunted "jobs" programs unequivocally destroyed jobs. Government "jobs" programs, such as the Works Progress Administration and the Civilian Conservation Corps, can only destroy private-sector jobs in order to "create" government make-work jobs. And since government bureaucrats spend the taxpayers' money much more inefficiently than the taxpayers themselves do, government jobs that are "created" usually destroy *several* private-sector jobs. For example, the federal government's own General Accounting Office has estimated that some federal jobs programs have provided $14,000-per-year jobs at a total cost of more than $100,000 *per job*, once one accounts for all the administrative expenses. Thus, in this case, about seven $14,000-per-year entry-level jobs must be destroyed in order to create one government job.

THE NEW DEAL PORK BARREL

Historians have perpetuated the myth that FDR spent the United States out of the Great Depression. There are two fundamental flaws in these assertions: First, as mentioned, it is impossible for government spending to *create* prosperity; only production can create prosperity. Second, the assumption behind the claims that government spending somehow ended the Depression is that FDR made spending decisions based on economic "need." That is, government spending programs are said to have targeted the neediest areas of the country.

There is no evidence of this. In fact, there is much evidence that New Deal spending was designed with one overriding objective: to use the money to buy votes in order to assure FDR's reelection, regardless of regional disparities in the degree of economic hardship. The South was the most devastated region of the country during the Great Depression, for example, but it received a disproportionately small amount of federal subsidies. John T. Flynn discusses how thoroughly politicized New Deal spending was by reporting the conclusions of a 1938 Official Report of the U.S. Senate Committee on Campaign Expenditures. Among the findings of the report:[52]

- In one Works Progress Administration (WPA) district in Kentucky, 349 WPA employees were put to work preparing forms listing the electoral preferences of every employee on work relief. Many of those who stated that they did not intend to vote for Roosevelt were laid off.
- In another Kentucky WPA district, government workers were required, as a condition of employment, to pledge to vote for the senior senator from Kentucky, who was an FDR supporter. If they refused, they were thrown off the relief rolls.
- Republicans in Kentucky were told that they would have to change party affiliations if they wanted to keep their WPA jobs.
- Letters were sent out to WPA employees in Kentucky instructing them to donate 2 percent of their salaries to the Roosevelt campaign if they wanted to keep their jobs.

- In Pennsylvania, businessmen who leased trucks to the WPA were solicited for $100 campaign contributions.
- As in Kentucky, Pennsylvania WPA workers were told to change their party affiliation if they wanted to keep their jobs. Many people refused and were fired.
- Government employment was increased dramatically right before elections. In Pennsylvania, "employment cards" were distributed that entitled holders of the cards to "two to four weeks of employment around election time."
- A Pennsylvania man who had been given a $60.50-per-month white-collar job was transferred to a pick-axe job in a limestone quarry after refusing to change his voter registration from Republican to Democrat.
- Tennessee WPA workers were also instructed to contribute 2 percent of their salaries to the Democratic Party as a condition of employment.
- In one congressional district in Cook County, Illinois, the WPA instructed 450 of its employees to canvass for (Democratic) votes around election time in 1938. The men were all laid off the day after the election.

The U.S. Senate report surveyed only four states, but there is every reason to believe that similar practices occurred in all the states. Economist Gavin Wright conducted a more systematic examination of WPA spending patterns and concluded that, in general, "WPA employment reached peaks in the fall of election years, and the pattern is most pronounced when employment is measured relative to indices of need."[53] In a 1939 magazine article entitled "The WPA: Politicians' Playground," historian Stanley High observed, "In states like Florida and Kentucky—where the New Deal's big fight was in the primary elections—the rise of WPA employment was hurried along in order to synchronize with the primaries."[54]

More recently, economic researchers have uncovered governmental data depicting the distribution of New Deal spending, which has enabled them to examine more fully the extent to which programs such as the WPA were motivated by politics—namely, the reelection of Franklin D. Roosevelt. In general, the relatively well-off western states tended to receive the lion's share of New Deal subsidies, whereas the southern states, where the Depression was most severe, received the least. The average resident of a western state received 60 percent more in federal subsidies than did the average southerner.[55] This is sharply at odds with the New Deal rhetoric of compassion and "relief" for the most "downtrodden."

As soon as these data were discovered (in 1969), pro-FDR academics began constructing excuses and rationales for the pattern of New Deal spending. The cost of living was much lower in the South, they said, so naturally there would have been less spending there. Cost-of-living differences existed but were rather small—for example, the annual cost-of-living estimate for Jacksonville, Florida, in 1938 was $1,260.44, while the corresponding estimate for Buffalo, New York, was $1,283.81.[56] In contrast, the differences in the distribution of spending on a regional basis were very large.

A second rationale offered by New Deal apologists is that since standards of living were so low in the South, it didn't take much to satisfy southerners. But this rationale is clearly at odds with all the "compassionate" rhetoric of the New Deal.

A third excuse for the New Deal's odd spending patterns has to do with matching requirements. The argument is that since some New Deal programs had matching requirements—that is, state and local governments had to match federal subsidies—it should be expected that more affluent states (especially in the West and Northeast) would receive more in subsidies, since they could afford greater matching amounts. But the key question is: if the New Deal programs were truly motivated by a desire to help those who most needed economic assistance, why were such matching requirements implemented in the first place? Surely Roosevelt's vaunted "Brain Trust" knew that the requirements would skew the distribution of subsidies in this way.[57]

In contrast to these questionable excuses, a number of economists have begun to examine the notion that politics may have been a more reliable and consistent explanation for the pattern of New Deal spending than "compassion" or "need." And in fact these economists have found little statistical support for the claim that economic need determined New Deal spending. For example, a 1991 study by Gary Anderson and Robert Tollison found that electoral votes per capita were indeed an important determinant of how New Deal spending was allocated. They also determined that congressional districts whose representatives were members of House or Senate appropriations committees received disproportionate New Deal subsidies.[58]

In *The Political Economy of the New Deal*, Jim F. Couch and William F. Shughart II explain how the Roosevelt administration considered politics above all else in handing out federal money. According to Couch and Shugart, the western states were showered with New Deal money because they were critical to the Democrats' political ambitions:

> The support of these states was instrumental in securing Franklin Roosevelt's nomination as the Democratic Party's standard-bearer in 1932. History might have played out very differently had "favorite son" candidates William Gibbs McAdoo of California and Speaker of the House (and soon-to-be vice presidential nominee) John Nance Garner of Texas not released the delegates pledged to them and thrown their sup-

port behind FDR on the convention's fourth ballot. Two years later, the West was again of the highest political importance to the New Dealers because of crucial senatorial races involving Democratic incumbents in Utah, Arizona, Montana, and in other states where they hoped to gain a seat: Nebraska, Wyoming, New Mexico, Washington, and California.[59]

Politics also explains why the South received so little federal aid. Since the War Between the States, the South had been solidly Democratic; few southerners could bring themselves to vote for the "party of Lincoln," and Roosevelt had won southern states handily in 1932. Thus, FDR knew that he had little need to buy the electoral votes of the southern states with federal funds. He needed only to throw the South enough crumbs to avoid a political revolt. His main priority was to use tax dollars to buy votes in those states where his electoral margins were slimmer.

Couch and Shughart found the "perverse" result that during the Great Depression "states with healthier economies received proportionately more federal aid in the form of [New Deal] grants *they were not expected to repay* while repayable loans were directed in slightly greater amounts to their harder-hit sisters [emphasis in original]."[60] They also concluded that "New Dealers allocated significantly more funds to states where the nation's most valuable . . . farms were located. . . . Little flowed to sharecroppers and other tenants or to farm laborers."[61] In addition, Couch and Shughart's research challenges the New Dealers' claims of special sensitivity to the hardships of blacks during the Great Depression: "States where blacks accounted for larger percentages of the farm population received fewer New Deal dollars."[62] Finally, these authors determined that Roosevelt quickly rewarded those states that served him well in 1932: "The states that gave Franklin Roosevelt larger percentages of the popular vote in 1932 were rewarded [shortly afterward] with significantly more federal aid than less-supportive constituencies. . . . A one percentage point increase in support of FDR in the 1932 presidential election translated into nearly $300 in additional per-capita federal aid over the 1933–1939 period."[63] Thus, FDR left no political stone unturned: he used government funds to bribe voters to vote for him when he needed them and also rewarded his supporters with further governmental largesse.

In light of all these findings, Couch and Shughart conclude:

> The distribution of the billions of dollars appropriated by Congress to prime the economic pump was guided less by considerations of economic need than by the forces of ordinary politics. Perhaps the New Deal failed as a matter of economic policy because it was so successful in building a winning political coalition: FDR was reelected overwhelmingly in 1936 and again in 1940 in part due to the support of the big-city machines, organized labor, and other constituencies which benefited disproportionately from New Deal largesse. Insofar as the region was "safe" for the Democrats, the administration's comparative neglect of the nation's number one economic problem—the South—can likewise be explained by politics.[64]

As David Gordon has written, Franklin Roosevelt was a most ordinary and familiar kind of politician. That is, he "was a vain, intellectually shallow person whose principal interest was to retain at all costs his personal power" and whose priorities were the "total subordination of his country's welfare to his personal ambition."[65] The effects of Roosevelt's self-serving interventionist economic scheme have been devastating. Indeed, were it not for FDR's crippling and long-lasting interventions, the American economy today would be much healthier than it is.

CHAPTER ELEVEN

Did Capitalism Cause the Energy Crisis?

As an economist, whenever I hear the word "shortage" I wait for the other shoe to drop. That other shoe is usually "price control."

—Thomas Sowell, *Capitalism* magazine (Jan. 11, 2001)

PRESIDENT Franklin Roosevelt's New Deal was devastating not just in the direct effect it had on the American economy of the 1930s. One of its most damaging side effects has been that it created the *expectation* that government will step in to "solve" any economic crisis—it has fostered the myth that government intervention is necessary to counter the exploitative nature of capitalists. Thus, government regulations now handcuff almost all industries, and virtually every day we hear calls for further regulation.

The energy industry in this country is a prime example of the industries that have been burdened by unnecessary government regulations and demonized by anticapitalist mythmakers. As seen in Chapter 7, the American oil industry started out in a laissez-faire environment in which there was little, if any, government regulation and no income taxation. Entrepreneurs like John D. Rockefeller were able literally to create one of the most important industries in world history from nothing. In doing so they transformed the world, made the machine age possible, improved the standard of living for millions, created hundreds of thousands of jobs, and invented management practices that would be emulated by other capitalists around the world. Capitalism, or market entrepreneurship, is what created all of these economic benefits. But from the early twentieth century on, the oil industry has been a regulated industry and has become less and less capitalistic. Today the industry is heavily regulated—strangled, some would say—by government. And inevitably, government regulation—not the capitalistic nature of the industry—causes high prices, shortages, and other problems.

Still, the myth persists that the industry's capitalistic nature is precisely what creates problems. Indeed, virtually every time there is a jump in gasoline prices the oil companies are accused of "price gouging," their profits are reported on the front pages of America's newspapers, and, more often than not, some congressional committee commences an investigation or holds hearings to look into the matter. During the so-called energy crisis of the 1970s the accusations against the oil companies were most strident, as the seven largest companies—"the seven sisters," as they were called—were accused of somehow orchestrating a shortage to boost their own profits. But on the face of it, the notion that a price-fixing conspiracy can periodically increase gasoline prices makes no sense. If oil companies are able to raise prices in such a manner, why don't they do it all the time? Why only every several years? Why do they throw all that money away by holding prices down? And why are they incapable of stopping oil prices from *falling*? (During the 2000 presidential election vice presidential candidate Dick Cheney appeared on *Meet the Press* to say that oil and gas prices were *too low* and that some kind of government "price stabilization program" was needed. At the time, he had just left his position as a top oil industry executive.) The obvious answer to these questions is that the oil companies do *not* have the price-fixing powers that the mainstream media—and anticapitalist intellectuals—ascribe to them.

Nevertheless, regulation has become a reality in the energy industry. Much of this regulation, in fact, has been supported by industry executives themselves. Such executives have been some of capitalism's worst enemies.

ENDLESS INTERVENTIONISM

The first attack on the capitalist system that built the oil industry came, of course, when the federal government found the Standard Oil Company to be in violation of the Sherman Act and broke it up into several separate companies. Barely a half dozen years later, however, the same federal government that prosecuted Standard Oil, supposedly for its monopolistic practices, created a *legal* oil industry cartel. Ironically, one of the men the government brought in to operate the cartel was A. C. Bedford, the chief executive officer of Standard Oil.[1] The occasion was World War I, and the government decided that it needed to "collaborate" with industry to eliminate "wasteful competition" and to set prices. In other words, laissez-faire was abandoned and the industry became centrally planned; it was not unlike the "experiment" being conducted economy-wide at the time in the Soviet Union.

Petroleum industry central planning was supposed to be a wartime measure, but industry executives decided that they rather liked having the government act as cartel enforcer. After the war they supported President Calvin Coolidge's Federal Oil Conservation Board, which mandated reductions of oil supplies within states. Such a tactic would have been illegal under the antitrust laws if done privately, but since government exempts itself from antitrust laws (and many others), such blatant price-fixing schemes were legal. The government cynically used "conservation of resources" as an excuse to create the cartel, as though its main concern was environmental protection. In this way, it could claim that the whole scheme was "in the public interest."

The industry also supported higher tariffs on imported petroleum to further protect it from international competition. Consequently, crude oil prices rose more than sevenfold—from ten cents a barrel to eighty-five cents—between August 1931 and June 1932, at the outset of the Great Depression.[2] The American manufacturing industries suffered quite severely, since virtually every manufactured product involves the use of some kind of crude oil product as an energy source.

Then, in the 1950s, import quotas were imposed. Thus, by 1960 the industry was fully cartelized, with the government acting as cartel enforcer.

But competition can never be completely eliminated. There was still considerable competition from other countries, especially ones in the Middle East. Oil production in the Persian Gulf region eventually made it impossible for American oil companies to control supplies and prices, even with all the cartel-creating regulations that had been put into place. Oil prices fell as the Persian Gulf countries increased their production substantially.

In the early 1970s, the Organization of Petroleum Exporting Countries (OPEC) imposed an embargo—that is, a sharp reduction in supply. At the same time, the U.S. government's barrage of environmental regulations had sharply reduced the domestic supply of petroleum and petroleum products. For example, the vast reserves of oil on the outer continental shelf off the coast of California were put off-limits to drilling for fear of oil spills that would despoil the coastline. In addition, a great deal of the land owned by the federal government—a substantial amount, since the government owns more than half of all the land west of the Mississippi River—was placed off-limits to oil exploration for environmental reasons. Meanwhile, the hundreds of new regulations that had been imposed on oil refineries made it much more costly, if not unprofitable altogether, to build them.

It was in this climate that the "energy crisis" developed. OPEC was not the only group responsible for the reduction in the oil supply; America's own government had done the same by overregulating the industry. On top of all this, in 1971 the Nixon administration had imposed wage and price controls in a failed attempt to control inflation—or at least to pretend to be controlling inflation just before the 1972 election. The controls were always intended to be temporary, and they were lifted in 1974 on all products *except* petroleum. With increased demand for petroleum due to a growing population, combined with regulation-induced supply reductions, price controls could only produce shortages. Holding prices below free-market levels artificially stimulated consumer demand but also made it less profitable to increase supply. The results were entirely predictable, and the shortages were there for all the world to see during the 1970s in the form of long lines at gasoline stations. The government responded with futile attempts at energy conservation, such as California's law that one could purchase gasoline on certain days if one's license plate ended with an even number, and on other days if the plate ended with an odd number.

All of this would have been avoided without price controls. When OPEC began its embargo, driving up the price of oil, domestic oil producers would have had extra incentives to introduce more supply onto the market. At the same time, the higher prices would have signaled consumers that it was prudent to conserve more. A new market equilibrium would have been reached without any shortages or misallocations, and the OPEC cartel would have been broken, as it eventually was, by increased domestic supplies brought on by free-market prices.

Instead, the federal government created the Federal Energy Administration, which became the Department of Energy (DOE) in 1977. This new bureaucracy quickly put into place an absurd collection of price controls and allocation rules, so that the U.S. energy industry soon rivaled any of the Soviet Union's centrally planned industries in its complexity—and inefficiency. The head of the new energy department was even given a Russian-sounding title by the media: energy czar. The Washington, D.C., bureaucracy was bursting with enthusiasm over its newly created central planning role in such a crucial industry. But the first energy czar, William E. Simon, called the whole operation a "disaster":

> As for the centralized allocation process itself, the kindest thing I can say about it is that it was a disaster. Even with a stack of sensible-sounding plans for even-handed allocation all over the country, the system kept falling apart, and chunks of the populace suddenly found themselves without gas. There was no logic to the pattern of failures. In Palm Beach suddenly there was no gas, while 10 miles away gas was plentiful. Parts of New Jersey suddenly went dry, while other parts of New Jersey were well supplied. Every day, in different parts of the country, people waited in line for gasoline for two, three, and four hours. The normal market distribution system is so complex, yet so smooth that no government mechanism could simulate it.[3]

The striking thing about this passage is that the spectacle of arbitrary supply allocations and long waiting lines is identical to how *every* industry operated in the socialist countries like the Soviet Union at the time. For more than a half century these governments had tried precisely the kinds of central planning schemes that were being implemented in the U.S. oil industry, and with unmitigated failure in every instance. Yet tremendous hubris on the part of the federal government led American politicians and bureaucrats to believe that they would somehow make better central planners than the Russians did. This hubris, unfortunately, was based on a complete misunderstanding of markets, and especially of their spontaneous, voluntary nature. Suppliers and consumers will always balance out their respective plans if they are only given the freedom to do so, free of price controls, allocation controls, and other regulatory restrictions on their behavior. (A popular joke at the time was that if the DOE were put in charge of the Mojave Desert, there would be a sand shortage.)

Simon continued with his explanation of the central planning disaster in the oil industry during the 1970s:

> As the shortages became more erratic and unpredictable, people began to "top off" their tanks. Instead of waiting, as is customary, to refill the tank when it is about one quarter full, all over the country people started buying 50 cents' worth of gas, a dollar's worth of gas, using every opportunity to keep their tanks full at all times. And that fiercely compounded the shortages and expanded the queues. The psychology of hysteria took over. Essentially the allocation plan had failed because there had been a ludicrous reliance on a little legion of government lawyers, who drafted regulations in indecipherable language, and bureaucratic technocrats, who imagined that they could simulate the complex free-market processes by pushing computer buttons. In fact, they couldn't.[4]

As discussed in Chapter 1, this notion—that a group of government "planners" could impose rules and regulations that could simulate a market economy—was properly labeled the "pretense of knowledge" by Nobel laureate Friedrich Hayek. Ironically, Hayek was awarded the Nobel Prize in 1974, at precisely the same time the newly empowered Federal Energy Administration bureaucracy was steadfastly ignoring his life's work and imposing an Americanized central planning regime on the oil industry.

Did Capitalism Cause the Energy Crisis?

Although some (not all) top oil industry executives had endorsed, if not lobbied for, such interventions as tariffs, quotas, and state prorationing regulations, it is also true that, from at least the end of the nineteenth century, the federal government had waged a propaganda campaign on behalf of effectively nationalizing the industry. In 1909 the U.S. Geological Survey (USGS) ominously warned that if the U.S. petroleum industry continued "the present rate of increase in production, the supply would be exhausted by about 1935."[5] In 1922 the same agency forecast that oil supplies would dry up by 1942 at the latest. In fact, the federal government routinely issued such erroneous forecasts almost from the day oil was discovered in Titusville, Pennsylvania, in 1866. In that year the U.S. Revenue Commission assured the nation that "synthetics" would be available when oil production ended, as the government fully expected it to do.[6]

The government continually underestimated the vast reserves available in the United States alone. In 1885 the USGS said there was little or no chance of finding oil in California; more than 8 billion barrels have been pumped since that date. Also, in 1891 it said there was little or no chance of discovering oil in *Texas!* In 1908 the USGS forecast the maximum future oil supply as 22.5 billion barrels, an estimate that has been off by tens of billions of barrels to date.

In 1914 the U.S. Bureau of Mines got into the false forecasting business and warned that there were only 5.7 billion barrels of oil left. In 1939 the U.S. Department of the Interior predicted that the United States would run out of oil by 1952, and sure enough, in 1949, the secretary of the interior warned that the "end of U.S. oil supplies is in sight." But in 1951 that forecast suddenly had to be revised, as the Department of the Interior predicted that oil reserves in the ground would last only another thirteen years. The Department of State also sounded the alarm, warning in 1947 that "sufficient oil cannot be found in the U.S."

There is a method to all this false forecasting madness. Namely, the government long ago recognized the importance of petroleum to the economy and has sought to control the industry, either through outright nationalization or pervasive regulation. Control of the petroleum industry is a tremendous source of power and revenue to the federal government.

The forecasts all ignore the basics of supply and demand as well. Whenever any resource becomes more scarce, the price will rise, causing consumers to conserve and stimulating the exploration for and development of new supplies. The higher price also provides a financial incentive to discover and market alternatives to the scarce resource. Thus, by ignoring these economic realities, government forecasters have systematically exaggerated the "threat" of running out of energy in an attempt to gain greater control over the industry. They accomplished this goal in the 1970s, and it was an unmitigated disaster for the industry and for consumers. It was a boon to governmental power, however; the Department of Energy still exists and is better funded than ever.[7]

Having created the energy crisis with its own interventions, the federal government did not eliminate the interventions that caused the crisis in the first place but instead vastly expanded its powers over the oil industry. This bold interventionist initiative, billed as Project Independence and introduced in November 1973, was supposed to make America independent of foreign oil sources by 1980. To achieve this goal, the government said it would subsidize new synthetic fuel industries, increase oil tariffs, store huge quantities of oil in a "petroleum reserve," and concentrate on conservation measures, such as more government spending on mass transit.[8]

As was to be expected, however, the government's initiatives only further impaired domestic oil producers' ability to supply more oil and make America less dependent on OPEC. In fact, even as the government was pursuing Project Independence in the late 1970s, it enacted a punitive tax on the oil companies known as the Windfall Profits Tax. Writing in 1980, William Simon explained just how counterproductive this tax was:

> An increase in profits for the suppliers (and potential suppliers) of a suddenly scarce commodity should be welcomed. Only when profits rise can companies amass the immense amounts of capital necessary for new exploration. Only then will outsiders be given the incentives to undertake the substantial costs of entering the oil business. So, the faster profits rise, the faster new oil will come into the market and the faster OPEC's stranglehold will be removed. A tax will hinder this beneficial process, either slowing down energy independence or making the consumer pay more for it. In other words, it is Big Government which is ripping us off, not Big Oil.[9]

Project Independence suffered from the same inefficiencies that always plague Big Government initiatives. In 1979 the federal government created a Synthetic Fuels Corporation as a "quasi-governmental entity" (in the convoluted language of Washington, D.C.) that would make low-interest loan guarantees to companies developing synthetic fuels. As with all government programs, however, the indirect subsidies were distributed according to whichever members of Congress had the most clout and could funnel the subsidies into their home districts or states, not according to whatever firms held the most promise in developing synthetic fuels. In other words, it was a giant political pork barrel.

The government promised to be producing 500,000 barrels of synthetic fuel per day by 1987, but it never supplied more than 10,000 barrels. Moreover, the loan guarantees were limited to those companies that had such poor prospects that they could not obtain private funding. In other words, only the most unprofitable companies qualified.

There is even evidence that the Synfuels Corporation *impeded* the development of synthetic fuels. Energy industry analyst Milton Copulos explains that "virtually all lending [by investment banks] for alcohol fuel plant construction came to a halt as the banking community waited to see what the federal programs would eventually include." As a result, says Copulus, "construction of alcohol plants came to a virtual halt."[10] Thankfully, the whole program was scrapped in 1986.

Project Independence was also a veiled form of protectionism, as it increased tariffs on imported oil. The Strategic Petroleum Reserve was another ridiculous project, for to this day it has never contained enough oil to make much of a difference in oil markets. Once the reserve was established, the DOE bureaucrats began crowing about what an insightful element of planning it was. There was one problem, however: they forgot to install pumps to get the oil out of the caves in which it was being stored. Embarrassed by this oversight, the DOE hastily installed a pumping system that later had to be taken out because it didn't work.[11]

The Carter administration then resorted to the tried and true tactic of having a government agency produce a "forecast" warning about energy shortages ahead. In this case, the agency was the CIA, and the forecast claimed that the United States would experience severe energy shortages by 1985 unless drastic governmental measures were taken to conserve energy. The Carter administration therefore proposed a series of annoying regulations. The fifty-five-mile-per-hour speed limit became law as part of these energy-conserving efforts, but other proposed regulations were too ridiculous ever to take effect. For example, the proposal to establish a new federal thermostat police to enforce certain mandated thermostat settings in homes never got off the ground. Even the speed limit was never really obeyed.

Did Capitalism Cause the Energy Crisis?

THE GOVERNMENT-CREATED NATURAL GAS CRISIS

Just as it has done with the oil industry, the federal government has burdened the natural gas industry with unnecessary regulations and interventionist schemes. The federal government assumed regulatory power over natural gas producers as a result of a 1954 U.S. Supreme Court decision. In *Phillips* v. *Wisconsin,* the court gave the Federal Power Commission (FPC) the power to regulate the well-head price of natural gas sold in interstate commerce. A dual market was created: gas sold in interstate commerce was subject to a price ceiling, but natural gas produced and sold within any state was unregulated.

Predictably, the interstate market experienced periodic shortages in the late 1950s and 1960s, which induced the federal government to implement an allocation scheme for gas, just as it would for petroleum in the 1970s. The shortages became severe enough and the allocation scheme inequitable enough that Congress was pressured to do something about them. The Natural Gas Policy Act of 1978 liberalized the price controls on interstate gas sales, but at the same time it brought intrastate gas under its control. The central planners at the FPC created thirty different classifications for natural gas wells, each of which had its own controlled price. The natural gas flowing from the wells was all identical—there is no product more homogeneous than natural gas—but the FPC bureaucrats supposedly detected a number of distinguishing characteristics. Consequently, the price one received for one's natural gas depended on such things as how, when, and where the wells were drilled. Price ceilings were imposed in all markets, which threw the market for natural gas into a state of government-created chaos: natural gas shortages developed everywhere, and bureaucrats responded to the shortages with even more creative central planning scenarios. The price controls were completely arbitrary, ranging from 21 cents to $11 per cubic foot.[12]

As with petroleum regulation during the same period, the natural gas producers faced diminished incentives to explore for and develop new natural gas sources, since the price (and profit potential) was being held down with the FPC's price controls. Because so-called deep wells went unregulated, for instance, natural gas producers had incentives to invest only in such wells, even though they were not necessarily the most economical to develop.

It was obvious to any observer at the time that where there was no price regulation, natural gas supplies were plentiful; where prices were controlled, there was chaos. To the FPC, this did not mean that deregulation was desirable, however. Instead, the commission declared a "crisis" and adopted *more* rationing schemes by forcing large natural gas users to reduce their consumption. This is typical of regulators in any industry: they thrive on crises, real or imagined. And when there is no genuine crisis, they are quite adept at creating one. Government-induced market chaos always benefits government bureaucrats by increasing the perceived demand for them to "solve" the crisis, not to mention giving a boost to their agency budgets.

Most of the controls imposed on natural gas markets in the 1970s were phased out by the mid-1980s, but many remain and continue to hamper the natural gas market.

DEREGULATION: THE RETURN TO CAPITALISM

In 1980, facing another government-induced energy crisis, President Jimmy Carter finally began the deregulation of oil and gas prices, and President Ronald Reagan accelerated the process the next year. Not surprisingly, deregulation ended the energy crisis: a sharp turn in the direction of free-market capitalism was all that was needed.

Did Capitalism Cause the Energy Crisis?

Economics teaches that price controls usually cause prices to be *higher* than they otherwise would be in the long run because they stifle supply, and this is exactly what happened with the oil and gas price controls the U.S. government imposed in the 1970s. Because of the OPEC oil embargo, crude oil prices skyrocketed from $3 per barrel in 1972 to $12 by 1974; by 1981 crude oil prices had risen even further, to $35 per barrel. OPEC was in a strong position, and the U.S. government's price controls on domestic oil and natural gas stifled domestic production and therefore made American consumers even more dependent on OPEC oil. But economic theory also holds that eliminating price controls will prompt an initial jump in prices and will stimulate supply, which will cause prices to moderate, perhaps even to fall below the precontrol price level. Again, this is exactly what happened with the U.S. energy industry. Price deregulation created the largest production boom in the history of the American petroleum industry. As a result of the increased supply, by 1985 the price of crude oil had plummeted to $10 a barrel and lower, and there was talk of a "depression" in Texas and Oklahoma.[13] Deregulation directly benefited the American consumer, as the cost of gasoline dropped significantly. The average nationwide price of unleaded regular gasoline peaked in 1981 at $1.38 (up from 66 cents in 1976, the first year for which the U.S. Department of Energy has data on unleaded gasoline prices) and then fell to $1.30 in 1982, $1.21 in 1984, and 93 cents in 1986. Adjusting for inflation, in real 1996 dollars, the price of regular unleaded gasoline fell by 47 percent (from $2.21 to $1.18) from 1981 to 1988. The price fluctuated for several years, but by 1998 the real price of unleaded regular had declined to $1.03, less than half what it was on the eve of deregulation.[14] There were no longer any signs of shortages and no need for heavy-handed bureaucratic "allocation controls." The price of natural gas was also deregulated, but it was phased in over a twelve-year period, not being completed until 1993.

In essence, the deregulation of oil and gas prices, and the dismantling of the DOE's bizarre, central planning–style allocation schemes, reintroduced a strong dose of capitalism into the oil and gas industries. The natural consequence was an almost immediate end to the "energy crisis" that had been fabricated purely by government policy. Once again, capitalism saved America from the follies of interventionism.

CALIFORNIA'S REGULATION-INDUCED ENERGY CRISIS

Sadly, our government often fails to heed the lessons of the past. Sure enough, in the late 1990s government officials created yet another energy crisis with their foolish regulatory policies. And once again they wrongly blamed the problem on deregulation.

The electric power crisis that plagued California beginning in the late 1990s is commonly cited in calls for further government regulation. After all, the anticapitalists say, California began experiencing rolling blackouts because in 1996 the state government passed a law deregulating the electricity industry. But that 1996 law deregulated only the *wholesale* price of electricity purchased by electric power distributors within the state; it maintained price controls on retail prices and applied even more onerous regulations to the rest of the industry. Thus, California's power shortages were the direct result of the state's energy *regulation*.

The main problem was that the California government, pushed by the state's powerful environmental lobby, prevented energy producers from increasing the supply of electric power in the 1990s. No electric-power-generating plants had come online since around 1990; certainly no additional nuclear power had been permitted; and hydroelectric power had also been blocked because of the environmental lobby's purported concern for the health of snails, minnows, frogs, and other creatures that might have had their lifestyles disrupted by the building of dams. The government and the environmentalists even succeeded in dismantling some existing power plants.[15]

And as electric power *supply* in California was stagnant or even shrinking, power *demand* was rapidly increasing because of population growth and the increased use of electric power by the burgeoning Silicon Valley–based computer industry (personal computers use massive amounts of electricity). Under normal free-market conditions, increased demand coupled with stable supply would increase prices, which in turn would make it even more profitable for energy producers to increase the supply of electricity. No shortages would exist, and the increased supply would cause prices to fall. But regulation stood in the way of such supply increases.

It gets worse. By imposing price controls on retail electricity prices, the 1996 law guaranteed shortages. Why? Because prices that are legally held below free-market, equilibrium prices set by supply and demand artificially stimulate demand while stifling supply. In addition, the 1996 law forced California's electric utilities (most notably Southern California Edison and Pacific Gas and Electric) to sell off many of their electric-power-generating facilities, and as a result these companies lost the efficiencies that come with vertical integration (as discussed in Chapter 7). As economist Benjamin Zycher wrote in the *Los Angeles Times,* the law forced the utilities "into the role of mere middlemen."[16]

The California government further sabotaged the state's private electric power industry by forbidding the electric utilities from entering into long-term contracts, thus preventing them from reducing their risk by locking in electricity purchases when prices were low. Even worse, a state-sanctioned "independent system operator" controlled the transmission and distribution of electricity; like all government or government-sponsored agencies, it operated with all the efficiency of the post office and the charm of the IRS.

The state was so adamant about permitting no new electric power generation that when, in the summer of 2000, Pacific Gas and Electric offered to place a barge in San Francisco Bay with a generator that would provide a mere 95 megawatts of electricity to help alleviate some of the localized power outage problems, the state said no.[17] Once again, the environmental lobby played a key role in preventing California from addressing the true problem.

The end result of this regulatory morass was that California's power companies were forced to purchase electricity that was rising in price while the government's price controls forbade them from raising their own prices. Because of government regulation—which was brought on by the urging of the environmental lobby—the electric utilities were simply incapable of meeting the state population's growing demand for electric power.

And yet California's politicians and environmentalists blamed the whole mess—which *they* were responsible for—on greedy out-of-state energy suppliers. Such talk was completely irrational. In fact, although the same suppliers did business in many states besides California, no other state was the victim of such "greed."

California's energy crisis was perfectly predictable. Just as predictable were the cries from the environmentalists and many other anticapitalists that greedy capitalists were to blame for everything. Still, the anticapitalists have been remarkably successful in their propaganda campaign, since we so often hear the dubious claim that government deregulation is responsible for any sort of energy crisis. Indeed, in the immediate aftermath of the blackout that struck the northeastern United States in August 2003, nationally ambitious Democrats like John Kerry and Hillary Clinton were quick to blame the Republican administration for focusing on deregulation.[18]

Such claims are, of course, bogus. But as long as the anticapitalists can continue to perpetrate such hoaxes, Americans will have to endure similar fiascos in the future.

The Never-Ending War on Capitalism

Resentment is at work when one so hates somebody for his more favorable circumstances that one is prepared to bear heavy losses if only the hated one might also come to harm. Many of those who attack capitalism know very well that their situation under any other economic system will be less favorable.

—Ludwig von Mises, *The Anti-Capitalistic Mentality* (1972)

THROUGHOUT this book we have seen how government intervention in the economy more often than not makes things worse rather than better, whether it is antitrust laws, price controls, the minimum wage, corporate subsidies, or any of the government's other interventionist schemes. Worse, once intervention creates a problem like unemployment or supply shortages of some important product, the problem is incorrectly blamed on capitalism. At that point, the government and its intellectual supporters in academe and elsewhere begin clamoring for even more government intervention. If they succeed, they inevitably make things even worse, and the cycle of interventionism repeats itself.

Thus, interventionism creates a permanent ball and chain around the neck of capitalism, so to speak. Capitalism would work much better, and we would all have a higher standard of living, without it.

The accumulation of so many forms of government intervention into the U.S. economy has caused some astute scholars of capitalism to become depressingly pessimistic. As long ago as 1978 the well-known economists Michael Jensen and William Meckling predicted a very gloomy future for capitalism. "The most spectacular period of economic growth in our history is over," they wrote, because "government is destroying two vital instruments of that growth—the system of contract rights and the large corporation."[1] Politicians, they noted, no longer felt constrained in waging crusades against various businesses or industries in order to make themselves more politically popular. The result was that politicians and government regulators had severely eroded property rights, freedom of contract, and freedom of association—some of the cornerstones of American capitalism.

Their argument is well taken. Government has increasingly taken decision-making powers away from business owners and investors. Whenever politics takes precedence over economics in business decision making, the result is a less productive economy and a lowered standard of living. Indeed, government regulators exert great influence over virtually all aspects of business decision making. They influence the hiring, firing, and promotion of employees through labor regulation and the National Labor Relations Board. The Securities and Exchange Commission's several thousand regulations cast a net around the capital markets. The Federal Trade Commission reserves the right to regulate and control any and all business practices, from advertising to product pricing, contract design, and even orange juice labeling.

Every law firm that practices labor law must have access to literally hundreds of thousands of pages of laws and regulations that affect every imaginable aspect of labor relations and must spend thousands or tens of thousands of dollars annually just to keep up with all the new laws and regulations.

No two companies can merge without the permission of state attorneys general, the Federal Trade Commission, and the antitrust division of the U.S. Justice Department, all of which have the power to regulate mergers and acquisitions. Federal, state, and local tax authorities require all businesses, large and small, to supply them with mountains of paperwork. The Occupational Safety and Health Administration (OSHA) enforces more than four thousand regulations that affect all aspects of virtually every workplace. It even regulates the shape of toilet seats and the height of ladders. It has had no positive discernible effect on job safety, however, since accidents are inevitably caused by human error. But that doesn't stop it from instructing nursing homes where to store bottles of Windex, or telling construction workers the kind of work shoes they may legally wear.

The Environmental Protection Agency is arguably the biggest government bureaucracy in world history, now that the Soviet Union is no more. No new drugs may be produced or marketed without first spending years jumping through the regulatory hoops created by the Food and Drug Administration. "Drug lag" that postpones the introduction of lifesaving drugs has caused the premature deaths of thousands of Americans.

The Federal Reserve Board, the Federal Deposit Insurance Corporation, and the Comptroller of the Currency regulate nearly every aspect of banking. They also compel banks to make bad loans to uncreditworthy borrowers under the Community Reinvestment Act.

State and local governments can be just as oppressive, imposing heavy taxes on business owners, zoning them out of business, harassing them with costly and senseless environmental regulations, and making it almost impossible to find educated employees because of the sorry performance of so many public schools.

THE BUREAUCRATIZATION OF CAPITALISM

As a result of this hyperregulation of American capitalism, American businesses are no longer free to base their decisions on profit-and-loss considerations. As Ludwig von Mises explained more than four decades ago:

> The bureaucratization of privately-owned enterprises that we see going on about us everywhere today is purely the result of interventionism, which forces them to take into account factors that, if they were free to determine their policies for themselves, would be far from playing any role whatsoever in the conduct of their business. When a concern must pay heed to the political prejudices and sensibilities of all kinds in order to avoid being continually harassed by various organs of the state, it soon finds that it is no longer in a position to base its calculations on the solid ground of profit and loss.[2]

Increasingly, businesses must replace economic considerations with political ones, which means that they become less efficient and, in an aggregate sense, we all become poorer. The poor are especially harmed, for they need capitalism—and the jobs and economic opportunity that it alone can create—more than anyone.

In 1995, economist Murray Weidenbaum, who served as the chairman of the president's council of economic advisers under President Reagan, compiled a list of sixteen laws passed in the preceding two decades that have one thing in common: they all interfere with property rights—specifically, with a business's right to make use of its resources to its best advantage (see Table 12.1).

These laws are just a few recent examples of why American corporations must spend an inordinate amount of time complying with

TABLE 12.1: GOVERNMENT INFRINGEMENTS ON PROPERTY RIGHTS OF BUSINESS OWNERS, 1974–1993

LAW	PROPERTY RIGHTS OBSTRUCTION
1974 Warranty Improvement Act	Government mandates warranties (which interfere with a business's ability to determine what products and services the business will and will not offer)
1975 Energy Act	More government control over the energy industry
1976 Hart-Scott-Rodino Antitrust Amendments	Require companies to notify Department of Justice of planned mergers
1976 Toxic Substances Act	Restricts use of chemicals
1977 Energy Act	Creates the Department of Energy
1977 Surface Mining Act	Federalizes mining regulation
1978 Age Discrimination Act	Federalizes the retirement age
1980 Superfund Act	Socializes cost of environmental cleanups
1984 Insider Trading Act	Criminalizes securities trading with vague and undefined "nonpublic information"
1986 Superfund Amendments	Require companies to report emissions to the government

LAW	PROPERTY RIGHTS OBSTRUCTION
1986 Age Discrimination Act	Further federalizes labor policy
1990 Clean Air Act Amendments	Broaden the EPA's powers (the laws have been shown to have actually worsened air pollution)
1990 Americans with Disabilities Act	Defines over 70 new areas of "disability," including alcoholism
1990 Pollution Prevention Act	Mandates mountains of paperwork
1991 Civil Rights Act	Further legalizes workplace discrimination in favor of politically favored groups
1993 Family and Medical Leave Act	Gives employees an "entitlement" to take time off with "job reinstatement rights"

Source: Murray Weidenbaum, *Business and Government in the Global Marketplace* (Englewood Cliffs, NJ: Prentice Hall, 1995), 48–52.

government paperwork, rules, and regulations instead of making better and lower-priced products or introducing new products. Profits are reduced, and, subsequently, the stock market is depressed, further depriving millions of American investors of the ability to accumulate wealth for their own retirement or for the general benefit of themselves and their families.

Investors are understandably more leery about investing, since the future profitability of the companies they may be investing in is so cloudy. Consequently, many corporations are deprived of the capital they need to expand or to become more productive and more competitive in global competition. Being less competitive than they would otherwise be, they ultimately will employ fewer workers and pay lesser salaries, further lowering the American standard of living.

Some argue that certain laws and regulations that restrict the operation of free-market capitalism in America are necessary to provide various benefits to the American people, such as job and food safety or a cleaner environment. But there have been hundreds—probably thousands—of scholarly studies of the effectiveness of government regulation, and these studies show that usually regulation either is ineffective or makes a problem *worse*. Many of these studies have been published in the prestigious, peer-reviewed *Journal of Law and Economics*, published by the University of Chicago Law School. The onetime-editor of the *Journal*, Nobel laureate Ronald Coase, summed it up:

> There have been more serious studies made of government regulation of industry in the last fifteen years or so, particularly in the United States, than in the whole preceding period. These studies have been both quantitative and nonquantitative. . . . The main lesson to be drawn from these studies is clear: they all tend to suggest that the regulation is either ineffective or that when it has a noticeable impact, on balance, the effect is bad, so that consumers obtain a worse product or a higher-priced product or both as a result of regulation. Indeed, this result is found so uniformly as to create a puzzle: one would expect to find, in all these studies, at least some government programs that do more good than harm.[3]

One manifestation of the bureaucratization of American capitalism is that American universities rarely teach anything about the practices or philosophy of entrepreneurship—the kind of entrepreneurship practiced by John D. Rockefeller, James J. Hill, and many other successful capitalists. Instead, schools of business offer numerous courses on "business law," "administrative law," and "corporate social responsibility," which is mostly propaganda on behalf of even more regulation and higher taxation. In other words, American universities devote an inordinate amount of time and resources to teach potential business leaders not how to be capitalists but how to be corporate bureaucrats. This cannot be good for the future of American prosperity.

All this regulation of American capitalism has had the side effect of stifling free speech. Since every business in America is regulated in all aspects of its existence and must deal with regulators on a routine basis, seldom do businesses seriously criticize government regulation. Criticizing a regulator can lead to a regulatory crackdown, complete with heavy fines imposed on the outspoken businessperson. There can be no genuinely free speech in a heavily regulated economy where corporations are essentially blackmailed into silence.

POLITICAL EXTORTION

American politicians are fond of making speeches about how they would supposedly enact policies to help "the economy," meaning capitalism, but in reality they are capitalism's worst enemies. The reality is that most politicians, especially at the federal level, view businesses as cash cows to be plundered for the benefit of their own political careers. This phenomenon was explained at great length in a 1997 book by Northwestern University law professor Fred S. McChesney entitled *Money for Nothing: Politicians, Rent Extraction, and Political Extortion*.[4] In this Harvard University Press book Professor McChesney explains that not all government regulation is special-interest legislation, although there is certainly enough of that. Rather, his analysis focuses on how members of Congress often propose onerous legislation that would harm individual businesses or even entire industries and then sit back and wait to be bribed to withdraw or vote against the antibusiness legislation. "Because the state can legally take wealth from its citizens," McChesney writes, "politicians can extort from private parties payments *not* to expropriate private wealth."[5] In other words, many American politicians are skilled extortion artists, little different from the Mafia. McChesney shows how this "political extortion" works. Corporations are pressured into making campaign "contributions" to politicians, paying them for speaking appearances, throwing lavish parties for them, taking them (and their spouses or dates) on all-expenses-paid trips to exotic resorts, giving jobs to their friends and relatives, and various other forms of thinly veiled extortion payments. Rather than paying attention to the process or producing better and cheaper products and services, American businesses are forced to devote considerable time and money to the game of political extortion.

A favorite tool of the political extortionists is to threaten to impose price controls on an industry. When Congress threatened to impose price controls on the health-care industry in the early 1990s, a *New York Times* headline announced, "Medical Industry Showers Congress with Lobby Money." "As Congress prepares to debate drastic changes in the nation's health care system," the *Times* wrote, "its members are receiving vast campaign contributions from the medical industry, an amount apparently unprecedented for a non-election year."[6] The "contributions" were reportedly almost a third higher than in the prior nonelection year, with some individual members of Congress being given more than $1 million. Talk in Congress of price controls soon ended.

Frequently the political extortionists propose legislation that would increase the cost of doing business as a means to collect campaign cash. For example, financial institutions were threatened with legislation that would make paperwork and tax withholding very costly; the bill was eventually dropped after they "contributed" millions to the sponsors of the legislation. Congress also proposed "unisex" insurance premiums and benefits—and then dropped the idea after raking in additional millions. Every couple of years the beer industry is threatened with a higher excise tax on beer, which would cut into sales somewhat, and the industry is compelled to fork over large sums of money to members of Congress to avoid this additional taxation.

Every several years Congress proposes a major alteration of the income tax code, which usually becomes the Mother of All Political Extortion Rackets. As McChesney reports, in one such instance, after the Tax Reform Act of 1986 was proposed, "members of the tax-writing committees nearly tripled their take from political action committees during the first six months of this year."[7] The money came from insurance companies, drug companies, military contractors, and even horse breeders, all of whom were concerned about being negatively affected by the proposed tax legislation.

The practice of political extortion has become so commonplace in Washington, D.C., that members of Congress and their staffs refer to such legislation as "milker bills" or "juicer bills," since the legislation is designed to "milk" campaign contributions from corporations or "juice up" politicians' campaign coffers. In the end, the effect is the further bureaucratization and politicization of American capitalism, which can only lead to fewer jobs and a lowered standard of living in the long run.

THE GATES/ROCKEFELLER MYTH

The government restricts free-market capitalism not just through its thousands of regulations and its extortionate tactics but also by going after the most successful capitalists. Nothing demonstrates this more clearly than the federal government's handling of Bill Gates, founder and chairman of the Microsoft Corporation. Gates rose to political prominence in the 1990s and was referred to—often disparagingly—as a "new John D. Rockefeller," and like Rockefeller he would be attacked despite the many benefits he brought to Americans.

Gates dropped out of college to create what is arguably the most successful corporation in American history, and in so doing he became the richest man in the world. He devoted almost no time and money to playing the game of Washington, D.C., politics, which generated great resentment among the political elite. The Federal Trade Commission investigated Microsoft's business practices for four years in the early 1990s but eventually determined that his company had not violated antitrust laws. Nevertheless, the antitrust division of the U.S. Justice Department began its own investigation, and after several more years the federal government filed an antitrust lawsuit against Microsoft.

Once the lawsuit was filed, the attacks on Gates began in earnest. Even the federal judge assigned to the case, Judge Thomas Penfield Jackson, compared Gates to the gangster Al Capone in public interviews. For such obvious bias, the judge was eventually taken off the case by the same panel of three federal judges that had appointed him. More common was the comparison to Rockefeller, an analogy that became a staple of media reports. It is a good analogy, but the mainstream media and the anticapitalist intellectuals who generally made the comparisons were doing so for the wrong reasons: they meant to inform the public that, like Rockefeller, Gates was a monopolist. As seen in earlier chapters, Rockefeller was no monopolist but an entrepreneur who provided tremendous benefits to consumers, employees, and society in general by reducing the price and expanding the supply of petroleum products for decades. Gates can be considered the information-age version of John D.

Rockefeller. He and a few other entrepreneurs literally created the information age. His products are so popular that hundreds of millions of people all around the world use them. All of those who have bought Microsoft products have done so voluntarily, on the free market, not because they were coerced into buying the products.

The federal government never did make a case that Microsoft harmed consumers—supposedly the primary reason for all antitrust laws. Instead, it made the dubious argument that the company's expenditure of some $2.5 billion *annually* on innovation somehow stifled innovation by other companies, and that perhaps, someday, maybe, the result would be that some consumers would be harmed. In the end, good sense and justice for the most part prevailed: unlike Rockefeller's Standard Oil, Gates's Microsoft was not broken up.

This was the proper ruling, for as economists Stan Liebowitz and Stephen Margolis reveal, the various theoretical arguments made against Microsoft were unconvincing. In their book *Winners, Losers, and Microsoft*—perhaps the most impressive scholarly analysis of Microsoft's impact on competition in high-technology markets—Liebowitz and Margolis dismantle all the arguments that Microsoft acted as a monopoly.[8] Their most telling evidence of Microsoft's innocence is that without exception, whenever Microsoft entered a market, it caused the prices in that market to *decline*, as competitors were forced to cut their costs and prices. Examining fourteen different products, Liebowitz and Margolis find that "in those categories where Microsoft participates, directly or indirectly, prices have declined by approximately 60 percent, a far more dramatic drop than the 15 percent drop in markets completely devoid of Microsoft's influence."[9] They find similar results in many other markets that Microsoft competed in, from word processing and spreadsheet software to personal finance software to desktop publishing to Web browsers. Typically, Microsoft continued to cut its prices even in markets where it was clearly dominant because there were (and are) literally hundreds if not thousands of competitors in those markets, and because a number of other competitors could arise if Microsoft actually did charge monopolistic prices. Liebowitz and Margolis conclude that the explanation for Microsoft's success is very simple:

> Microsoft produces good products at low prices. Some, including the Department of Justice, have suggested that Microsoft did not earn its large market shares in [software] applications. Our data are at complete variance with this claim. Our data show that when Microsoft moved from a low to a high market share, its products were always of higher quality than the market leader's. When its products were not superior, it did not make inroads against the market leader. Our data . . . disprove the claim that Microsoft has used its monopoly position to keep prices high. As a matter of fact, we found that after Microsoft becomes dominant in a product category, prices in that market begin to fall. . . . In short, Microsoft's effect on the software markets has been to lower prices and improve product quality.[10]

So Microsoft has only helped consumers. But the federal government's lengthy case against Microsoft has had a profound and damaging effect. American consumers are almost always the losers with antitrust regulation, for even when a company is found innocent it usually has spent large sums—millions—on lawyers and has diverted thousands of hours away from its primary business of producing better and cheaper products for consumers to responding to all the demands and requests of government lawyers. The company inevitably becomes less competitive as a result.

THE ANTI-MICROSOFT CONSPIRACY

If the claim that Microsoft acted as a monopoly was unfounded, how did the antitrust case originate? In fact, the case against Microsoft was similar to almost all other antitrust cases in that it was instigated not to protect consumers but at the request of less successful rivals. These rivals could not, or would not, compete with Microsoft, either because they could not lower their costs and prices or because their products were inferior. Therefore they attempted to recruit the government to punish their most successful rival for their own benefit, at the expense of their consumers.

The true anticompetitive (and anticapitalist) nature of the government's persecution of Microsoft was revealed in a book by journalist John Heilemann entitled *Pride Before the Fall*.[11] In the book Heilemann shows that although Microsoft was sued by the U.S. Justice Department, the lawsuit was a direct result of a plot by Microsoft's competitors, who had a simple objective: "decapitating Microsoft."[12] Various Microsoft rivals, including Sun Microsystems and Novell, hatched the conspiracy in August 1997 during a two-day meeting in Silicon Valley, California. At that meeting the general counsels and publicists for the Microsoft competitors sat down with Senator Orrin Hatch—who represents Novell's home state, Utah—as well as staff members of the Senate Judiciary Committee. They initiated an anti-Microsoft lobbying and public relations effort at the meeting, giving it the Orwellian name of ProComp. The conspirators then invested some $3 million in something called Project Sherman, which recruited a bevy of $700-per-hour consultants to construct a mock legal case against Microsoft to be presented to Justice Department lawyers. The "political sensitivity" of the scheme was so high, says Heilemann, that the plot was "conducted in utmost secrecy." For if word got out that the Justice Department's case originated not with Justice but with Microsoft's rivals, the public would surely smell a rat, and it would be much more difficult to garner political support for the continued persecution of Microsoft.

The mock-trial case that Project Sherman presented was essentially the case that the government eventually put on. In his preliminary "finding of fact," after the trial had ended, Judge Thomas Penfield Jackson adopted the conspirators' claim that Microsoft was a "monopoly" even though in some markets, such as software applications, it had literally thousands of competitors. He claimed that Microsoft "coerced" its customers but did not explain what power Bill Gates had—or any businessperson has—to achieve such coercion on the free market. Judge Jackson also claimed, absurdly, that consumers were somehow harmed because Microsoft gave its Web browser away for free. In addition, he concluded that, although there was no evidence presented at trial of consumer harm, Microsoft could *in theory* harm consumers in the future if it decided to raise prices. (Under this theory, every business in America could potentially be found guilty of violating the antitrust laws.) Finally, he argued that impeding Microsoft's ability to spend billions annually on innovation would somehow *increase* computer industry innovation.

After issuing his irrational and counterfactual "finding of fact," Judge Jackson proposed a remedy that the anti-Microsoft conspirators had recommended to the Justice Department—and that gives a clear idea of how the U.S. government thinks capitalism in America ought to be structured. Among other things, the "remedy" would have prohibited Microsoft from offering "terms more favorable" to its biggest clients, a common business practice. It would have compelled Microsoft to offer all computer manufacturers "equal access" to discounts, technical support, license terms, and more. It would have created a paperwork nightmare for the company by requiring a report to be sent to the government after each and every agreement made with any software applications business.

Judge Jackson wanted to create a colony of spies among Microsoft employees by ordering the company to establish a means by which employees could report "potential violations" of the government agreement to the federal regulators. Government regulators would have been given the right to storm onto Microsoft's property during business hours to inspect all of its files, messages, and other documents. And the company would have been forced to share its computer source code with all of its rivals. This would be the equivalent of forcing Coca-Cola to publish the secret formula for Coke on the Internet. Finally, the judge wanted to break Microsoft up into at least three separate companies—again, the preferred position of Microsoft's rivals.

All of these "remedies" would have crippled Microsoft, which of course was their purpose. Thankfully, Judge Jackson was dropped from the case because of the gross bias he exhibited in media interviews. His "finding of fact" was mostly discarded, and his proposed "remedy" never came into fruition. His successor, Judge Colleen Kollar-Kotelly, approved a much more reasonable settlement between Microsoft and the Department of Justice that did not break the company up, Standard Oil–style, or cripple it, as Microsoft's Project Sherman competitors would have preferred.

The moral of the Microsoft antitrust story is that very few federal politicians have any respect for capitalism or capitalists despite all their "pro-business" rhetoric. Whenever the opportunity arises, they will threaten to ruin any corporation if they think such a crusade can help their political careers. Senator Orrin Hatch was merely the political errand boy for Novell, one of the largest corporations in his state of Utah. He was attempting to use the coercive powers of the U.S. Justice Department to protect a wealthy constituent from competition, with little or no regard to the effects of his efforts on the economy and the nation as a whole.

The Microsoft case also reinforces the point that certain capitalists are capitalism's worst enemies. The Novells and Sun Micro-systems of the world are neomercantilists who, when faced with stiff competition, lobby the government to cripple their rivals rather than going to work producing better and cheaper products for consumers.

LEGAL PLUNDER

One of the hallmarks of capitalism is freedom of contract. When buyers and sellers engage in a business transaction there is always at least an implicit contract (and many implicit contracts are upheld in court). Contracts define property rights, which, after all, are what are being exchanged in any business transaction: I give up property rights in some of my money, and in return you give up property rights in, say, your car.

But the freedom of contract has come under attack. No longer are Americans free to decide what transactions to partake in, what contracts to enter into. Until relatively recently, for example, it was up to each consumer to decide how safe his or her car was to be. The obvious choice was between a larger, heavier, *and safer* car, or a smaller, lighter, more fuel-efficient, and more dangerous one. But today, thanks to a virtual revolution in how the courts enforce liability law, product safety is no longer the exclusive responsibility of buyers and sellers. Lawyers, judges, juries, and regulatory agencies now mandate that *all* cars be "crashworthy," and indeed they mandate safety standards for all consumer products. As Peter Huber wrote in his landmark book *Liability:*

> A woman's choice of contraceptives was once a matter largely under the control of the woman herself, and her doctors, with the FDA in the background. . . . Today tort [personal injury] law has shifted that authority . . . from the doctor's office to the courtroom.

Balancing the risks and benefits of childhood vaccination was once a concern of parents, pediatricians, the FDA, and state health authorities. But here again, the views of the courts have become the driving force in determining what may be bought and sold.

Not long ago, workplace safety was something to be decided between employer and employees. . . . Today the courts supervise a free-for-all of litigation that pits employees against both employers and the outside suppliers of materials and equipment, the latter two against each other, and both against their insurers.[13]

A new "liability tax" has been created, says Huber, as the costs of all this litigation are at least partly passed on to the consumer. There has been "a wholesale shift from consent to coercion in the law of accidents," as today "we emphasize litigation after the fact" instead of deferring to individual choice and personal responsibility. For all practical purposes, "contracts are dead, at least insofar as they attempt to allocate responsibility for accidents, ahead of time."[14]

Product safety standards have effectively been socialized, and lawyers now have incentives to spend their lives digging up cases and evidence against corporations because some consumers stupidly misused their products. An infamous example that was widely publicized is of an elderly woman who put a cup of piping-hot McDonald's coffee between her legs while driving her car and scalded herself after making a sharp turn and spilling the coffee. She and her lawyers sued McDonald's, accepting no responsibility at all for her own foolishness, and a jury originally awarded her a multimillion-dollar settlement. The award was eventually reduced to a mere $200,000 or so, and McDonald's was apparently pleased to get off that cheaply. Once individual responsibility is denied, there can be no end to this kind of legalized plundering of corporations.

The Never-Ending War on Capitalism

Trial lawyers now routinely sue corporations for immense sums without ever intending to go to court to prove their case. Their hope, in many instances, is an out-of-court "settlement," which is essentially an act of extortion permitted by the legal system. The following examples, collected by the Manhattan Institutes website Overlawyered.com, illustrate the extent to which the American legal system condones this racket:

- Two Ohio carpet installers won an award of $8 million from an adhesive manufacturer after they used a flammable adhesive indoors and caused an explosion, burning themselves—even though the two men admitted in court that they had read the adhesive's label before using the product and had understood that the adhesive was flammable and should not be used inside.
- A class-action lawyer sued fast-food companies, arguing that if they are responsible for, say, 5 percent of obesity in the United States, then that's 5 percent of a $117 billion industry that should be awarded to him and his overweight clients.
- An Indiana man who described himself as a "compulsive gambler" sued a casino for failing to bar him from entering the casino and gambling away his savings—that is, for failing to protect him from himself. A judge threw out the case, but similar cases were subsequently filed. In addition, in 2002 a former Massachusetts attorney general who had sued the tobacco industry said that lawyers would soon target the gambling industry to secure compensation for addicts.
- A federal judge in East St. Louis, Illinois, awarded $19 million to a family who claimed that their physician's use of a vacuum extractor during labor had caused their child's cerebral palsy. No cause-and-effect was established in

court, and the family sued the U.S. Treasury, not their doctor, since he was employed by a hospital that received federal funds.

• California lawyers were discovered to have been mass-mailing letters to hundreds of small businesses in the state offering, for a modest fee of around $5,000, not to sue them under the state's "unfair competition law." The *Wall Street Journal* labeled the practice "the shakedown scandal" in "the shakedown state."

• Cosmetic companies accused of price fixing settled a class-action lawsuit by agreeing to provide the plaintiffs with a couple of tubes of free lipstick each—while the plaintiffs' lawyers were sure to benefit much more handsomely.

• A federal judge ruled that airline passengers who sit for hours without moving and develop blood clots could sue airlines even when they fully understood that lack of movement could lead to the condition.

• A jury awarded a New York City man $76.4 million in damages because he had been shot and paralyzed by a police officer. But substantial evidence supported the police officer's contention that he had fired in self-defense: the plaintiff admitted that he had been holding a semiautomatic weapon, ballistics reports confirmed that the plaintiff had fired the weapon, and the plaintiff was a member of a gang known as the Five Percenters, which "preaches hatred of police and advises its members to shoot rather than submit to arrest," according to Overlawyered.com. After a retrial the award was reduced to $51 million, and then in the summer of 2003 a judge reduced it even further, to $9.75 million.[15]

Thousands of similar examples could be listed here. One thing this explosion in liability lawsuits has done is to impose a new "tort tax" on the U.S. economy. This implicit tax has driven up the price and reduced the availability of products and services. Many hospital vaccines are no longer available because of the risk of liability: if one in ten million people administered a vaccine has a bad reaction, then a lawsuit could bankrupt the manufacturer of the vaccine. Many drugs and other products used for pregnancy and obstetrics are now unavailable because pregnancy itself is risky and the effects of the drugs are difficult to separate out from the normal risks of pregnancy—at least in the eyes of potential jurors. Many other medical products, such as heart valve replacements, are unavailable because of liability concerns. The medical profession itself is in jeopardy, for insurers are increasingly unwilling to offer medical liability insurance, even at astronomical rates. In January of 2003, thirty-nine West Virginia surgeons went on strike to protest rising medical malpractice insurance and the fact that most insurers in the state, recognizing the excessive risk that so many frivolous lawsuits create, do not even offer medical malpractice insurance.[16] Liability insurance is not just a problem for the medical profession, however; day-care centers and many other industries find such insurance to be more and more difficult to secure.

The "liability crisis" has also stifled innovation in numerous industries, since newer products carry with them more risk of lawsuits than do old, tried-and-true products. The result, says Huber, "is to ingrain a bias against innovation at all levels of the economy."[17] Ironically, this in turn produces *less* safety, since competitive businesses would normally strive to innovate and invent safer and safer products to satisfy the consuming public.

Anyone—whether a corporate executive or an ordinary citizen—should be held responsible for harming or injuring another human being. There is certainly a role for lawyers in suing for such damages. But the abandonment of individual responsibility in the area of liability law has led to a situation in which literally thousands of lawyers spend their days suing or threatening to sue businesses of all sizes not in pursuit of justice but to shake them down for out-of-court "settlements" in which the lawyers sometimes receive millions of dollars while their class-action clients receive very little. The end result is a further crippling of American capitalism and a further lowering of everyone's standard of living. And whenever the general standard of living is lowered, the poor are harmed the most, since they more than anyone need capitalism—and the jobs and incomes it creates.

THE WAR ON VICE

The attacks on individual responsibility in the field of liability law are part of a new kind of war on capitalism in America. Socialists of all stripes have always waged an ideological war against individual responsibility, for if it is true that sane, adult individuals cannot and should not be held responsible for their own decisions, then the argument can be made that the state should step in and control virtually all aspects of people's lives. If people can't make sensible decisions regarding the feeding and education of their own children, the state should step in. If they can't adequately earn a living, the state should step in. If they can't prepare for their own old age and that of their parents, then the state should do it. And on and on.

This attack on individual responsibility has grown more fierce in recent years. The first victim of this sort of political crusade was the tobacco industry. Everyone has known for decades that cigarette smoking causes cancer, lung disease, and other ailments, and that smokers are knowingly taking a very large health risk. Moreover, although smoking is "addictive," tens of millions of Americans have been able to kick the habit, in large part because they recognize the health risks involved in smoking. Thus, for some forty years juries did not award monetary damages to diseased smokers who sued tobacco companies; jurors understood that smokers recognize the health risks of their habit, are willing to accept them, and should take responsibility for the consequences. But "public health activists" and others who waged a decades-long crusade against the notion of individual responsibility, and who demonized the tobacco industry, eventually won out. As a result of their crusade, starting in the mid-1990s legislatures in a number of states passed laws that essentially prohibited the tobacco companies from defending themselves in court.

Florida was the first state to enact such legislation.[18] The Florida Medicaid Third-Party Liability Act destroyed traditional jurisprudence in several respects. To begin, it abolished the notion that defendants should be able to raise a defense. Because of the law, tobacco companies could no longer defend themselves by saying that smokers know the risks involved in cigarette smoking—in other words, by arguing that individuals are responsible for their own behavior, good or bad. According to the law, "assumption of risk" and "all other affirmative defenses normally available to a liable third party are to be abrogated."[19]

The Florida law overturned another cornerstone of the age-old system of Anglo-Saxon jurisprudence when it abandoned the idea that harm against an individual must be proven before that individual can be awarded damages in a liability case. Instead it stipulated that "statistical analysis" can be used to "prove" a consumer product's harm *to the state of Florida's budget*. This law established a dangerous precedent in American jurisprudence. To begin, one can never "prove" anything with statistical analysis, for such analysis allows one to speak only in terms of probabilities. More important, the law dictated that if a statistical correlation can be shown between the incidence of a smoking-related disease like lung cancer and the state's Medicaid expenditures, then the state can sue the tobacco companies to "recover" its expenses (presumably, Medicaid paid for part of the hospital expenses for the lung cancer victims). No argument even needs to be made that smoking, or smoking any particular brand of cigarettes, caused the disease, or that the victim was not responsible for his own foolish behavior. All that needs to be shown is a simple statistical correlation between disease incidence and Medicare expenditures, which can force companies producing the product to pay hundreds of millions, if not billions, of dollars to the state of Florida.

The Florida law also dictated that the state can seek recovery of payments based on an entire class of victims rather than individual ones, eliminated the statute of limitation, and provided that the state can pay private attorneys up to 30 percent of the amount collected for litigating the case.[20]

Soon after Florida passed its law, Maryland and a number of other states followed suit. In short, the states stacked the deck against the tobacco industry and created strong incentives for lawyers to file even more class-action lawsuits. The tobacco companies knew that they could no longer rely on the common sense of juries, especially since the litigants no longer had to prove that a company's product had harmed an individual or individuals. Therefore the tobacco companies agreed to a "settlement" with the state governments, promising to pay the states some $235 billion over twenty years. The trial lawyers involved in these cases profited handsomely for their work. In Maryland, for example, the tobacco industry's $4 billion settlement with the state meant a contingency fee of more than $1 billion for lawyer Peter Angelos. The state balked at paying Angelos that amount, so he sued the state to "recover" his full contingency fee. Eventually he settled for a mere $150 million.

The point here is not to defend smoking or the tobacco companies. The point is that the tobacco litigation and legislation of recent years has established a terrible precedent: when the notion of individual responsibility is abandoned, American corporations can be plundered by trial lawyers, politicians, and "public health activists" (who share in the loot as recipients of government grants funded by the "settlement" money). In principle, almost *any* manufacturer of *any* product can now be fair game. What happens, for example, when a skier is seriously injured while flying recklessly down a steep, ice-covered mountain in a snowstorm and playing catch with a football with fellow skiers? Can the ski manufacturer be blamed—and sued for all it is worth? The list of possibilities is endless.

Indeed, it was entirely predictable—and James Bennett and I did predict it in our book *The Food and Drink Police*—that the same tactics that were used in effect to extort billions of dollars from the tobacco industry would be used next on the beer, wine, liquor, and fast-food industries, among others. Almost as soon as the "settlement" with the tobacco companies was completed, the news media began reporting on a new "war on fat," with "Big Food" portrayed as the new national villain instead of "Big Tobacco." (What a relief it must be to the tobacco companies not to be the lone villain any longer.)

The class-action lawyers who filed lawsuits against McDonald's, Wendy's, Kentucky Fried Chicken, Burger King, and other fast-food chains presented "victims" like one Gregory Rhymes, a fifteen-year-old boy who was five feet six inches tall and tipped the scales at more than four hundred pounds.[21] Rhymes said he ate at McDonald's several times a day, and "I normally order the Big Mac, fries, ice cream and a shake. I like to supersize my orders."[22] Rhymes's lawyer, Samuel Hirsch, said that Rhymes and his other clients were "too dumb to know what's good for them."[23] Another typical participant in the class-action suits against the fast-food chains was fifty-six-year-old Caesar Barber, who claimed that these establishments were responsible for his medical problems, which stemmed from his obesity.[24] Nor has the fast-food industry been the only target in the campaign against "Big Food": a Washington State man sued the Safeway grocery store chain and Washington dairy farmers, claiming that his lifelong habit of drinking fresh milk was responsible for his clogged arteries.

All of these lawsuits—and many more that are bound to come—are based on the principle that individuals have no free will and are therefore not responsible for their own actions.

In recent years the federal government has begun relying on a new measure that exaggerates the extent of obesity in America. The now prevalent "body mass index" is a measure of one's weight that doesn't distinguish between muscle and fat. According to this index many physically fit people (including professional athletes) are seriously overweight or obese.[25] Armed with such information, and with the undeniable fact that obesity leads to health problems and premature deaths, public health activists are not only clamoring to sue the fast-food companies (in hopes that much of any settlement money will go to them and their organizations) but are also calling for "fat taxes." Professor Kelly Brownell of Yale University has long been advocating a "Twinkie Tax" on "unhealthy foods" to deter people from consuming them. The funds collected would in theory be used to fund "nutrition education" and "public exercise programs" (mandatory treadmill workouts?).[26] In general terms, Brownell talks of the "toxic food environment" in which Americans supposedly live.

Many of the same political activists who waged the war on tobacco now receive (through their respective "nonprofit" organizations) some of the tobacco money largesse, courtesy of donations by trial lawyers, and are using these funds to wage the war on food. Leading antitobacco/antifat activist John Banzhaf of George Washington University Law School has stated, "People are wondering if tactics used against the tobacco industry very successfully ... could be used against the problem of obesity."[27] Professor Marion Nestle of New York University concurs, saying, "It might be time to follow the lead of the legal tactics that smoked out Big Tobacco."[28] These activists have already held a "Fat Summit" in Washington, D.C.

WorldNetDaily writer Joel Miller predicts how the war on food will proceed:

> Ten years from now, spokesmen from Nabisco, Frito-Lay, McDonald's and Hershey are all going to be testifying in congressional hearings, "No, we did not know that fat was addictive. No, we did not deliberately manipulate fat levels to hook unwary consumers of our products." And then 10 years later, Congress and the "fat industry" will reach an "Historic Fat Accord," like the one reached with tobacco.[29]

This may sound far-fetched, but so did the notion that someone would sue McDonald's for being fat just a few years ago. The "war on fat" is part of the never-ending war on capitalism that continues to cripple America.

THE WAR GOES ON

One of the major salvos in the war against the fast-food industry came not in the form of a class-action lawsuit but in a best-selling book, Eric Schlosser's *Fast Food Nation: The Dark Side of the All-American Meal*, first published in 2001.[30] Here the author makes the remarkable discovery that a steady diet of french fries and McDonald's milk shakes will make you fat. Schlosser has nothing good to say about anything the fast-food industry does, despite the fact that millions of Americans express their disagreement with him every day by eating at these establishments. What Schlosser and others attacking the fast-food industry fail to acknowledge is that American consumers are as educated as they have ever been and can certainly judge for themselves where the best place to eat is. In other words, most Americans understand that a McDonald's double cheeseburger is not as low-cal as a soybean burger without the bun; they nevertheless exercise their free will by occasionally eating at fast-food restaurants. Moreover, for all of Schlosser's claims about health problems in the industry, the most important point is that government health regulators routinely inspect all fast-food establishments, and any genuine health problems would quickly spell the bankruptcy of any restaurant chain.

In fact, Schlosser's book is much more than an attack on the fast-food industry; it is part of the much larger war against capitalism in this country. Schlosser reveals his real agenda in the book's epilogue, where he sings the praises of "scientific socialists," a term that Lenin used to boast of the alleged accomplishments of Soviet socialism. He condemns capitalism in general and waxes eloquent about the alleged munificence of all kinds of government interventions and bureaucracies, from the job-destroying minimum wage to public works departments and government road-building programs, which are perhaps the most colossal example of government corruption. Schlosser ends his book by recommending further government intervention: more government job-training schemes; OSHA regulation; laws favoring labor unions; more food regulation; several new regulatory agencies to control the activities of ranchers, farmers, and supermarkets; advertising bans; and much more. If all this is accomplished, says Schlosser, the great day may arrive when restaurants sell "free-range, organic, grass-fed hamburgers."[31]

It is remarkable how Schlosser does little more than repackage some of the same old myths about capitalism that earlier generations of muckraking journalists perpetrated. Indeed, on the back of the paperback edition of *Fast Food Nation* is a blurb from the *San Francisco Chronicle* proclaiming that Schlosser is "channeling the spirits of Upton Sinclair and Rachel Carson." Sinclair was the early-twentieth-century socialist author of the book *The Jungle,* which turned out to be a wildly inaccurate and unfair portrayal of the beef industry. Rachel Carson's fable about the allegedly disastrous effects of pesticides, *Silent Spring,* became a classic of the environmental movement despite the fact that is was indeed a fable. Full of gross exaggerations, this enormously popular book was so influential that pesticides were banned in certain Third World countries, causing massive crop failures due to insect infestations and contributing to literally thousands of deaths. Nevertheless, *Silent Spring* served the political agenda of the anti-industry industry, just as Schlosser's book is obviously designed to do.

Schlosser's *Fast Food Nation* is just one of a number of anti-capitalist screeds that have reached the *New York Times* best-seller list in recent years. These books prove once again what is known as "Gresham's Law": bad ideas tend to drive out the good. (Since half-baked ideas are easy for lay people to understand and require little intellectual effort, they tend to drive out truths that require more sophisticated reasoning and historical understanding.)

Another of these best-selling anticapitalist tomes is *Nickel and Dimed: On (Not) Getting By in America*, by Ph.D. biologist Barbara Ehrenreich.[32] The author, who informs readers that she "married a Teamster Union organizer," claims to have written the book out of concern for the plight of people who were being phased out of welfare. Although she is an affluent author (she has written several books and is a contributor to *Time, Harper's,* the *New Republic,* the *Nation,* and the *New York Times Magazine*), she pretended to be an entry-level restaurant and hotel worker so she could write a book about her experiences. And guess what. She discovered that entry-level jobs don't pay very well!

She also discovered that many people who have left the welfare rolls to go to work have a tough time of it. What this proves is not that employers are stingy—the theme of Ehrenreich's sophomoric book—but that the welfare system itself does indeed destroy the work ethic. After all, why should one learn a trade or skill, act responsibly, continue to educate oneself, and do everything else necessary to succeed in the workplace if one can do well enough by collecting a welfare check?

The fact is, the typical entry-level job is called "entry-level" for a good reason: most people use their experience to move up to better and better jobs, as Chapter 6 explained. These jobs are only temporary, but Ehrenreich makes no mention of this in her book.

In general, she champions a socialist agenda but fails to see how her recommendations would only hurt the workers she purports to represent. For example, she advocates government-mandated wage increases that would drive thousands of entry-level employees out of work altogether. Also, she urges the government to build more housing projects "to house the poor," citing the fact that government expenditures on such projects slowed down during the 1990s. But it is no surprise that government spending on public housing fell during that time, for the 1990s were a time of vigorous economic growth and low unemployment. What's more, the significant increases in government spending that she calls for would only increase the tax burden for entry-level workers (and all others), which is hardly an ideal development for a group that is supposed to be having great difficulty making ends meet. Indeed, even while talking about the plight of entry-level workers, Ehrenreich completely ignores the fact that workers typically pay more in taxes than they do for food, clothing, shelter, and transportation *combined*.[33]

Authors like Ehrenreich and Schlosser are only part of the anticapitalist surge. Perhaps the author who has gained the most attention—and the most wealth—from denouncing capitalism and promoting socialism is the gadfly Michael Moore. Two of Moore's books—*Stupid White Men* and *Downsize This!*—have been *New York Times* best sellers even though they simply rehash many of the same old misguided and misinformed socialist complaints about capitalism. For example, in *Stupid White Men* Moore condemns "C-A-P-I-T-A-L-I-S-M" for weeding out businesses that have higher costs and prices and/or lower-quality products than their rivals.[34] But he completely misunderstands that *consumers,* not capitalists, ultimately decide the fate of companies. If consumers do not like what is being offered by ninety out of a hundred companies in an industry, then the people who run those ninety companies will be compelled to find other lines of work. Moore also misunderstands that when all of those poorly performing businesses go bankrupt, their more efficient rivals, as well as companies in different industries, can use the failed businesses' workers and other resources more productively. This is a sign of the *success* of capitalism.

Like many other anticapitalists, Moore points to a series of blackouts in this country, particularly in California, and blames "deregulation" in the electricity industry. Of course, his claim that "deregulation" has caused blackouts is extraordinarily sloppy, as discussed in Chapter 11, for in reality electricity in the United States is still very much hampered by government regulation, especially price controls. As part of his assault on supposed deregulation, Moore mindlessly champions government-run electric power monopolies despite the fact that such monopolies have proven to be spectacularly inefficient and wasteful wherever they have been put in place. The world learned of socialism's failure in 1989, but apparently Michael Moore has not yet been informed of it.

Though Moore claims to speak for the working class, the schemes that he advocates in *Stupid White Men* go *against* the interests of working people in this country, in large part because he simply doesn't understand how the employment relationship works under capitalism. Moore lambastes certain employers for not providing workers with a large menu of fringe benefits and for not significantly increasing their wages. But as we have seen, employers can pay workers only what is justified by their productivity. If a worker produces, say, $1,000 a week in goods and services for an employer, the employer will lose money when the government forces him to pay that worker more than $1,000 per week; the employer's only recourse is to fire (or not to hire in the first place) employees who don't produce enough to justify government-mandated wages.

In *Downsize This!* Moore similarly advocates strategies that actually hurt the very people whose welfare he claims to champion. For example, writing about the deep recession years of the 1970s, he condemns certain labor unions for "stupidly" agreeing to renegotiate their contracts to allow (temporarily) lower wages in return for job security.[35] But those unions that *refused* to accept the temporary wage reductions saw their employers go bankrupt and their members lose their jobs. Yet to the clueless Michael Moore, the unions that saved their members' jobs were the ones that acted "stupidly."

Downsize This! recycles other tired old myths, as well. Moore correctly criticizes various corporations for receiving corporate welfare, but he incorrectly calls this "capitalism." In reality, and as discussed in considerable detail throughout this book, corporate welfare is a characteristic of mercantilism, which is the opposite of capitalism. In addition, he blames capitalism for the sorry state of certain Indian reservations and for the fiscal condition of Washington, D.C. But Indian reservations have always been islands of socialism "managed" by the U.S. Department of the Interior's Bureau of Indian Affairs, not examples of capitalism. And Washington,

D.C., is one of the highest tax jurisdictions in the United States; it has the largest number of municipal employees of any city its size; its government-run school system is among the worst in America; its police are notoriously corrupt; and the phrase "public service" is considered to be a cruel joke by D.C. residents. In other words, Washington, D.C., is another island of socialism in a sea of capitalism.

Moore also condemns the Nike Corporation for employing workers in Indonesia who earn less than Americans do and bloviates on about why wages in Indonesia should be as high as in the United States. However, if government policy were to force this wage equalization, many employees would lose their jobs. And that would be a disaster for these Indonesians, who earn far higher wages at Nike than they could earn anywhere else. In fact, for many of these workers, the alternatives to working at Nike would include begging, crime, and grinding poverty. Wage equalization would only benefit American labor unions, since it would eliminate a source of lower-cost, competing labor.

As part of his relentless campaign in support of the labor unions, Moore spreads the myth that everything was going perfectly well for America's labor unions until President Reagan fired the federal air traffic controllers for their illegal strike in 1982. (Laws prohibit such government employees from going on strike because these employees effectively have a monopoly on the services they perform. Armed with this monopoly power, they can use the strike to force the government to increase taxes to pay them more. This is patently undemocratic, because it effectively transfers the power to tax from the voters to these politically powerful public employees.) Contrary to Moore's assertions, however, labor unions had begun losing members long before the 1980s; union membership as a proportion of the private-sector labor force had begun declining in the *1950s*.

By the time of the air traffic controllers' strike, the steel, automobile, and textile industry unions had lost hundreds of thousands of members.

Like Ehrenreich and other critics of capitalism, Moore recommends bigger and bigger government to solve the problems that capitalism has supposedly created, but of course he does not acknowledge how the higher taxes necessary to pay for his socialist schemes would make it even more difficult for American workers to make ends meet.

In short, the people who have bought these best-selling books by Michael Moore, Barbara Ehrenreich, and Eric Schlosser have been sold a bill of goods. But this is hardly a surprise, for anticapitalist activists have always perpetuated popular myths designed to cripple American capitalism. For generations these activists have been demonizing both individual industries and the capitalist system itself. This, of course, has enabled lawyers and politicians to employ their extortion-like schemes: their fat taxes, their class-action lawsuits, and their gun-under-the-table "settlements." It's always about money, although the campaigns against tobacco, fast food, milk, colas, and everything else are always cloaked in some kind of "public interest" rhetoric.

Anticapitalism is an ongoing crusade, and such a crusade, if successful, is always sure to destroy jobs, destroy economic freedom, and make us all poorer. But as a careful reexamination of this country's history makes abundantly clear, capitalism has been America's great blessing. Truth, in short, is not on the side of the anticapitalists. The more Americans come to understand the truth about capitalism, the more reason they will have to be optimistic for the future of their country.

NOTES

INTRODUCTION: THE UNTOLD STORY

1. Adam Smith, *An Inquiry into the Nature and Causes of the Wealth of Nations* (New York: Random House, 1937), 422.
2. Neela Banerjee and David Firestone, "New Kind of Electricity Market Strains Old Wires Beyond Limits," *New York Times*, August 24, 2003, 1.

CHAPTER ONE: WHAT IS CAPITALISM?

1. Adam Smith, *An Inquiry into the Nature and Causes of the Wealth of Nations* (New York: Random House, 1937), 422.
2. Ludwig von Mises, *Liberalism: In the Classical Tradition* (San Francisco: Cobden Press, 1985), 32.
3. Joseph Schumpeter, *Capitalism, Socialism, and Democracy*, 3rd ed. (New York: Harper and Row, 1962), 62.
4. Ludwig von Mises, *Human Action: A Treatise on Economics* (Auburn, AL: Ludwig von Mises Institute, 1998), 270.
5. Ibid., 272.
6. For the classic refutation of socialism as an economic system see Ludwig von Mises, *Socialism* (Indianapolis: LibertyClassics, 1981), first published in 1922. The mass murder and economic destruction that were the inevitable consequences of socialism—and that were predicted by Mises and others in the 1920s—are documented in Stephane Courtois et al., eds., *The Black Book of Communism* (Cambridge: Harvard University Press, 1999).

7. Ludwig von Mises, *The Free and Prosperous Commonwealth* (New York: Volcker Fund, 1962), 67.

8. Leonard Read, "I, Pencil," Foundation for Economic Education (http: 11209.217.49.168/vnews.php?nid=316).

9. Friedrich Hayek, "The Pretense of Knowledge: Nobel Lecture," *American Economic Review*, May 1975.

10. Hernando de Soto, *The Mystery of Capital: Why Capitalism Triumphs in the West and Fails Everywhere Else* (New York: Basic Books, 2000).

11. Ibid., 6.

12. Ibid.

13. Nathan Rosenberg and L. E. Birdzell Jr., *How the West Grew Rich: The Economic Transformation of the Industrial World* (New York: Basic Books, 1986), 116–17.

14. Israel Kirzner, *Competition and Entrepreneurship* (Chicago: University of Chicago Press, 1978), 81.

15. These can be viewed online at www.fraserinstitute.ca and www.heritage.org.

16. United Nations, *Human Development Report 2000* (New York: United Nations, 2001).

CHAPTER TWO: ANTICAPITALISM

1. F. A. Hayek, "The Intellectuals and Socialism," *University of Chicago Law Review*, vol. 3 (Spring 1949), 1.

2. Ibid., 16.

3. Thomas Sowell, *The Vision of the Anointed: Self-Congratulation as a Basis for Social Policy* (New York: Basic Books, 1995).

4. Murray Rothbard, "Egalitarianism as a Revolt Against Nature," in *Egalitarianism as a Revolt Against Nature and Other Essays*, 2nd ed. (Auburn, AL: Ludwig von Mises Institute, 2000), 8.

5. Charles Murray, *Losing Ground* (New York: Basic Books, 1984).

6. Hayek, "The Intellectuals and Socialism," 20.

7. Thomas J. DiLorenzo, "The Free-Market Revolution in Textbooks," *Policy Review*, Spring 1988.

8. Paul Hollander, *Political Pilgrims: Travels of Western Intellectuals to the Soviet Union, China, and Cuba, 1928–1978* (New York: Harper and Row, 1981).

9. Ibid., 4.

10. Ibid., 5.
11. Ibid., 8.
12. Ibid., 99.
13. William C. White, "Americans in Soviet Russia," *Scribner's Magazine*, February 1931, 171.
14. Hollander, *Political Pilgrims*, 106.
15. Ibid., 112.
16. Ibid.
17. Ibid., 113.
18. Theodore Dreiser, *Dreiser Looks at Russia*, 26, cited in Hollander, *Political Pilgrims*, 111.
19. Ibid., 123.
20. Ibid., 122.
21. Ibid., 117.
22. Ibid.
23. Ibid., 119.
24. Stephane Courtois et al., *The Black Book of Communism: Crimes, Terror, Repression* (Cambridge: Harvard University Press, 1999), 9.
25. Ibid., 170.
26. Ibid., 174.
27. Hollander, *Political Pilgrims*, 223.
28. Ibid.
29. Ibid., 224.
30. Ibid.
31. Ibid., 232.
32. Ibid., 229.
33. Ibid., 236.
34. Ibid., 239–41.
35. Ibid., 262.
36. Ibid., 277.
37. Ibid., 294.
38. Ludwig von Mises, *The Anti-Capitalistic Mentality* (New York: Van Nostrand, 1956; repr., Grove City, PA: Libertarian Press, 1972).
39. Ibid., 8.
40. Ibid., 10.
41. Ibid., 11.

42. Ibid., 12.
43. Ibid., 25.
44. Ibid., 40.
45. Adam Smith, *An Inquiry into the Nature and Causes of the Wealth of Nations* (New York: Random House, 1937), 625.
46. Thomas J. DiLorenzo, *The Real Lincoln: A New Look at Abraham Lincoln, His Agenda, and an Unnecessary War* (New York: Three Rivers Press, 2003), especially Chapter 4.
47. Murray Rothbard, "Mercantilism: A Lesson for Our Times?" in *The Logic of Action Two* (Cheltenham, UK: Edward Elgar, 1997), 43.
48. George Reisman, *Capitalism: A Treatise on Economics* (Ottawa, IL: Jameson Books, 1996), 65.
49. Ibid., 71.

CHAPTER THREE:
HOW CAPITALISM SAVED THE PILGRIMS

1. Tom Bethell, *The Noblest Triumph: Property and Prosperity Through the Ages* (New York: St. Martin's Press, 1998).
2. Warren M. Billings, ed., "George Percy's Account of the Voyage to Virginia and the Colony's First Days," in *The Old Dominion in the Seventeenth Century: A Documentary History of Virginia, 1606–1689* (Chapel Hill: University of North Carolina Press, 1975), 22–26, cited in Bethell, *The Noblest Triumph*, 33.
3. Ibid., 28.
4. Ibid.
5. Philip A. Bruce, *Economic History of Virginia in the Seventeenth Century* (New York: Macmillan, 1907), 212.
6. Gary M. Walton and Hugh Rockoff, *History of the American Economy*, 8th ed. (New York: Dryden Press, 1998), 30.
7. Bethell, *The Noblest Triumph*, p. 35.
8. Mathew Page Andrews, *Virginia, The Old Dominion*, vol. 1 (Richmond, VA: Dietz Press, 1949), 59, cited in Bethell, *The Noblest Triumph*, 35.
9. Ibid., 32.
10. Bethell, *The Noblest Triumph*, 38.
11. William Bradford, *Of Plymouth Plantation, 1620–1647*, with an introduction by Samuel Eliot Morison (New York: Knopf, 2002), 116.
12. Ibid., 119.

13. Ibid., 120.
14. Ibid., 121.
15. Ibid.
16. Ibid.
17. Samuel Eliot Morison, *The Story of the "Old Colony" of New Plymouth* (New York: Knopf, 1960).
18. Larry Schweikart, *The Entrepreneurial Adventure: A History of Business in the United States* (New York: Harcourt Brace, 2000), 37.
19. Ibid., 38.
20. Jeremy Atack and Peter Passell, *A New Economic View of American History*, 2nd ed. (New York: Norton, 1994), 50.
21. Ibid., 51.

CHAPTER FOUR: AMERICA'S CAPITALIST REVOLT

1. Susan Previant Lee and Peter Passell, *A New Economic View of American History* (New York: Norton, 1979), 29.
2. Charles Adams, *For Good and Evil: The Impact of Taxes on the Course of Civilization*, 2nd ed. (New York: Madison Books, 1999), 302.
3. Lee and Passell, *A New Economic View of American History*, 30. The foregoing discussion is drawn from this source.
4. Ibid.
5. Larry Schweikart, *The Entrepreneurial Adventure: A History of Business in the United States* (New York: Harcourt Brace, 2000), 47.
6. Ibid., 304.
7. Adams, *For Good and Evil*, 305.
8. Ibid.
9. Ibid., 308.
10. Schweikart, *The Entrepreneurial Adventure*, 48.
11. Adams, *For Good and Evil*, 311.
12. Schweikart, *The Entrepreneurial Adventure*, 48.
13. C. F. Adams, ed., *The Works of John Adams*, vol. 6 (Boston: Little, Brown, 1850), 9.
14. Gottfried Dietze, *America's Political Dilemma: From Limited to Unlimited Democracy* (Baltimore: Johns Hopkins University Press, 1968), 67.
15. Charles Beard, *An Economic Interpretation of the Constitution* (New York: Macmillan, 1913).

16. Forrest McDonald, *We the People: The Economic Origins of the Constitution* (Chicago: University of Chicago Press, 1958).

17. Dietze, *America's Political Dilemma*, 67.

18. F. Thornton Miller, introduction to John Taylor, *Tyranny Unmasked* (Indianapolis: Liberty Fund, 1992), xvi.

19. Taylor, *Tyranny Unmasked*, 11.

20. Ibid., 19.

21. Miller, introduction to Taylor, *Tyranny Unmasked*, xxi.

22. Thomas J. DiLorenzo, *The Real Lincoln: A New Look at Abraham Lincoln, His Agenda, and an Unnecessary War* (New York: Three Rivers Press, 2003); and Forrest McDonald, *States' Rights and the Union* (Lawrence: University Press of Kansas, 1999).

23. James J. Kilpatrick, *The Sovereign States* (Chicago: Henry Regnery, 1957), 130.

24. Henry Adams, *Documents Relating to New-England Federalism, 1800–1815* (Boston: Little, Brown, 1877), 376.

25. Ibid.

26. Robert V. Remini, *Andrew Jackson and the Bank War* (New York: Norton, 1967).

27. Kilpatrick, *The Sovereign States*, 152.

28. Chauncey Boucher, *The Nullification Controversy in South Carolina* (New York: Greenwood Press, 1968), 1.

29. Ibid., 183.

30. Robert A. McGuire and T. Norman Van Cott, "The Confederate Constitution, Tariffs, and the Laffer Relationship," *Economic Inquiry* 40, no. 3 (Summer 2002): 428–38.

31. See DiLorenzo, *The Real Lincoln*.

CHAPTER FIVE: HIGHWAYS OF CAPITALISM

1. Alexander Hamilton, *The Report on Manufactures*, reprinted in Michael Lind, ed., *Hamilton's Republic* (New York: Free Press, 1997), 31.

2. Carter Goodrich, *Government Promotion of American Canals and Railroads, 1800–1890* (Westport, CT: Greenwood Press, 1960), 19.

3. Ibid., 28.

4. Ibid., 28–29.

5. Robert Allen Rutland, *The Presidency of James Madison* (Lawrence: University of Kansas Press, 1990), 205.

6. John Quincy Adams, letter to Charles W. Upham, February 2, 1837, in Walter Lafeber, ed., *John Quincy Adams and American Continental Empire* (Chicago: Quadrangle Books, 1965), 146–47.

7. Ibid.

8. Ibid.

9. "Farewell Address of Andrew Jackson," in Joseph L. Blau, ed., *Social Theories of Jacksonian Democracy* (New York: Hafner, 1947), 305.

10. Daniel B. Klein, "The Voluntary Provision of Public Goods? The Turnpike Companies of Early America," *Economic Inquiry*, October 1990, 788–812.

11. Ibid., 797–98.

12. Benjamin De Witt, "A Sketch of the Turnpike Roads in the State of New York," in *The New American State Papers*, vol. 1 (Wilmington, DE: Scholarly Resources, Inc., 1972), 215, cited in Klein, "The Voluntary Provision of Public Goods?" 795–96.

13. Klein, "The Voluntary Provision of Public Goods?" 798.

14. Alexis de Tocqueville, *Democracy in America* (New York: Vintage Books, 1945), 114.

15. *Congressional Globe*, 37th Congress, 2nd Session, 2808.

16. Dee Brown, *Hear That Lonesome Whistle Blow: The Epic Story of the Transcontinental Railroads* (New York: Holt, 1977), 49.

17. Ibid., 58.

18. Ludwig von Mises, *Human Action: A Treatise in Economics,* scholar's edition (Auburn, AL: Mises Institute, 1998), 307.

19. John Bach McMaster, *A History of the People of the United States*, vol. 6 (New York: Appleton, 1914), 628.

20. Goodrich, *Government Promotion of Canals and Railroads, 1800–1890,* 138.

21. Ibid.

22. Ibid., 139.

23. Ibid., 143.

24. William Herndon and Jesse Weik, *Life of Lincoln* (New York: Da Capo Press, 1983), 161.

25. Ibid.

26. Cited in Paul Angle, *The Lincoln Reader* (New York: Da Capo Press, 1947), 100.

27. Goodrich, *Government Promotion of Canals and Railroads, 1800–1890,* 145.

28. Ibid., 147.

29. Ibid., 158.

30. Ibid., 231.
31. Marshall L. DeRosa, *The Confederate Constitution of 1861* (Columbia: University of Missouri Press, 1991), 94.

CHAPTER SIX: HOW CAPITALISM
ENRICHED THE WORKING CLASS

1. Ludwig von Mises, *Human Action: A Treatise on Economics*, scholar's edition (Auburn, AL: Mises Institute, 1998), 615.
2. Gary Walton and Hugh Rockoff, *History of the American Economy* (New York: Dryden Press, 1998), 242.
3. Ibid., 408.
4. Michael Cox and Richard Alm, *Myths of Rich and Poor* (New York: Basic Books, 1999), 23.
5. Walton and Rockoff, *History of the American Economy*, 42–44.
6. Cox and Alm, *Myths of Rich and Poor*, 55.
7. Ibid.
8. Ibid., 57.
9. Federal Reserve Bank of Dallas, *2000 Annual Report* (Dallas: Federal Reserve Bank of Dallas, 2000), 6.
10. Cox and Alm, *Myths of Rich and Poor*, 70–71.
11. Ibid., 70–75.
12. Ibid., 76.
13. Ibid., 88.
14. Morgan Reynolds, *Power and Privilege: Labor Unions in America* (New York: Universe Books, 1984), 62.

CHAPTER SEVEN: THE TRUTH
ABOUT THE "ROBBER BARONS"

1. Burton W. Folsom Jr., *Entrepreneurs vs. the State: A New Look at the Rise of Big Business in America, 1840–1920* (Herndon, VA: Young America's Foundation, 1987), 22.
2. Albro Martin, *James J. Hill and the Opening of the Northwest* (New York: Oxford University Press, 1976), 411.
3. Ibid., 410.
4. Albro Martin's *James J. Hill and the Opening of the Northwest* is an excellent biography of Hill, as is Michael P. Malone's *James J. Hill: Empire Builder of the Northwest* (Norman: University of Oklahoma Press, 1996). Hill also

wrote an autobiography, *Highways of Progress* (New York: Doubleday, 1910).

5. Malone, *James J. Hill*, 36.

6. Ibid., 37.

7. Ibid.

8. Ibid., 53.

9. Folsom, *Entrepreneurs vs. the State*, 27.

10. Ibid., 90.

11. Ibid., 91.

12. Ibid., 99.

13. Ibid., 28.

14. Ibid.

15. Malone, *James J. Hill*, 102.

16. James Stover, *American Railroads* (Chicago: University of Chicago Press, 1961), 67.

17. Folsom, *Entrepreneurs vs. the State*, 18.

18. Ibid., 19.

19. Ibid., 20–21.

20. Ibid., 34.

21. Ibid., 35.

22. Grace Goulder, *John D. Rockefeller: The Cleveland Years* (Cleveland: Western Reserve Historical Society, 1972), 26–27. See also Allan Nevins, *Study in Power: John D. Rockefeller* (New York: Scribner's, 1953).

23. Folsom, *Entrepreneurs vs. the State*, 84.

24. Dominick Armentano, *Antitrust and Monopoly: Anatomy of a Policy Failure* (New York: Wiley, 1982), 58.

25. Ida Tarbell, *The History of the Standard Oil Company* (New York: Peter Smith, 1950).

26. Ibid., 240, cited in Armentano, *Antitrust and Monopoly*, 65–66.

27. Armentano, *Antitrust and Monopoly*, 58.

28. Ibid., 59.

29. Nevins, *Study in Power*, vol. 1, 296.

30. Folsom, *Entrepreneurs vs. the State*, 87.

31. John S. McGee, "Predatory Price Cutting: The Standard Oil (N.J.) Case," *Journal of Law and Economics* 1 (October 1958): 144–58.

32. See Armentano, *Antitrust and Monopoly*, 68–73.

33. Ibid., 74.

34. Ibid., 75.
35. Ibid.
36. Ibid., 76.
37. Folsom, *Entrepreneurs vs. the State*, 2.
38. Ibid.
39. Ibid., 7.

CHAPTER EIGHT: ANTITRUST MYTHS

1. Richard Posner, *Antitrust Law: An Economic Perspective* (Chicago: University of Chicago Press, 1976), 23.
2. Thomas Hazlett, "Interview with George Stigler," *Reason*, January 1984, 46.
3. Marshall Howard, *Antitrust and Trade Regulation* (New York: Prentice Hall, 1983), 1.
4. On the Republican Party as the party of protectionism, see Thomas J. DiLorenzo, *The Real Lincoln: A New Look at Abraham Lincoln, His Agenda, and an Unnecessary War* (New York: Three Rivers Press, 2003); and Charles Adams, *When in the Course of Human Events: Arguing the Case for Southern Secession* (New York: Rowman & Littlefield, 2000).
5. William Letwin, *Law and Economic Policy in America: The Evolution of the Sherman Antitrust Law* (Chicago: University of Chicago Press, 1965), 67.
6. Robert Gray and James Peterson, *Economic Development in the United States* (New York: Irwin, 1965), 57.
7. Sanford D. Gordon, "Attitudes Toward Trusts Prior to the Sherman Act," *Southern Economics Journal* 20 (June 1963): 158.
8. Robert Bork, "Legislative Intent and the Policy of the Sherman Act," *Journal of Law and Economics* 9 (October 1966): 16.
9. Thomas J. DiLorenzo, "The Origins of Antitrust: An Interest-Group Perspective," *International Review of Law and Economics* 5, no. 1 (June 1985): 73–90.
10. *Congressional Record*, 51st Congress, 1st Session, House, June 20, 1890, 4, 100.
11. *New York Times*, October 1, 1890, 2.
12. Ibid.
13. Thomas J. DiLorenzo, "The Origins of Antitrust: Rhetoric vs. Reality," *Regulation*, Fall 1990, 27.
14. Ibid.
15. Ibid., 28.

16. Ibid., 29.
17. Yale Brozen, *Concentration, Mergers, and Public Policy* (New York: Macmillan, 1982), 14.
18. Dominick Armentano, *Antitrust and Monopoly: Anatomy of a Policy Failure* (New York: Wiley, 1982).
19. Armentano, *Antitrust and Monopoly*, 271.
20. Ibid., 91.
21. Ibid., 92.
22. Ibid., 93.
23. Ibid., 89.
24. Ibid., 91.
25. Ibid.
26. Ibid., 103.
27. *United States* v. *Aluminum Company of America et al.*, 44 F. Supp. 427.
28. Ibid.
29. Armentano, *Antitrust and Monopoly*, 112.
30. See Dominick Armentano, "Competition, Antitrust, and the Ready-to-Eat Cereals Case," Cato Institute *Policy Report*, February 1981, 1–5.
31. Armentano, *Antitrust and Monopoly*, 242.
32. Ibid., 244.
33. Ibid.
34. John Steele Gordon, "Read Your History, Janet," *Forbes*, February 23, 1998.
35. Armentano, *Antitrust and Monopoly*, 273.
36. Roger L. Faith, Donald R. Leavens, and Robert D. Tollison, "Antitrust Pork Barrel," *Journal of Law and Economics* 25 (October 1982): 329–42.

CHAPTER NINE: DID CAPITALISM
CAUSE THE GREAT DEPRESSION?

1. Major L. Wilson, *The Presidency of Martin Van Buren* (Lawrence: University Press of Kansas, 1984), 39.
2. James D. Richardson, ed., *A Compilation of the Messages and Papers of the Presidents* (New York: Bureau of National Literature, 1922), vol. 2, 1,561, cited in Jeffrey Hummel, "Martin Van Buren: The American Gladstone," in John Denson, ed., *Reassessing the Presidency* (Auburn, AL: Mises Institute, 2001), 178.
3. Ibid., 1,547.

4. Ibid.
5. Hummel, "Martin Van Buren," 186.
6. Ibid., 188.
7. Ibid.
8. Joan Hoff Wilson, *Herbert Hoover: Forgotten Progressive* (Boston: Little, Brown), 80.
9. Ibid.
10. William J. Barber, *From New Era to New Deal: Herbert Hoover, the Economists, and American Economic Policy, 1921–1933* (New York: Cambridge University Press, 1985), 15.
11. Ibid., 87.
12. Friedrich Hayek, "Competition as a Discovery Procedure," in Chiaki Nishiyama and Kurt R. Lenbe, *The Essence of Hayek* (Stanford, CA: Hoover Institution Press, 1984), 254–65.
13. Friedrich Hayek, *The Fatal Conceit: The Errors of Socialism* (Chicago: University of Chicago Press, 1991).
14. Ibid., 95.
15. Ibid., 24.
16. Ibid., 102.
17. Ibid., 22.
18. Wilson, *Herbert Hoover*, 118.
19. Barber, *From New Era to New Deal*, 41.
20. Acceptance speech at the Republican National Convention, August 11, 1932, cited in Murray N. Rothbard, *America's Great Depression* (Auburn, AL: Mises Institute, 2000), 187.
21. Ibid., 212.
22. Ibid., 213.
23. Hoff Wilson, *Herbert Hoover*, 146.
24. Ibid.
25. Rothbard, *America's Great Depression*, 287.
26. Ibid., 227.
27. Ibid., 230.
28. Ibid., 234.
29. Wilson Brown and Jan Hogendorn, *International Economics: Theory and Context* (New York: Addison-Wesley, 1994), 192.
30. Ibid., 193.

31. Charles Kindleberger, *The World in Depression: 1929–1939* (Berkeley and Los Angeles: University of California Press, 1973).

32. Brown and Hogendorn, *International Economics,* 193.

33. Rothbard, *America's Great Depression,* 297.

34. Ibid., 317.

35. Ibid., 93.

36. Frank W. Fetter, "Tariff Policy and Foreign Trade," in J. G. Smith, ed., *Facing the Facts* (New York: Putnam, 1932), 83, cited in Rothbard, *America's Great Depression,* 140.

37. Rothbard, *America's Great Depression,* 162.

CHAPTER TEN: HOW THE NEW
DEAL CRIPPLED CAPITALISM

1. I consider myself somewhat of an expert on the subject of government lies. See James T. Bennett and Thomas J. DiLorenzo, *Official Lies: How Washington Misleads Us* (Alexandria, VA: Groom Books, 1992).

2. Cited in Robert Higgs, "How FDR Made the Depression Worse," *The Free Market Newsletter,* February 1995 (Mises Institute, Auburn, AL).

3. Benjamin M. Anderson, *Economics and the Public Welfare: A Financial and Economic History of the United States, 1914–1946* (Indianapolis: Liberty Press, 1979), 474.

4. Robert Higgs, "Regime Uncertainty: Why the Great Depression Lasted So Long and Why Prosperity Resumed After the War," *Independent Review,* Spring 1997, 561–90.

5. Ibid.

6. Richard K. Vedder and Lowell E. Gallaway, *Out of Work: Unemployment and Government in Twentieth-Century America* (New York: Holmes & Meier, 1993), 129.

7. Robert Higgs, "Wartime Prosperity? A Reassessment of the U.S. Economy in the 1940s," *Journal of Economic History,* March 1992, 41–60.

8. U.S. Department of Commerce, *Historical Statistics of the United States* (Washington, D.C.: U.S. Government Printing Office, 1961), 711.

9. Higgs, "Regime Uncertainty," 586.

10. John T. Flynn, *The Roosevelt Myth* (New York: Devin-Adair, 1948).

11. Henry Hazlitt, "The Fallacies of the N.R.A.," *The American Mercury,* Dec. 1933, 422.

12. Flynn, *The Roosevelt Myth*, 45.
13. Ibid., 44.
14. Henry Hazlitt, "The Fallacies of the N.R.A.," 421.
15. Robert Higgs, *Crisis and Leviathan: Critical Episodes in the Growth of American Government* (New York: Oxford University Press, 1987), 178.
16. Ibid., 179.
17. Hazlitt, "The Fallacies of the N.R.A.," 422.
18. Flynn, *The Roosevelt Myth*, 49.
19. David E. Conrad, *The Forgotten Farmers* (Urbana: University of Illinois Press, 1965).
20. William E. Leuchtenberg, *Franklin D. Roosevelt and the New Deal* (New York: Harper and Row, 1963), 45.
21. "Trading with the Enemy Act," United States Code, Title 50: War and National Defense, October 6, 1917, Ch. 106, 40 Stat. 411. See www.access.gpo.gov/uscode/title50a/50a_2_1_.html.
22. "Report of the National Recovery Review Board," *New York Times*, May 21, 1934.
23. Flynn, *The Roosevelt Myth*, 43.
24. Fausto Pitigliani, *The Italian Corporative State* (New York: Macmillan, 1934).
25. Ibid., 93.
26. Luigi Villari, *Bolshevism, Fascism, and Capitalism* (New Haven: Yale University Press, 1932), 107.
27. Benito Mussolini, *Fascism: Doctrine and Institutions* (Rome: Adrita Press, 1935), 8.
28. Ibid., 29.
29. Richard Washburn Child, foreword to Benito Mussolini, *My Autobiography* (New York: Scribner's, 1928), xi, xix.
30. Cited in Charles Beard and Mary Beard, *America in Midpassage* (New York: Macmillan, 1932), 100.
31. Martin Fausold and George T. Mazuzan, *The Hoover Presidency: A Reappraisal* (Albany: State University of New York Press, 1974), 107.
32. Stuart Chase, "A Ten Year Plan for America," *Harper's*, June 1931, 2.
33. Rexford Tugwell, Thomas Munro, and Roy E. Stryker, *American Economic Life* (New York: Harcourt, Brace, 1930), 707.
34. Ibid., 709.
35. Ibid., 711.
36. Ibid., 712.

37. Ibid.

38. Ibid., 716.

39. Rexford G. Tugwell, "The Principle of Planning and the Institution of Laissez Faire," *American Economic Review*, May 1932, 79.

40. Ibid., 82.

41. Charlotte Twight, *America's Emerging Fascist Economy* (New Rochelle, NY: Arlington House, 1975), 13–29.

42. *Congressional Record* 78th Congress, 1st Session, House, 1934, 402–403.

43. Morgan Reynolds, *Power and Privilege: Labor Unions in America* (New York: Universe Books, 1984), 265.

44. Friedrich A. Hayek, *The Constitution of Liberty* (Chicago: University of Chicago Press, 1960), 267.

45. Howard Dickman, *Industrial Democracy in America: Ideological Origins of National Labor Relations Policy* (La Salle, IL: Open Court, 1987), 287.

46. Vedder and Gallaway, *Out of Work*, 134.

47. Ibid., 139.

48. Ibid., 141.

49. Ibid.

50. Flynn, *The Roosevelt Myth*, 132.

51. U.S. Department of Commerce, *Historical Statistics of the United States*, 711.

52. Cited in Flynn, *The Roosevelt Myth*, 133–37.

53. Gavin Wright, "The Political Economy of New Deal Spending: An Econometric Analysis," *Review of Economics and Statistics*, February 1974, 35.

54. Stanley High, "The WPA: Politicians' Playground," *Current History*, May 1939, 23–25.

55. Jim F. Couch and William F. Shughart II, *The Political Economy of the New Deal* (Northampton, MA: Edward Elgar, 1998), 130.

56. Ibid., 139.

57. Ibid., 143.

58. Gary Anderson and Robert Tollison, "Congressional Influence and Patterns of New Deal Spending," *Journal of Law and Economics*, April 1991, 161–75.

59. Ibid., 145.

60. Couch and Shughart, *The Political Economy of the New Deal*, 187.

61. Ibid.

62. Ibid., 192.

63. Ibid., 188.

64. Ibid., 228.

65. David Gordon, "Power Mad," *The Mises Review*, Spring 1999, 7–12.

CHAPTER ELEVEN: DID CAPITALISM
CAUSE THE ENERGY CRISIS?

1. Dominick Armentano, *Antitrust and Monopoly: Anatomy of a Policy Failure* (New York: Wiley, 1982), 74.

2. Ibid., 75.

3. William E. Simon, *A Time for Truth* (New York: McGraw-Hill, 1978), 53.

4. Ibid.

5. U.S. Department of Interior, U.S. Geological Survey, *Papers on the Conservation of Mineral Resources* (Washington, D.C.: U.S. Government Printing Office, 1909), 45–46.

6. This and the following government forecasts are from U.S. Congress, House Committee on Interstate and Foreign Commerce, *Presidential Energy Program, Hearings Before the Subcommittee on Energy and Power*, 94th Congress, 1st Session, 1975, 643.

7. According to the Department of Energy's Office of Management, Budget, and Evaluation, the DOE's budget for fiscal year 2003 was $21.9 billion. See www.mbe.doe.gov/budget/03budget/content/highlite/highlite.pdf.

8. James P. Gannon, "All Roads Are Steep in U.S. Drive to Achieve Energy Independence," *Wall Street Journal*, March 12, 1974.

9. William E. Simon, "Tilting at Windfall Profits," *Policy Review* 11 (Winter 1980): 21.

10. Milton R. Copulos, "Reagan's Fading Energy Agenda," Heritage Foundation *Backgrounder* No. 204 (Washington, D.C.: Heritage Foundation, August 17, 1982), 9.

11. Walter S. Mossberg, "When U.S. Set Up That Oil Reserve, It Left One Thing Out," *Wall Street Journal*, March 15, 1979.

12. Milton R. Copulos, "How to Keep Natural Gas Supplies Short and Prices High," Heritage Foundation *Issues Bulletin* no. 108 (Washington, D.C.: Heritage Foundation, June 12, 1984), 1.

13. "Oil Price History and Analysis," *Energy Economics Newsletter.* See www.wtrg.com/prices.htm.

14. U.S. Department of Energy, "Retail Motor Gasoline and On-Highway

Diesel Fuel Prices, 1949–2001." See www.eia.doe.gov/emeu/aer/txt/ptb0522.html.

15. George Reisman, "California Screaming, Under Government Blows," *Mises Institute Daily Article*, December 22, 2000 (www.mises.org/fullarticle.asp?control=575&id=64).

16. Benjamin Zycher, "Don't Blame the Power Crisis on Deregulation," *Los Angeles Times*, December 28, 2000.

17. Ibid.

18. Referring to the Bush administration, Hillary Clinton told Larry King, "They have continued to try to push deregulation and privatization, and to try to undo a lot of the systems in changes that many of us thought were important and necessary that we tried to work on during the Clinton administration. . . . I don't think the federal administration under this president is really focused on making sure we don't have these problems in the future" (*Larry King Live*, CNN, August 14, 2003). John Kerry, meanwhile, condemned the Bush administration for its "obsession with giveaways to their friends in the oil business" and declared that "these blackouts also expose some of the failures of this administration's energy policies" (quoted on *Meet the Press*, NBC, August 17, 2003).

CONCLUSION: THE NEVER-ENDING
WAR ON CAPITALISM

1. Michel Jensen and William Meckling, "The Future of Capitalism," *Financial Analyst's Journal*, May 1978, 1.

2. Ludwig von Mises, *Liberalism: In the Classical Tradition* (Irvington, NY: Foundation for Economic Education, 1985), 102.

3. Ronald Coase, "Economists and Public Policy," in J. Fred Weston, ed., *Large Corporations in a Changing Society* (New York: New York University Press, 1975).

4. Fred S. McChesney, *Money for Nothing: Politicians, Rent Extraction, and Political Extortion* (Cambridge: Harvard University Press, 1997).

5. Ibid., inside cover.

6. Ibid., 57.

7. Ibid., 63.

8. Stanley J. Liebowitz and Stephen E. Margolis, *Winners, Losers, and Micro-*

soft: Competition and Antitrust in High Technology (Oakland, CA: Independent Institute, 1999).

9. Ibid., 139.

10. Ibid., 228.

11. John Heilemann, *Pride Before the Fall* (New York: HarperBusiness, 2002).

12. Ibid., 88–89.

13. Peter Huber, *Liability: The Legal Revolution and Its Consequences* (New York: Basic Books, 1988), 8.

14. Ibid.

15. These examples are taken from the website www.overlawyered.com.

16. "W. Va. Doctors Strike Over Insurance Costs," CNN.com, January 1, 2003.

17. Huber, *Liability*, 15.

18. Robert A. Levy, "Tobacco Medicaid Litigation: Snuffing Out the Rule of Law," Cato Institute Policy Analysis No. 275 (Washington, D.C.: Cato Institute, June 20, 1997).

19. Ibid.

20. Ibid., 6.

21. Ralph Reiland, "McDonald's Made Me Fat," *Capitalism*, January 16, 2003.

22. Ibid., p. 1.

23. Ibid.

24. Ralph Reiland, "Legal Man Takes On the 'Fat Pushers.' Who's Next? Krispy Kreme?" *Capitalism*, August 4, 2002.

25. See, for example, "The Surgeon General's Warning on the Health Consequences of Being Overweight or Obese"; www.ez-weightloss.com/ez-weightloss/articlesurgeongeneraloverweight.html.

26. Larry Elder, "Coming Soon: The Fat Tax," *Capitalism*, November 9, 1999.

27. Michael Park, "Lawyers See Fat Payoffs in Junk Food Lawsuits," Fox News.com, January 23, 2002. See www.foxnews.com/story/0,2933,43735,00.html.

28. Ibid.

29. Joel Miller, "Waging War on Fat," WorldNetDaily, September 20, 1999. See www.worldnetdaily.com/news/article.asp?ARTICLE_ID=16201.

30. Eric Schlosser, *Fast Food Nation: The Dark Side of the All-American Meal* (New York: HarperCollins, 2002).

31. Ibid., 269.

32. Barbara Ehrenreich, *Nickel and Dimed: On (Not) Getting By in America* (New York: Holt, 2001).

33. Amity Shlaes, *The Greedy Hand: How Taxes Drive Americans Crazy and What to Do About It* (New York: Random House, 1999).

34. Michael Moore, *Stupid White Men . . . and Other Sorry Excuses for the State of the Nation!* (New York: ReganBooks, 2001), 55.

35. Michael Moore, *Downsize This! Random Threats from an Unarmed American* (New York: HarperPerennial, 1997), 141.

ANNOTATED BIBLIOGRAPHY

Adams, Charles. *For Good and Evil: The Impact of Taxes on the Course of Civilization.* New York: Madison Books, 1999.

A fascinating account of the profound effect taxes have had on world civilization beginning with ancient Egypt up through the end of the twentieth century.

Armentano, Dominick. *Antitrust and Monopoly: Anatomy of a Policy Failure.* New York: Wiley, 1982.

The author examines fifty-five of the most famous federal antitrust cases in history (as of 1982) and finds that, in each and every case, companies were prosecuted for dropping prices, improving their products or services, and expanding production. He concludes that antitrust regulation has always been harmful to competition and should be abolished.

Bailey, Ronald. *Eco-Scam: The False Prophets of Ecological Apocalypse.* New York: St. Martin's Press, 1993.

Bailey exposes the many environmentalist myths, including the biggest myth—that capitalist economic progress is bad for the environment. He proves that, for the most part, "environmentalism" is more interested in crippling capitalism than in improving the natural environment.

Bethell, Tom. *The Noblest Triumph: Property and Prosperity Through the Ages.* New York: St. Martin's Press, 1998.

A scholarly and well-written history of the role of private property in the economy from ancient times to the present day. Throughout history, famine, starvation, and poverty have been caused by the lack or absence of private property.

Bork, Robert. *The Antitrust Paradox: A Policy at War with Itself.* New York: Basic Books, 1978.

> The former Yale University law professor, federal judge, and U.S. solicitor general explains why nearly every antitrust doctrine and law is harmful to industrial competitiveness.

Bovard, James. *The Fair Trade Fraud.* New York: St. Martin's Press, 1991.

> One of America's top investigative journalists exposes the fraud, corruption, and economic harm done by protectionist trade policies.

Brozen, Yale. *Concentration, Mergers, and Public Policy.* New York: Macmillan, 1982.

> A lucid explanation of how large businesses have historically become large by pleasing their customers better than their competitors do, and how public policies designed to break up big businesses are inherently harmful to consumers. A state-of-the-art survey of the relevant economics literature.

Carson, Clarence B. *Organized Against Whom? The Labor Union in America.* Alexandria, VA: Western Goals, 1983.

> Carson exposes the greatest myth about labor unions—that they defend workers from their employers. In reality, unions are organized against nonunion labor and use force, coercion, and special-interest legislation to benefit themselves at the expense of the rest of society.

Couch, Jim F., and William Shughart II. *The Political Economy of the New Deal.* Northampton, MA: Edward Elgar, 1998.

> The authors make a very strong case that New Deal policies were driven by political opportunism and careerism, not a desire to improve the economy.

DeSoto, Hernando. *The Mystery of Capital: Why Capitalism Triumphs in the West and Fails Everywhere Else.* New York: Basic Books, 2000.

> DeSoto explains why government intervention prohibits capital accumulation—a prerequisite for capitalism—in much of the Third World and is therefore a major reason for the poverty there.

DiLorenzo, Thomas J. "The Origins of Antitrust: An Interest-Group Perspective." *International Review of Law and Economics,* vol. 5, 1985.

> This article shows that the businesses that were first accused of monopolizing American industry through the formation of trusts in the late 1880s were in fact the most competitive industries in America and were expanding

output and dropping prices rapidly. Antitrust law was a protectionist law from the very beginning and has always been harmful to competition.

———. *The Real Lincoln: A New Look at Abraham Lincoln, His Agenda, and an Unnecessary War.* Paperback ed. New York: Three Rivers Press, 2003.

Abraham Lincoln devoted his twenty-eight-year political career prior to becoming president to agitating for the Whig Party agenda of mercantilism, but this agenda was not adopted in any significant degree until the 1860s—when Lincoln himself became president.

DiLorenzo, Thomas J., and Jack C. High. "Antitrust and Competition, Historically Considered." *Economic Inquiry*, vol. 26, July 1988.

When the first federal antitrust law was passed in 1890, the economics profession was almost unanimously against it, believing that it was inherently in conflict with dynamic, rivalrous competition.

Flynn, John T. *The Roosevelt Myth.* New York: Devin-Adair, 1948.

The most hard-hitting critique of FDR's economic policies by one of his top contemporary critics.

Folsom, Burton W., Jr. *The Myth of the Robber Barons.* Herndon, VA: Young America's Foundation, 1996.

Folsom portrays America's early capitalist heroes such as James J. Hill, who literally created entire industries without any governmental assistance. He also explains how the real "robber barons" were other men who gained great wealth through political connections rather than free-market capitalism.

Friedman, Milton, and Rose Friedman. *Capitalism and Freedom.* Chicago: University of Chicago Press, 1962.

This is the Friedmans' classic defense of capitalism on philosophical as well as economic grounds. More capitalism means more freedom, and vice versa. Moreover, political and economic freedom are inseparable.

———. *Free to Choose: A Personal Statement.* New York: Avon Books, 1979.

One of the best-written and best-informed explanations of free-market capitalism ever published. The Friedmans explain first how free markets work and then how interventionism inevitably makes society worse off by interfering in the spontaneous order of markets.

Greiner, Donna, and Theodore B. Kinni. *Ayn Rand and Business.* New York: Texere, 2001.

These authors apply Ayn Rand's unabashed defense of capitalism and her objectivist philosophy to modern business practices.

Annotated Bibliography

Hayek, Friedrich A. "The Intellectuals and Socialism." *University of Chicago Law Review*, vol. 3, Spring 1949.

    Hayek explains why so many intellectuals have been infatuated by socialism despite its failures.

————. "The Pretense of Knowledge: Nobel Lecture." *American Economic Review*, May 1975.

    The Nobel laureate explains why a socialist economy could never efficiently utilize the information necessary for rational economic decision making.

Hazlitt, Henry. *Economics in One Lesson*. New York: Arlington House, 1946.

    The best introduction to economics ever written. Although the book was first published in 1946, most of Hazlitt's examples and illustrations are timeless.

Hessen, Robert. *In Defense of the Corporation*. Stanford, CA: Hoover Institution Press, 1979.

    Hessen shatters the myth that "big business" is necessarily bad for society, showing how businesses grow by satisfying large numbers of consumers. He also destroys the anticapitalist arguments of such gadflies as Ralph Nader.

Heyne, Paul. *The Economic Way of Thinking*. 9th ed. Upper Saddle River, NJ: Prentice Hall, 2000.

    One of the very best contemporary introductory economics textbooks.

Higgs, Robert. "Regime Uncertainty: Why the Great Depression Lasted So Long and Why Prosperity Resumed after the War." *Independent Review*, Spring 1997, 561–90.

    Higgs shows how Franklin Roosevelt's administration's relentless political attacks on capitalism and capitalists caused business investment to dry up, and how the Great Depression ended only after World War II, when the size and scope of government were dramatically curtailed.

Hollander, Paul. *Political Pilgrims: Travels of Western Intellectuals to the Soviet Union, China, and Cuba, 1928–1978*. New York: Harper and Row, 1981.

    Hollander shows how socialist dictators around the world made fools of so many Western intellectuals who blindly embraced socialism because of their hatred of capitalism.

Hood, John M. *The Heroic Enterprise*. New York: Free Press, 1996.

Hood defends capitalism and capitalists against the forces of political correctness who want businesspeople to give away more and more of their (and their shareholders') money to various liberal political causes in the name of "corporate social responsibility." He explains in great detail why "corporate social responsibility" is socially irresponsible.

Hoppe, Hans-Hermann. *The Economics and Ethics of Private Property*. Boston: Kluwer Academic Publishers, 1993.

A lucid discussion of the ethical and economic case in favor of private property and free-market capitalism.

Huber, Peter. *Liability: The Legal Revolution and Its Consequences*. New York: Basic Books, 1988.

Huber describes the causes and consequences of America's crazy liability law system, in which people with deep pockets are often sued regardless of whether they are liable for harming anyone.

Hutt, William H. *The Theory of Collective Bargaining*. Washington, D.C.: Cato Institute, 1974.

Hutt challenges the notion that workers are better off with collective bargaining instead of individual bargaining over wages and working conditions. He also exposes numerous myths about labor unions, such as the myth that unions are necessary to raise the living standards of workers.

Kirzner, Israel. *Competition and Entrepreneurship*. Chicago: University of Chicago Press, 1978.

The author explains the role of entrepreneurship in the economy, something that most other economists ignore.

Irwin, Douglas A. *Against the Tide: An Intellectual History of Free Trade*. Princeton, NJ: Princeton University Press, 1996.

A comprehensive history of free-trade doctrines and theories, beginning with the seventeenth century.

Liebowitz, Stanley J., and Stephen E. Margolis. *Winners, Losers, and Microsoft*. Oakland, CA: Independent Institute, 2001.

The authors use economic theory and evidence to show that the Microsoft Corporation has always been a boon for competitiveness, contrary to the claims by the company's sour-grapes competitors and résumé-building government antitrust attorneys.

Locke, Edwin A. *The Prime Movers: Traits of the Great Wealth Creators*. New York: AMACOM, 2000.

Locke catalogues the personal and business-practice traits of those who have been pioneers of industry and wealth creation in America.

Manne, Henry G. *The Modern Corporation and Social Responsibility.* Washington, D.C.: American Enterprise Institute, 1972.

One of the founders of the "law and economics" movement explains how businesses can best be "socially responsible" by steadfastly concentrating on profit maximization.

Martin, Albro. *James J. Hill and the Opening of the Northwest.* New York: Oxford University Press, 1976.

An excellent biography of the man who, without any governmental assistance, built a transcontinental railroad, better and more profitably than his subsidized rivals.

McGee, John S. "Predatory Pricing: The Standard Oil (N.J.) Case." *Journal of Law and Economics,* vol. 1, October 1958.

The classic article exposing the "predatory pricing" myth and proving that John D. Rockefeller's Standard Oil Company was never so foolish as to attempt such a strategy.

Mises, Ludwig von. *The Anticapitalistic Mentality.* Grove City, PA: Libertarian Press, Inc., 1972.

The famous Austrian School economist explores the various reasons why intellectuals, journalists, Hollywood, and popular culture in general vilify capitalism.

———. *Human Action: A Treatise on Economics,* scholars ed. Auburn, AL: Mises Institute, 1998.

A comprehensive treatise on economics by the great Austrian School economist.

———. *Liberalism: In the Classical Tradition.* Irvington, NY: Foundation for Economic Education, 1985.

The best philosophical defense of capitalism ever written.

———. *Socialism.* Indianapolis: Liberty Classics, 1981.

Originally published in 1922, this is Mises's comprehensive explanation of why socialism could never work as an economic system.

Nishiyama, Chiaki, and Kurt R. Leube. *The Essence of Hayek.* Stanford, CA: Hoover Institution Press, 1984.

A good introduction to the social and economic thought of Friedrich A. Hayek, the Nobel laureate Austrian School economist.

Petro, Sylvester. *The Labor Policy of the Free Society*. New York: Ronald Press, 1957.

A classic defense of unregulated labor markets. Petro describes how the regulation of labor relations benefits special interests at the expense of the rest of society while diminishing personal freedom.

Powell, Jim. *FDR's Folly*. New York: Crown Forum, 2003.

Powell summarizes decades of economic research on how virtually every New Deal economic policy made the Great Depression worse and caused it to last longer than it otherwise would have.

Rand, Ayn. *Atlas Shrugged*. New York: Random House, 1957.

Rand's spectacularly successful novel is one of the most influential arguments ever made in defense of individualism, capitalism, and freedom.

———, ed. *Capitalism: The Unknown Ideal*. New York: Signet, 1967.

A collection of articles by Rand, Alan Greenspan, Robert Hessen, and Nathaniel Brandon that explains and defends many aspects of capitalism, from the gold standard to private property to patents and copyrights. The anticapitalist mentality is also scrutinized.

Reisman, George. *Capitalism: A Treatise on Economics*. Ottawa, IL: Jameson Books, 1996.

A major treatise on the economics of capitalism that draws on the Austrian School, neoclassical economics, and the philosophy of Ayn Rand. The book is in the category of Mises's *Human Action* and Rothbard's *Man, Economy, and State*.

Reynolds, Morgan. *Power and Privilege: Labor Unions in America*. New York: Universe Books, 1984.

Reynolds argues that labor unions are essentially labor monopolies and that the legislation and regulation propping up those monopolies are harmful to nonunion workers, consumers, and society in general. He also shows that unions are inherently harmful to productivity and industrial competitiveness.

Rosenberg, Nathan, and L. E. Birdzell Jr. *How the West Grew Rich: The Economic Transformation of the Industrial World*. New York: Basic Books, 1986.

A scholarly history of the evolution of capitalism, from the Middle Ages to the present day.

Rothbard, Murray N. *America's Great Depression*. Auburn, AL: Mises Institute, 2000.

Rothbard proves that Herbert Hoover's unprecedented interventionism, along with Federal Reserve policy, caused America's Great Depression.

————. *The Ethics of Liberty*. Atlantic Highlands, NJ: Humanities Press, 1982.

A classic defense of the philosophy of liberty and its importance to a free and prosperous society. Rothbard also explains in great detail why government intervention is the enemy of liberty and economic progress.

————. *Man, Economy, and State*. Mission, KS: Sheed, Andrews and McMeel, 1962.

A treatise on economic theory by one of the twentieth century's pre-eminent Austrian School, free-market economists.

————. 1977. *Power and Market: Government and the Economy*. Menlo Park, CA: Institute for Humane Studies.

An excellent and comprehensive exposition of the economics of government interventionism.

————. *What Has Government Done to Our Money?* Santa Ana, CA: Rampart College, 1974.

An explanation of why the gold standard is consistent with free-market capitalism but fractional reserve banking is not.

Schweichart, Larry. *The Entrepreneurial Adventure: A History of Business in the United States*. New York: Harcourt Brace, 2000.

A history of entrepreneurship in America from the colonial era up through the age of Microsoft.

Simon, Julian L. *The Ultimate Resource*. Princeton, NJ: Princeton University Press, 1981.

Simon brilliantly shows how human ingenuity has always been the driving force of economic progress, as long as a high degree of economic freedom—i.e., capitalism—exists. He also shows how dangerously wrong-headed the "zero population growth" wing of the environmentalist movement is.

Smith, Adam. *An Inquiry into the Nature and Causes of the Wealth of Nations*. New York: Random House, 1937.

Adam Smith's classic critique of mercantilism and explanation of how freedom of exchange—i.e., capitalism—is the source of wealth creation.

Sowell, Thomas. *Basic Economics: A Citizen's Guide to the Economy*. New York: Basic Books, 2000.

Second only to Henry Hazlitt's *Economics in One Lesson* as an outstanding introduction to economic theory and its applications to the modern world.

Vedder, Richard K., and Lowell Gallaway. *Out of Work: Unemployment and Government in Twentieth-Century America*. New York: Holmes & Meier, 1993.

A very scholarly analysis and explanation of why government intervention is the cause of unemployment and how free-market capitalism is the cure.

Younkins, Edward W. *Capitalism and Commerce: Conceptual Foundations of Free Enterprise*. New York: Lexington Books, 2002.

A well-written survey of the various philosophies in defense of capitalism as well as of the "obstacles to a free society," such as collectivism, environmentalism, antitrust, protectionism, and inflationism.

ACKNOWLEDGMENTS

I would first like to thank David Richardson, my former editor at Prima Publishing, for urging me to write a book in defense of capitalism that takes a historical perspective. He believed there would be a need for such a book in light of the slew of anticapitalistic books that were sure to be published in the wake of the Enron scandal, and he was right. Many of these books have argued that the sins of a few are an inherent feature of capitalism and not just minor aberrations. This book proves what hokum that argument is.

Jed Donahue, my new editor at Crown Forum, has also been a great source of advice and editorial commentary throughout the process and deserves a great deal of thanks.

I would also like to thank my associates at the Ludwig von Mises Institute in Auburn, Alabama, especially Lew Rockwell and Jeff Tucker, for providing me with a constant source of ideas, research materials, constructive criticisms, and a platform for expressing many of my ideas. I consider the Institute to be the premier educational institution in the world devoted to the study of capitalism and am proud to be associated with it.

Finally, my wife, Stacey, has been a strong source of support, as always, for my habit of spending endless hours in front of a computer, writing chapter after chapter, book after book. She makes it possible for me to be a writer as well as an economic educator, for which I am eternally grateful.

INDEX

Index

Index

Index

Index

Index

Index

Thomas J. DiLorenzo is a professor of economics in the Sellinger School of Business and Management at Loyola College in Maryland and a member of the senior faculty of the Mises Institute in Auburn, Alabama. He is the author or coauthor of twelve books, the last of which is *The Real Lincoln,* and is widely published in academic economics journals as well as such national publications as the *Wall Street Journal, Barron's, Reader's Digest, USA Today,* and the *Washington Post.* DiLorenzo lives in Clarksville, Maryland.

Printed in the United States
by Baker & Taylor Publisher Services